Tamás Czövek's *Challenging the Beast* brings a fresh and original reading of the Bible's Primeval History (PH), Genesis 1–11, and especially its concluding narrative, the Tower of Babel story. Building on the current, but not universal, consensus that PH, in its final form, emerged from Judah's sixth-century Babylonian captivity, Czövek anchors PH in a polemic against the concept of empire reflected in Babylon's capital city, its kingship, and its ziggurat temple. The alternative, a commonwealth of "commoners" that will emerge from God's call of Abraham, is the ultimate context of the story, but in Czövek's view the unique features of PH, especially chapter 11, cannot be explained by traditional readings.

New readings of Genesis 1–11 will continue as long as Old Testament scholars wrestle with Israel's fascinating account of both its own, and creation's, origins. Not all will agree with such a focus on the sixth-century provenance. But, in a day when synchronic studies have, often refreshingly, replaced earlier diachronic studies, Tamás Czövek's fresh and close reading of this ancient text will be required reading for anyone seriously interacting with Genesis 1–11. It will also help that this academic treatise is both well-argued and eminently readable.

Carl E. Armerding, PhD
Emeritus Professor of Old Testament,
Regent College, Canada
Senior Fellow, Oxford Centre for Mission Studies, UK

In his book, Tamás Czövek presents an impressive concept for the understanding of the Primeval History. Dealing with a wide range of current German- and English-language scholarly literature and building especially on the work of David A. Clines, he interprets the Primeval History, in a synchronic approach, as a radical questioning of the Mesopotamian mythological tradition. While the focus there is on kingship, city, and temple, Czövek works out the power-critical function of the Primeval History, in which the focus is instead on the commoners, the land, and the justice – thus challenging the empire. This contribution to the historical-critical understanding of the Primeval History is well worth reading and of great contemporary political relevance.

Benjamin Ziemer, PhD
Faculty of Theology, Old Testament,
Martin-Luther-Universität, Halle-Wittenberg, Germany

Challenging the Beast, Challenging Empire

A Literary-Critical, Comparative, and Theological Reading of the Primeval History

Tamás Czövek

ACADEMIC

© 2025 Tamás Czövek

Published 2025 by Langham Academic
An imprint of Langham Publishing
www.langhampublishing.org

Langham Publishing and its imprints are a ministry of Langham Partnership

Langham Partnership
PO Box 296, Carlisle, Cumbria, CA3 9WZ, UK
www.langham.org

ISBNs:
978-1-83973-989-7 Print
978-1-78641-293-5 ePub
978-1-78641-294-2 PDF
DOI: https://doi.org/10.69811/9781839739897

Tamás Czövek has asserted his right under the Copyright, Designs and Patents Act, 1988 to be identified as the Author of this work.

All rights reserved. No part of this publication may be reproduced, stored in a retrieval system or transmitted, in any form or by any means, electronic, mechanical, photocopying, recording or otherwise, without the prior written permission of the publisher or the Copyright Licensing Agency.

Requests to reuse content from Langham Publishing are processed through PLSclear. Please visit www.plsclear.com to complete your request.

All Scripture quotations, unless otherwise indicated, are taken from the Holy Bible, New International Version®, NIV®. Copyright ©1973, 1978, 1984, 2011 by Biblica, Inc.™ Used by permission of Zondervan.

Scripture quotations marked (ESV) are from The Holy Bible, English Standard Version® (ESV®), copyright © 2001 by Crossway, a publishing ministry of Good News Publishers. Used by permission. All rights reserved.

Scripture quotations marked (RSV) are from Revised Standard Version of the Bible, copyright © 1946, 1952, and 1971 National Council of the Churches of Christ in the United States of America. Used by permission. All rights reserved.

Scripture quotations marked (AT) are the author's own translation.

British Library Cataloguing-in-Publication Data
A catalogue record for this book is available from the British Library

ISBN: 978-1-83973-989-7

Cover & Book Design: projectluz.com

Langham Partnership actively supports theological dialogue and an author's right to publish but does not necessarily endorse the views and opinions set forth here or in works referenced within this publication, nor can we guarantee technical and grammatical correctness. Langham Partnership does not accept any responsibility or liability to persons or property as a consequence of the reading, use or interpretation of its published content.

To my mother,
and to the memory of my father

Contents

Acknowledgments ix

Abbreviations xi

Chapter 1 1
   Context and Method
      Context 1
         City 3
         Kingship 6
         Shrine 11
         Commoners 13
         Myths and Genealogies 14
         Rites 18
         Reading the Primeval History against a
            Babylonian Backdrop 20
      Literature Survey 21
         Synchronic Approaches 21
         Comparative Approaches 32
      The Narrator's Literary Strategy 37
      Methodology 40

Chapter 2 47
   The Primeval History: An Alternative to Babylon's Metanarrative
      Dethroning Marduk: The Beginnings (1:1–3:24) 47
         Cosmogony (1:1–2:3) 48
         Anthropogony (2:4–25) 61
         In the Garden (3:1–24) 76
      Challenging Imperial Hegemony: The Multiplication of
         Humankind and the Beginning of Civilization (4:1–5:32) 90
         A Diverse Culture of Commoners: God's Image and
            Knowing Good and Evil (4:1–26) 90
         An Egalitarian World of Commoners: The Ten
            Generations (5:1–32) 106
         A Diverse Creation and Society: "According to Their
            Kinds" – Excursus 112
      The Flood: A New Beginning by Destruction (6:1–9:19) 118
         Before the Flood: Of Demigods, Giants, and Heroes (6:1–8) ...118
         The Flood (6:9–8:19) 128
         God's Covenant (8:20–9:19) 137

    The Multiplication of Humankind: A New Beginning
        (9:20–10:32) 142
            Noah's Stupor (9:20–29) 143
            The Genealogy of Noah's Sons (10:1–32) 147
    Things Gone Awry: Babylon and Shem (11:1–26) 153
        Challenging Imperial Royal Politics: The City of Babylon
            (11:1–9) 154
            Shem's Genealogy (11:10–26) 169

Chapter 3 171
Prospects: A New Genealogy and Beyond
    Terah's Genealogy (11:27–32) 171
    Abraham's Story: Genesis 12:1 and Beyond 172

Chapter 4 177
Conclusions
    General 177
    City 178
    Kingship 179
    Shrine 182
    A Universal Vision and Politics 183
    The Primeval History as a Parable: Israel's Trauma 186
    The Theme of the Primeval History 190
    Relevance and Implications 191

Bibliography 195

Acknowledgments

In 2008, I attended a missiology conference in Hungary. On hearing that I was an Old Testament scholar, a South African missiologist kindly drew my attention to recent interpretations of the Tower of Babel story that see the builders' sin in horizontal rather than vertical terms. My interest was raised and I felt the enormous challenge to tackle this passage. I quickly realized though that it can correctly be interpreted only by studying both its narrower and wider contexts, that is, by studying the whole of Primeval History (PH). Little did I know at the time, fortunately, that, according to one Tyndale House estimation, on average, two studies a day are completed on PH. It is an over-researched topic, one whose secondary literature is so enormous that no one can dream of reading all of it. In addition, proposing a new thesis of how to read PH is extremely difficult.

My actual research started at Princeton Theological Seminary in 2010. It was a good start and I spent the three summer months in the excellent library of the seminary whose self-advertising motto, spelled out in seminary banners and its mission statement, was "diversity." In 2012, I spent six weeks in the friendly environment and superior library of Wheaton College, then, another three months in Halle, Germany where, with the kind assistance of Professor Ernst-Joachim Waschke, I studied the German secondary literature. Next year, I worked at the Protestant Theological Faculty of Charles University, Prague, then, in a friend's house near Prague surrounded with all sorts of books, the complete works of Marx-Engels and Lenin among them. Whether or not this circumstance contributed to my thesis of seeing PH as an anti-empire document I leave for further research to determine.

This research has been sponsored by John Wesley College and the Pentecostal Theological Seminary, Budapest, DAAD, Germany, and Langham

Partnership. I am grateful to them as well as to principals Gábor Iványi at John Wesley College and Paul Gracza at the Pentecostal Theological Seminary for supporting my research. An earlier version of the manuscript was read by Professor Bernard F. Batto who kindly drew my attention to weaknesses in my argument, studies to read, or neglected aspects. Neither he nor any who read and made observations on the manuscript are of course accountable for the end product.

My wife and four children have bravely put up with my long physical and mental absences. Without their assistance and forbearance, I would not have succeeded. I dedicate this study to them.

Abbreviations

ANE	Ancient Near East
BCS	Babylonian creation story
MKL	Mesopotamian king lists
MT	Masoretic Text
NT	New Testament
OT	Old Testament
P	Priestly writer/source
PH	Primeval history
SFS	Sumerian flood story
SKL	Sumerian king list
WSL	West Semitic list

CHAPTER 1

Context and Method

Context

"It is abundantly clear today that, of the two major centres of civilization in the area, it was distant Mesopotamia and not neighbouring Egypt that left the deeper cultural impress upon Israel."[1] Even though it was over half a century ago that Ephraim Speiser made this statement his view has become scholarly consensus. Of the dependence of Genesis on Mesopotamian myths, Jacobsen claims that the Priestly writer/source (referred to from here as P) knew and admired Mesopotamian records that inspired him to imitation.[2] The various cultures of ancient Mesopotamia adopted each other's cultural heritage, revered and cherished for centuries. Myths were assigned particular significance in worldview and politics.

With the first chapters of Genesis, we enter the world of ancient Near East (ANE) myths. In the Primeval History (PH), we can see numerous clear and quite a few oblique references to Mesopotamian mythology – primordial events, mythic heroes, and concepts all contributing in their own way to how society was expected to function. Those myths usually originated in ancient times but still played a significant role in Neo-Babylonian society, religion, and politics. This context inevitably impacted the Jewish people, who, exiled to Babylonia, were governed by the interests and rules of imperial politics, and witnessed to Babylonian religious festivals and rites.

---

1. Speiser, "Biblical Idea of History," 209; cf. Clifford, "Hebrew Scriptures," 520.
2. Jacobsen, "Eridu Genesis," 528–29.

This study is an attempt to read Genesis 1–11 to see its theology against a Babylonian background. I will first discuss the socio-cultural context of PH, then provide a literature survey before outlining the narrator's literary strategy and my methodology in detail. The major bulk of this study is devoted to exegesis, the thesis being that PH is a counter-narrative to that of Babylon, criticizing Babylon's hierarchical society, imperial politics, and culture and advocating an egalitarian world.[3] This world involves the rejection of city-, kingship-, and sanctuary-based religion in favor of a society based on commoners. This aspect has not been fully appreciated before.

In studying the biblical text, I will not deal with genetic questions of how and when the text was formed. Despite its long textual pre-history, I will read PH as a self-contained literary unit, the introduction to Genesis and the Pentateuch. To be sure, there have been studies on PH as the introduction to Genesis, the Pentateuch, or the Old Testament (OT).[4] However, synchronic studies have paid little attention to the Mesopotamian background. Diachronic studies, on the other hand, tend to study PH as an accumulation of sources. Even though the Mesopotamian background is well-known, I know of no synchronic study on PH making use of this background to the extent it seems necessary.

J. R. Isaac has shown that the Joseph narrative reflects motifs of the kingship rituals of the *akītu* festival.[5] Her conclusion is pertinent to my theme:

> Examination of some of the myth, ritual and symbolic elements in the Joseph story makes a persuasive argument that the literature of Mesopotamia was also the literature of Israel and Judah, and may have been used in a variety of ways with the assumption that the audience knew the literature and would recognize the references made to the myths, whether direct or oblique.[6]

---

3. Crüsemann, *Torah*, 246–47, states concerning Deuteronomy, "The sovereignty of the people underlying the law compels us to speak of something like a democracy." PH's values, explicit or implicit, compel us to speak of something like democracy too. Thus, I sometimes use the terms "democracy" and "democratic" at the risk of being anachronistic.

4. See Turner, *Announcements of Plot*; Clines, "Theme in Genesis 1–11," 483–507; Schüle, *Prolog*.

5. Isaac, "Here Comes this Dreamer," 239–40.

6. Isaac, 246.

Along these lines, and with a number of OT scholars, I regard sixth-century Babylon as the context of the origin of PH.[7] This context is a significant factor for interpretation. Even though Israel had encountered polytheism and ANE mythology in the land of Canaan, and Israelite religion had had syncretistic elements, in Babylonia they came across Babylonian religion, culture, and politics in all their manifestations – rites, festivals, architecture, social stratification, politics. It was the worldview and the narrative of the world empire that destroyed their land and culture.

In Mesopotamia, the most important concepts fundamental for the society were kingship, city, and temple. They were correlated but, for the sake of a transparent argument, I will discuss them separately. The significance of each member of the "triad" for Mesopotamian society has been recognized and studied. However, considering them as a "triad" constitutive for PH is novel.[8] The perceived insignificance of commoners in Mesopotamia is noteworthy too.

City

In Mesopotamia, the capital city was not only the center of a country but also the nexus between the human and divine worlds. Therefore, creation in Mesopotamia was closely linked with cities. The city was regarded as sacred because the gods chose that particular location, designed it, and laid its foundations.[9] City walls were conceived of as keeping out not just military danger, but "In the Mesopotamian view, within the walls there is order, outside them is chaos. The countryside is the place where enemies, barbarians, animals, and ghosts live, all to be kept out. The walls provide that security, clearly delineating the two spheres."[10]

---

7. See Smith, *Priestly Vision of Genesis*, 78–82, 124–27. Since this study is concerned with PH against the backdrop of Neo-Babylonian Mesopotamia, I will not specify time references when referring to BC/BCE.

8. McDowell concludes her study on the image of God by stating "that the nature of the divine-human relationship as it is presented in Gen 1 had three major components which were intimately related to one another: kinship, kingship and cult" (McDowell, *Image of God*, 207). It is tempting to correlate the city-kingship-shrine triad with McDowell's "three major components" and elaborate on this correlation. The latter two concepts definitely qualify but city and kinship hardly.

9. Westenholz, "Theological Foundation," 43–44.

10. Van de Mieroop, "Reading Babylon," 265.

Cities were often known by their shrines "thus reflecting the early amalgam of the city and divinity. These cities were conceived as sacred rather than political settlements, built in pure places. . . . The glorification of the city and its temples was a major theme in the hymns which were addressed to a city or its temple."[11] The city was the sacred symbol of the society because it was the outward sign by which citizens distinguished themselves from others.[12] "The cities themselves were property of the gods and thereby holy. In many cases not only the temples, but also the holy cities, were regarded not as human-made, but rather built by the gods" or, at least, sanctioned by them.[13]

From Hammurabi's time on, Babylon achieved a crucial role so that, by the close of the second millennium, Babylon's kings had managed to promote their city and their tutelary god Marduk into the front ranks of the cosmos by creating a theological and cosmological basis for their elevation. To this end, they used myths, epics, hymns, and historiographic texts. Babylon was often identified with the archetypal primeval cities of Eridu and Nippur.[14]

> Sumerian religion crystallized in city states, each with its particular gods and cults. Mutual tolerance was manifested in a generally accepted hierarchical order of the chief gods from the different cities. While Hammurabi welded the same cities into a single Babylonian state, religion continued its city-bound organization, though quite substantial changes gradually took place in the official hierarchy. And in all matters the 1,100 years between Hammurabi and Nebuchadnezzar II witnessed tremendous development. Yet, to the end, despite the political unity based on the city of Babylon, matters of thought still reflected local attachments.[15]

The fifty-one epithets of Babylon in the Topography of Babylon, Tintir, originating probably in the twelfth century, are summarized by A. R. George:

---

11. Westenholz, "Theological Foundation," 46.
12. Westenholz, 44; cf. Clifford, *Creation Accounts*, 21–22.
13. Schaudig, "Cult Centralization," 148.
14. Hallo and Simpson, *Ancient Near East*, 49.
15. Lambert, "New Look," 289–90.

> They portray the city as a place of prosperity and happiness, of justice, freedom and beauty, whose foundation is primeval, created by the gods and chosen by them as their home; on this account it is a sacred city, a fount of life and a source of wisdom, the religious and cosmological centre of the universe, given over to the celebration of festivals and exercising control over kingship and the divine decrees which rule mankind.[16]

It seems that Tintir was designed to demonstrate that Babylon had replaced Nippur as the religious center of Babylonia just as, in the Babylonian creation story (BCS), Enlil had ceded power to Marduk.[17] The Praise of Babylon, probably composed under Sargon II,[18] extols Marduk and his sanctuary:

> May months and years bless sublime Esagila,
> May its brickwork give blessing to noble Marduk.
> At the month of life, (at?) the New Year's festival, let a
>   celebration be held,
> Let the four world regions gaze fixedly upon his features,
> May he bestow a satisfying life upon the shepherd who
>   provides for him. (lines 5–9)[19]

BCS takes as much pains to explain Babylon's origin as it does to proclaim Marduk's supremacy in the pantheon. Babylon, under Nebuchadnezzar II, reached the apex of what a city could be. It aspired to embody, with its city walls, buildings, and Marduk's sanctuary, an ordered place in a chaotic world. It housed all the gods that provided universal order; indeed, the city was a complete universe on its own.[20] J. G. Westenholz has observed that the Mesopotamian theology emphasized the divine origin of the city thus legitimating "the urban character of civilized society."[21] City, its sanctuary, and the divine realm had a close interrelationship; the city's well-being depended on the right relationship to the city's god.[22]

---

16. George, *Babylonian Topographical Texts*, 8.
17. George, 6.
18. Foster, *Before the Muses*, 876.
19. Foster, 754.
20. Van de Mieroop, "Reading Babylon," 273.
21. Westenholz, "Theological Foundation," 51.
22. Westenholz, 51.

Since "city" was a theologically loaded concept in Mesopotamia, founding a city entailed, more often than not, imperial attitudes, tendencies of supremacy, and proneness to rivalry. From Sargon on, all the

> kings shared a common vision: to realize, no matter, how briefly or ephemerally, the perennial ideal of Mesopotamian unity. Whether they succeeded or perished in the attempt, their memory apparently intrigued later generations beyond that of the more typical, but duller, periods of fragmentary petty statism that intervened.[23]

This view of cities had the consequence that urban life was seen as superior to the nomadic. Nomads were regarded as uncivilized, a threat to society. "Mesopotamian theology that is reflected in most of the mythology of Babylon and Assyria has an urbanized society as its foundation."[24] Cities were governed by kings, making kingship another significant concept.

Kingship

Kingship and capital cities in the Sumerian king list (SKL) and other works are intimately interrelated.[25] A. L. Oppenheim hits the nail on the head by considering them "The institutionalization of the desire for continuity in Mesopotamia."[26] Once elective kingship was replaced by hereditary kingship in Mesopotamia, the tendency of kings to claim divine backing was inevitable. "Achievement of this end required a firm alliance of royal and religious interests, including a whole new ideology, or theology, of kingship."[27]

In Mesopotamia, a kingless society was one in which humans were without guidance, thus leading a miserable life;[28] this is also suggested by a reconstructed part of the Sumerian flood story (SFS).[29] The purported significance of kings is tangible in genealogies. Genealogy was a "royal genre." King

---

23. Hallo and Simpson, *Ancient Near East*, 46.
24. Walton, " Mesopotamian Background," 165.
25. Miller, "Eridu, Dunnu, and Babel," 237–38.
26. Oppenheim, *Ancient Mesopotamia*, 79.
27. Hallo and Simpson, *Ancient Near East*, 46.
28. Cf. Speiser, "Ancient Mesopotamia," 50.
29. See Jacobsen, "Eridu Genesis," 516.

lists testified to unity and authority.³⁰ Not just that, since the Amorite ethos emphasized genealogy and ancestor worship genealogy was employed to political ends.³¹ The underlying agenda of the SKL was geographical power.³² Akkadian lists show a genealogical interest with genealogies serving similar ends. The SKL's reference to kingship's heavenly origin implied that the office was of divine origin and not the office-holder.³³ The "basic ideology of the Sumerian King List involves more than a zealous theory; we may be dealing with a current norm of political thought, a widely accepted political idea which cherished the concept of long-continued unification of the land."³⁴ In Mesopotamia, genealogies were never used to structure narratives or link narrative units.³⁵ Segmented genealogies, seldom stretching beyond three generations, were much less frequent and were hardly preserved and used politically.³⁶

In Babylon, history began with kings.³⁷ In creation accounts kings are "created separately in order to oversee the human race's service of gods."³⁸ Batto notes that, "in Mesopotamian myth at least, kingship was a necessary part of – even the apex of – the creation of humankind."³⁹ Not surprisingly, "the builders and rulers of the great cities were remembered in the tradition as either kings, or gods, or both."⁴⁰ Thus, as Westermann comments, "This is the reason why in Egypt and Mesopotamia, after the genealogies of the gods, it is

---

30. Hallo, "Royal Hymns," 175–76.
31. Hallo, "Royal Ancestor Worship," 400.
32. See Wilcke, "Genealogical and Geographical," 557–71.
33. See Wilson, *Genealogy*, 81.
34. Hartman, "Some Thoughts," 27. Regarding the early kings in SKL, Jacobsen claims that it was compiled at the inauguration of the Neo-Sumerian period at Uruk. With their independence from the Guti re-established, Sumer sought to express national feelings and unity by reflecting on its past and the restoration of kingship (Jacobsen, *Sumerian King List*, 140–41). Disagreeing with Jacobsen, Kraus dates it at the beginning of the Old-Babylonian dynasty (Kraus, "Zur Liste der älteren Könige," 46–51). Be that as it may, the origin of SKL is bound up with the beginning and legitimizing of a new era.
35. Wilson, *Genealogy*, 135.
36. Wilson, 196.
37. See Lambert and Millard, *Atra-Ḫasis*, 15.
38. Clifford, *Creation Accounts*, 143.
39. Batto, "Divine Sovereign," 179.
40. Miller, "Eridu, Dunnu, and Babel," 240.

the genealogies of the kings that are of importance, that is, merit being part of tradition. After the origin, the only real history is the history of the kings."[41]

In the late Assyrian epic Creation of the King, the creation of a king is narrated in the fashion of the creation of the first humans.

> Belet-ili fashioned the king, the counsellor-man,
> They [the gods] gave the king warfare on behalf of the [great] gods.
> Anu gave his crown, Enlil ga[ve his throne],
> Nergal gave his weapon, Ninurta gave [his splendor],
> Belet-ili gave [his] fea[tures],
> Nusku commissioned a (wise) counsellor and he stood in attendance upon him.
> He who shall speak [lies and falsehood] to the king,
> Be [he important, he shall die violently],
> [Be he rich, he will become poor].
> [He who shall harbor evil against the king in his heart],
> [Erra will call him to account in a plague].
> [He who shall think disrespectful thoughts of the king,
> a whirlwind shall crush him,
> his accumulated goods shall be a puff of wind].
> [The gods of heaven and netherworld assembled],
> [They blessed the king, the counsellor-man],
> [They delivered the weapon of combat and battle into his hand],
> [They gave him the people of this land, that he serve as their shepherd]. (lines 36–52)[42]

In the epic The Return of Lugalbanda, King Enmerkar of Uruk lays siege to Aratta. After a long, futile siege, he complains to his tutelary goddess, Inanna by recounting how he built his capital city Uruk.

> Once upon a time my noble sister, Holy Inana,
> From her bright mountain chose me in her holy heart
> And made me enter Kulab [possibly Uruk], the Brickwork.

---

41. Westermann, *Genesis 1–11*, 8.
42. Foster, *Before the Muses*, 496–97.

> Unug [i.e., Uruk] then was a mere marsh, oozing water.
> Where there was dry land Euphrates poplars grew.
> Where there was a reed thicket old and young reeds grew together.
> Enki, king of Eridug,
> Made me tear out the old reeds and made me drain the water.
> Fifty years I was building, fifty years I was working.
> So now, if eventually in all of Sumer and Akkad
> The Martu, who know no grain, should rise up,
> There stands the wall of Unug, extended across the desert like a bird net! (lines 294–305)[43]

Then comes the complaint proper,

> But here, in this place, my power seems to be finished!
> My troops are bound to me as a calf to its mother.
> Yet, like a child that hates its mother and leaves the city
> My noble sister, Holy Inana,
> Has run back to Kulab, the Brickwork!
> Could she love her city, yet hate me?
> She should link the city to me!
> Could she hate her city, yet love me?
> She should link the city to me!
> Should the n u – g i g [i.e., Inana]—as happened to the Anzud chick—
> Reject me in person
> And abandon me by keeping to her holy chamber . . . (lines 306–18)[44]

The king's question is rhetorical with a firm answer in the negative expected. City, kingship, and tutelary deity are closely interrelated. City is as much linked to the king, and vice versa, as the love of the patron deity to the city. A claim to a tutelary deity was a power claim as well.

The king performed cultic duties as intermediary between the gods and the people; he represented the entire nation. He was a corporate personality and

---

43. Vanstiphout, *Epics of Sumerian Kings*, 151, 153.
44. Vanstiphout, 153.

functioned as an intermediary between the divine and the political spheres.[45] "He is the personification of the kingdom, and his kingdom is the image of heavenly dominion; accordingly, the king is seen as the 'perfect likeliness [sic] of the god.'"[46] Akkadian texts do not demonstrate that the subjects "are the primary concern of royal dominion. That has to be proved in the temples, at court, and in impressive deeds of warfare and building activities."[47] Spieckermann argues that,

> Pondering all these entities essential for royal dominion, one cannot avoid the conclusion that the king's responsibility for a people or a nation does not hold an influential position neither under the ideological aspect of kingship nor in reality. Subjects are necessary to exercise kingship. However, they are not the primary concern of royal dominion. They testify to the fact that a king has been bestowed with dominion according to divine will.[48]

As a consequence of centralized government, the general public were disenfranchised. Commoners were but cogs in the machine of a society founded on and made functioning by royal figures. In Mesopotamia, we can see a steady process of centralization of power in city states ruled by an individual who was the supreme commander of the armed forces, administrator of the main sanctuary, and lawgiver authorized by the gods. At the beginning, this idea manifested itself in city states. Later on, however, it compelled cities to subdue each other and form a single centralized state – an empire.[49]

There is no sign of democratic ideas and institutions gaining ground.[50] No wonder that in the developing monarchies of ANE, kings were increasingly responsible to gods instead of the general public.[51] Over time, this state of affairs entailed gradually imperialistic politics and religion. "The conclusion

---

45. See Frankfort, *Kingship and the Gods*, 251–61.

46. Spieckermann, "God and His People," 349–50. Holloway notes that this leads to a blurring of the distinctions between gods and kings (Holloway, *Aššur is King!*, 178–93). He concludes that "we must accept the existence of divinized royal images of living kings in the Neo-Assyrian temple system, and elsewhere" (Holloway, 187).

47. Spieckermann, "God and His People," 350–51.

48. Spieckermann, 351.

49. Jacobsen, "Primitive Democracy," 159–60.

50. Jacobsen, 165; cf. Jacobsen, "Political Institutions," 65–66.

51. Jacobsen, "Early Political Development," 126.

seems warranted that ancient Mesopotamia experienced all but one of what has been called the five basic stages of Greek constitutional development: only democracy failed to appear."[52]

Since kingship and religion in Sumer (and in larger Mesopotamia) were intricately interrelated, for the sake of both, I will turn my attention to shrine.[53]

Shrine

> Nebuchadnezzar, the righteous king, faithful shepherd who leads the peoples, director of the regions belonging to Bel, Šamaš, and Marduk, the contented, seeker after wisdom, regardful of life, exalted one who wearies not, caretaker of Esagila and Ezida, son of Nabopolassar king of Babylon am I.
>
> When Marduk, the great lord, exalted me over the kingdoms of the land and gave me many peoples to shepherd, before Marduk, my divine creator, in fear I bowed; to bear his yoke I bent my neck. His numerous monthly offerings, his pure free will ? offerings, I rendered greater than before. [. . .]
>
> E-temin-anki, *zikkurat* of Babylon, in joyful gladness I built. As to Babylon, the city of the great lord Marduk, Imgur-Bêl, its great wall, I finished. Upon the thresholds of the great gates mighty bulls of bronze and terrible serpents [*mušḫuššu*] standing upright I placed. Its moat I dug and reached the water level; therein I built with mortar and burnt brick.[54]

This part of the inscription, dating between 600–593 BCE and representative of Neo-Babylonian inscriptions, contains various references pertaining to my discussion.[55] Here, Nebuchadnezzar II lists his achievements. Foremost among them are those related to religion. In Sumer, temple building was associated with creation. The temple was considered "the concrete expression of the finality of the creation."[56] Therefore, temple construction was seen as a

---

52. Bailkey, "Early Mesopotamian Constitutional Development," 1235. The five stages being, monarchy, oligarchy, tyranny, democracy, and a return to tyranny (Bailkey, 1211).
53. Hallo, "Sumerian Religion," 93–111.
54. Langdon, *Building Inscriptions*, 83, 85.
55. Langdon, 21–22.
56. Clifford, *Creation Accounts*, 26, 61.

major duty of kings as the head of a state and servants of gods.[57] Indeed, no "greater service could be rendered to a god than the building of his house."[58] Constructing temples was commenced with festive rituals, carefully and usually executed by kings, and there were ceremonial feasts when they were dedicated.[59] In Babylon, it was not any different.

Under Nabupolossar and Nebuchadnezzar II, the "ancient cradle of the North Semitic races became once more, under the leadership of Babylon, the centre of the Semitic world, and the ancient shrines became the object of even greater veneration than they had been in the days of Assyrian dominion."[60] Owing to the diverse capabilities attributed to him, Marduk had achieved a dominant and decisive status in the Babylonian pantheon by the first millennium with his supremacy reaching its final and highest climax under Nebuchadnezzar II.[61] By the sixth century, Marduk was seen as the savior of the universe and creator of humankind.[62]

Marduk's son, Nabu also played a prominent role in Neo-Babylonian culture. The god of wisdom and science, he gained a prestigious status under Nabupolossar. Owing to his influence on human destiny in particular, Nabu was venerated in Babylonia and beyond. When mentioned along with Marduk, he always precedes his father.[63] This does not seem to have changed under Nebuchadnezzar's reign. The "holy triad" of city-kingship-temple was spectacularly underpinned by Nebuchadnezzar who created a center for his empire in Babylon by reconstructing the Etemenanki and building his palace: one god, one king, one temple, one palace.[64]

City, king, and shrine were always the beginning of Mesopotamian city states. Thus, Frankfort's claim that in Mesopotamia there was no "reference

---

57. With no attempt at comprehensiveness, George, *House Most High*, lists more than 1,200 temple names in Sumerian and Akkadian literary works.

58. Frankfort, *Kingship and the Gods*, 267.

59. See Hurowitz, *I have Built You an Exalted House*, 39–41. Cf. King Gudea's plan to build a temple to his patron deity Ninĝirsu and Gudea's consultation with various deities to implement the plan; see Black, Cunningham, Robson, and Zólyomi, *Literature of Ancient Sumer*, 44. After the divine approval, "In our city there was perfection" (Black, Cunningham, Robson, and Zólyomi, 45).

60. Langdon, *Building Inscriptions*, 1.

61. Sommerfeld, "Marduk," 362, 366.

62. See Black, "New Year Ceremonies," 40.

63. Langdon, *Building Inscriptions*, 4.

64. Schaudig, "Cult Centralization," 159–61.

to a primeval plan, an order established at the time of creation"[65] is only half true. It is certainly correct that, as opposed to Egypt, Mesopotamia did not view the universe as static. Also true is that in Mesopotamia "the gods had decreed justice as the order of society. They desired their elected ruler to be a just king and persecuted injustice wherever it occurred."[66] Still, one finds little sign of this divine concern as translated into social practice. Religion and piety were manifestations of the divine world order in which divine intention and action were attributed much more significance than human initiative.[67] This latter was subordinated to the divine. In general terms, the vertical aspects of religion were overemphasized at the cost of the horizontal. This is only partly explained by the fact that "the Mesopotamian did not presume that the gods themselves were bound by any order which man could comprehend."[68] Still, Mesopotamia's dynamic worldview was, to a considerable degree, rendered static by the significance of cities, kings, and temples assigned to them by virtue of their primeval origin. Having discussed the concepts of city, kingship, and religion, I will discuss the role of commoners.

Commoners

The word "commoner," I use in the sense of an individual belonging to the lower classes in Mesopotamian society. The briefness of my discussion is due to the perceived insignificance of commoners in Mesopotamian society. A. R. George highlights this:

> Palaces and temples were the chief patrons of both arts and letters in Sumer and Akkad – and then as now, he who pays the piper calls the tune. As a result we unfortunately know less than we would like about the common man: his concerns, his aspirations, his reactions to life. These matters figure in literature only or chiefly in proverbs and other types of so-called wisdom texts, numerically a relatively small literary genre.[69]

---

65. Frankfort, *Kingship and the Gods*, 270.
66. Frankfort, 278.
67. See Frankfort, 270,
68. Frankfort, 270. Strikingly, Frankfort's discussion of "Cosmic Powers and Social Justice" (277–81) contains very little of what a modern reader would expect.
69. Hallo, "Birth of Kings," 223; cf. Hallo, "Sumerian Religion," 664.

Apart from gods and demigods, it was kings, and sometimes sages and priests, who gained relevance in society and culture – they were the organizing and sustaining powers of society. No narrative on commoners has come to light; no significance was attributed to them.

Myths and Genealogies

The fabric of Mesopotamian society was sewn up by mythic epics, hymns, and genealogies, providing for the ideological cohesion of society. The Israelite exiles would inevitably get acquainted with them in sixth-century Babylonia. The BCS was a narrative authorized by the empire at the New Year festival in Babylon where it was recited and enacted, with royal participation. The Gilgamesh epic had gained a status of holy script by this time. Gilgamesh was known as a king and demigod, or superhuman force of evil, as late in antiquity as 200 CE and beyond.[70] The Epic of Gilgamesh deals with universal questions like friendship, mortality, heroism, and achievement in life. In this respect, Genesis, and PH in particular, proves an appropriate counterpart to the epic. Judging on the basis of extant manuscripts, the BCS and Gilgamesh were the most popular Mesopotamian epics at the time of the exile.[71] Atrahasis too was well-known.[72]

The narratives of PH are mythical.[73] The mythic genre of PH means that, as opposed to the genre of historical narrative from 11:27,[74] not every detail begs questions for explanation. In myths, "any single act can be unmotivated and unreasonable in itself, provided it is effective in setting up the explanation of the ensuing acts."[75] Indeed, we are model readers of Genesis 1–11, to use Umberto Eco's phrase,[76] if we do not want to know where evil came from in God's world created good, how the serpent could talk, where on earth could Cain acquire a wife, etc. For this very reason, we ask in vain why Cain and Abel sacrificed to God since they had not received any cultic instruction;

---

70. See George, *Babylonian Gilgamesh Epic*, vol. 1, 54–70.
71. See George, 39.
72. For the historical dependence of the Genesis flood story on Atrahasis and Gilgamesh, see Kvanvig, *Primeval History*, 224–33, with a nice list and discussion of parallels.
73. I also like "protohistory" coined by Wenham, "Genesis 1–11 as Protohistory," 85–88.
74. See Blenkinsopp, *Creation, Un-Creation*, 1.
75. Liverani, "Adapa," 6.
76. Eco, *Role of the Reader*.

what known command Cain transgressed by killing his brother, or how God can be revered by our reverence for life (see 9:6) as God himself had asked for nothing of this kind in the narrative.[77] In myth, many an odd detail is taken for granted and left unexplained in order to give an account of why the world is like it is.

Whereas myths are implicit building stones of PH, genealogies are explicit and a quite extensive part, some three chapters are dedicated to genealogy. Even though commentaries discuss at length the names in the genealogies, and the general situation has changed since Westermann's statement in 1972 (German edition), one has still the impression that the genealogies themselves have "no determining theological significance."[78] There were two sorts known in ancient Mesopotamia, vertical (or linear) and segmented genealogies.

Let us start with Wilson's observation. He notes a change in the use of genealogy during the Old Babylonian dynasty.

> The Amorites may have once used segmented genealogies for political purposes. However, when Amorite kings came to power in the heartland of Mesopotamia, these segmented genealogies ceased to function politically in the new monarchical context. Linear genealogies, through which the kings justified their right to rule, replaced segmented genealogies.[79]

Mesopotamian genealogies, Mesopotamian king lists (MKLs) and SKLs included, were mostly linear.[80] In contrast, West Semitic lists (WSLs) were most often segmented,[81] sometimes combined. Malamat gives a helpful account of the role of each:

> Vertical, one-dimensional patterns record only "genealogical depth" and sequence of generations, while the two-dimensional pattern forms points of segmentation; that is, it encompasses nodal eponyms from which stem several descendants who in turn may act as founding ancestors of peoples, tribes and clans,

---

77. Miles, *God*, 41, 44.
78. Westermann, *Genesis 1–11*, 3.
79. Wilson, "Between 'Azel' and 'Azel,'" 17.
80. Wilson, *Genealogy*, 57.
81. See Levin, "Understanding Biblical Genealogies," 12.

such as Terah, Abraham, Isaac, Jacob, and his twelve sons, in the Bible. This segmentation, with its wide range of primary and secondary lineages, is the foremost concept in the genealogical positioning of the individual and in the ascertaining of kinship, whether on a broad ethnographic plane or within a more restricted tribal circle.[82]

The Pentateuch uses "linear genealogies to define chronologies, and segmented genealogies to define ethnicity and the relationships between Israel and the nations."[83] Not just that, nearly all longer ANE genealogies are concerned with "office holders, usually kings but also priests and scribes."[84] In PH, however, all genealogies list common people. Thus, these genealogies are an indicator of how PH, as opposed to Mesopotamia, views culture, kingship, and society.

In Genesis, we have both segmented and linear genealogies, often but not always introduced by the ancestor, that focus on the descendants of a certain character.[85] It may cautiously be stated that segmented genealogies represent family lines, whose members will cease to play any significant role after the genealogy; whereas linear genealogies point ahead, their final member will be the protagonist in the next narrative. This is not to say that characters of segmented genealogies do not count. They indeed do by representing generations of the earth hence providing a universal outlook.[86] Still, they present inorganic material for the plot, and do not explicitly contribute to it. The lines of Cain (4:17–24), Ham, Japhet, and Shem (10:1–32), Ishmael (25:12), and Esau (36:1, 9) are dead ends. The exception to the rule, through Shem's linear genealogy, is Terah, whose line produces Abram, predecessor of Israel, and Lot, predecessor of Ammon and Moab (11:27–32). In contrast, Seth's line (ch. 5) produces Noah, savior of humankind. It is true that Lot gets his share as Abram's sidekick, but he exits the scene after his semi-genealogy in 19:37–38. In 29:31–30:24, Jacob's genealogy is segmented, implying an emphasis on his family – henceforth the focus is on Israel as a family and, from Exodus on, as

---

82. Malamat, "King Lists," 164; cf. Wilson, " Old Testament Genealogies," 169–89.
83. Levin, "Understanding Biblical Genealogies," 40.
84. Hess, "Genealogies of Genesis," 247.
85. See Carr, "Βίβλος γενέσεως Revisited (Part One)," 163.
86. See Carr, "Βίβλος γενέσεως Revisited (Part Two)," 328.

a nation (cf. Exod 1:1–5 and Num 3:1).[87] Noah (6:9), Isaac (25:19), and Joseph, (37:2) receive the focus by their respective *toledot* formulas. Note that Seth's, Isaac's, and Jacob's "genealogies" are preceded by the dead-end genealogies of Cain, Ishmael, and Esau, that happen to be those of the older brothers.[88]

By the application of the *toledot* formula it is emphasized that Abraham, and through him the people Israel, are linked to the creation of heaven and earth. The first of these formulas in 2:4, "This is the genealogy of heaven and earth" (AT) reports the creation of Adam whose genealogy leads to Noah, whose genealogy in turn leads to the forefather of Israel. This is a shrewd renunciation of royal genealogies like SKL that claim heavenly origins. In Genesis, humankind in general has heavenly origins albeit in a different sense than in other ANE accounts.

The *toledot* formula is a colophon, a heading of a new tablet. While a colophon in the Neo-Babylonian period only occasionally gives the name of the owner of the tablet, it almost always contains its scribe, along with their genealogy.[89] In this light, it is remarkable that the colophons of PH (i.e. the *toledot*) refer to neither of these but instead state, "This is the *toledot* of N," with the genealogy following not that of the scribe but of N.

Last but not least, Richard Hess cautions,

> Even the formal study of the biblical genealogies is not completely adequate. It is at once too broad and too narrow. It is too broad in that it ignores the basic components which form the genealogies, the personal names themselves. It is too narrow in that it fails to examine the narrative context of Gen 1–11 and how the genealogies fit therein.[90]

I will interpret the PH genealogies against their ANE background as well as their canonical context.

---

87. See Carr, "Βίβλος γενέσεως Revisited (Part One)," 171.
88. See Carr, 166.
89. Leichty, " Colophon," 151.
90. Hess, "Genealogies of Genesis," 253.

Rites

The most important occasion reflecting and defining society and religion in Babylon was the New Year or *akītu* festival.[91]

> The rituals involving the renewal of the king, the crucial role of the high priest in the ceremonies, and the two days of "determining of the destinies" functioned more to reinforce the ideology and agenda of the monarchy and the priesthood than to instill religious sentiment. Ostensibly dealing with the renewal of charter for kings, the *akītu* also involves aspects of legitimization of the Mesopotamian kings. The celebration of the *akītu* was an integral component in royal politics, both domestic and foreign. The continuity and the widespread dissemination of the festival throughout Mesopotamian history attest to its religious, political, and sociological import.[92]

It was increasingly politicized in the Neo-Babylonian era and maintained class distinction by providing the monarch a divinely ordered opportunity to boast of his own wealth and his own military achievements. The *akītu* was the most popular festival in Mesopotamia.[93]

In the festival, religious, political, and social aspects went hand in hand. The *akītu* provided the king with a golden opportunity publicly to demonstrate his concern for the wider populace of Babylon. Through the rituals of the *akītu*, the king reaffirmed to the entire society their inclusion even though in reality he was promoting the interests of the elite only. But in this way the *akītu* created social cohesion – sanctuary and kingship together provided the symbol of unity in Babylon. The BCS was enacted at the *akītu* and demonstrated that social reality was rooted in the cosmogonic myth.[94]

In the BCS, Marduk forms the world from the corpse of Tiamat the chaos monster. The world thus contains traces of primordial chaos, personified by Tiamat, as well as order, imposed on it by Marduk. In light of this aspect of the

---

91. The New Year festival took place in Neo-Babylonian times, 625–539, perhaps dating back to as early as 750; Lambert, "Myth and Ritual," 106. As a reference point in PH, this may also support PH's Babylonian provenance.

92. Bidmead, *Akītu Festival*, 2.

93. Bidmead, 5.

94. Bidmead, 170–72.

BCS, the *akītu* festival does not simply commemorate a primordial triumph over chaos, for chaos always lurks latently in the world. Rather, the festival sets into motion the ongoing victory over disorder. The disorder inherent in the world created from Tiamat's corpse did not evenly affect the cosmos: order was particularly present in the Esagila, while the area outside Babylon was conceived ritually as a domain of chaos.[95] Marduk's journey outside the city walls to the *akītu* house allows chaos to return to the city, while

> his return to the city at the end of the festival represents the triumph of order. Thus in the Babylonian Akitu the processions away from and back to the city on the eighth through eleventh of Nisan serve the same function as the events of the fifth: they recalled Marduk's original and ongoing victory over chaos as narrated in *Enuma Elish*.[96]

In the *akītu* itself, only citizens of status were allowed to participate in the procession, with the common citizens looking on.[97]

Another significant rite was the *mīs pî* or mouth washing ritual. The ritual is summarized by Schüle. (1) In the workshop of the city temple, craftsmen shape the wooden image and cover it with gold and precious stones. When finished, its mouth is washed and opened, then the image is set on a base. (2) From the workshop the image is carried through the desert to the river and from the river to a garden. (3) Arriving at the garden, the central place of the ritual, a place of plants and animals, a series of mouth washings is performed. It spends the rest of the day, the night, and a good part of the next day in the garden. The gods come there to accept the image. They spend the night in its company so providing perfect purity by which it is rid of any trace of human work. (4) Finally, it has to reach its final destination, the holy of holies in the temple where it will from now on reside. The ritual's significance for the creation of humankind in Genesis 2 will be discussed in due course.[98]

---

95. Pongratz-Leisten, *Ina šulmi īrub*, 77–78, 73–74.
96. Sommer, "Babylonian Akitu Festival," 81–95, 89–90.
97. Bidmead, *Akītu Festival*, 171.
98. Schüle, "Made in the 'Image of God,'" 12–13; Schüle, *Prolog*, 161–63; cf. Berlejung, *Theologie der Bilder*, 178–283; Walker and Dick, "Induction of the Cult," 68–72; McDowell, *Image of God*, 43–85.

Reading the Primeval History against a Babylonian Backdrop

The dividing of PH into creation, multiplication of humankind, and flood draws on ancient Sumerian-Akkadian traditions that belonged to the worldview of Mesopotamians but became obsolete after the collapse of Babylon. Similarly, the significance of genealogies like the SKL and, along with it, of numerology finds no echo in a post-Babylonian audience. Accounts and themes like creation or flood and motifs such as the tree of life, the serpent, the rainbow are modeled on Babylonian parallels – most important among them being the BCS, Atrahasis, Gilgamesh, and, to a lesser extent, Adapa, with explicit or implicit references to them. The sophistication of the number system along with the significance accorded to numbers and mathematics in Babylonia points in the same direction. Thus, we see themes and motifs that imply a Neo-Babylonian origin.

Kingship and state were in crisis at several points in Mesopotamian history, producing various sorts of literature envisaging a better future. Still, the "hypostatic" significance of the city-kingship-temple triad based on Babylonian ideology is a product of the earlier, Assyrian-Babylonian period only. The PH is not just envisaging a better future, it is much more systematic, comprehensive, and coherent. I will demonstrate how PH endorses values by reconstructing an alternative world to that based on the Mesopotamian triad.

In my view, PH obtained its nearly final shape during the Neo-Babylonian period. Assessing the evidence, this conclusion seems compelling. The allusions and references to Babylonian mythology suggest a Babylonian origin. We can see this in the first creation story already, traditionally assigned to the priestly source.[99] By its allusions, Genesis 1 polemicizes with the Babylonian worldview and world order as presented by the BCS. PH was drafted in order to confront Babylon. Having said this, I do not claim that PH, Genesis, or the Pentateuch was not reedited in post-exilic times. Indeed, it went through a process of editorial work in the post-Babylonian era.[100]

---

99. There is a general agreement on the dating of P "that the bulk of it was written in the exile or early post-exilic period" (Carr, *Hebrew Bible*, 216).

100. Cf. Carr, *Introduction to the Old Testament*, 207–22; see also Carr, *Formation*. Croatto argues for Persian provenance of the Pentateuch as a "counter-text." The data he lists, however, concern Babylonian religion and worldview, not Persian (Croatto, "Reading the Pentateuch," 383–400). After surveying the evidence, Uehlinger, comes to the conclusion that the reference

Literature Survey

Scholars concerned with the theology of PH have made compelling arguments for PH's exilic provenance, so this view is adopted here.[101] It is also my conviction that, without the comparative material of ANE myths, rituals, and concepts, PH cannot be interpreted. For this reason, both synchronic and comparative studies will be used and discussed. In addition, I consider it heuristic if not indispensable to read the narrative in a way that is sensitive to its political values, whether overt or covert. A story composed by those vanquished and exiled by a world empire can be expected to express their views on that empire.

Synchronic Approaches

In what follows, I will survey synchronic studies on the plot and, then, on the structure of PH.

The Theme/Plot of the Primeval History

Until recently, PH was generally seen as a collection or montage of narratives, genealogies, sources, traditions of diverse origin, with no unitary theme or purpose attributed to it. Summing up the overall approach up to the mid-1970s, Gary Smith is on the mark: "because of the variety of literary *genres* and the broad scope of divergent topics, few have treated the unit as a structural whole."[102] Indeed, the impression one gets by reading commentaries from

---

to kiln-fired brick and tar (11:3) implies a Neo-Babylonian context, probably the reign of Nebuchadnezzar II (Uehlinger, *Weltreich*, 360–72). But the story attained its final shape and import as a failed attempt at world dominion in the Persian era (572–83). Schüle deems the lack of reference to Persia in ch. 10 as a matter of course as Elam and Media, the neighbor countries are there (Schüle, *Prolog*, 371–72). This is the more baffling as he concludes that the subtext of the genealogy concerns itself with "the role of empires and Israel's relationship to other people" (Schüle, 372). To be sure, this silence can be attributed to the editors' more amicable attitude to Persian administration; see Carr, *Formation*, 205–207. Persia is neither implicitly nor explicitly referred to in PH nor mentioned in the genealogies. Even (possible) Arabian and Armenian tribes and Elam are referred to but not Persia. Thus, this procedure demonstrates a methodological fallacy. J, for instance, does not know the "image of God" formula thus has a different theological concept. Exodus tradition does not know of creation, therefore it has a different concept. P is unaware of the conquest, therefore it has a different concept. On the other hand, PH's unawareness of Persia does not posit a non-Persian background. This sort of argument is fallacious.

101. E.g. Batto, *Slaying the Dragon*, 73–101; LaCocque, *Trial of Innocence*; Smith, *Priestly Vision of Genesis*.

102. Smith, "Structure and Purpose," 310; his emphasis.

before that time is that PH is dealt with, even when stated to the contrary, as a patchwork of unrelated traditions or sources. One finds no answer to questions such as Why did the author pick these sources/traditions? In what way did these stories relate to his putative context?[103] What story did he want to tell? What is PH all about? In what way does PH introduce Genesis and the Pentateuch?[104]

Starting in the mid-1970s, the approach to PH changed. Without denying diverse sources or traditions, there has since been an increasing tendency to read PH as a coherent narrative with a theme addressing a particular existential situation. After considering biblical scholarship's proper concern with the origins and background of different units and their ANE parallels, Sasson notices this shift by stating that

> it is equally important a task to outline the frameworks of overarching, architectonic structure within Biblical narratives and to seek therein evidence for the theological presuppositions and the hermeneutical perspectives of those redactors who, by gathering the hoary traditions, by sifting from among them those which suited didactic purposes, and by shaping as well as by arranging and welding them in a manner which promoted their ideals, created a compilation of Genesis which approximates our very own.[105]

This change has come about as a result of emerging synchronic approaches and the search for the theology inherent in the narrative.

A little noticed 1975 paper by Isaac Kikawada seems to be the first attempt to make sense of the whole of Genesis 1–11 as one coherent narrative. He sees in the primeval narrative of humankind, threatened by annihilation three times but never fully realized, a pattern from Atrahasis utilized by Genesis.[106] In his 1981 article, he applies the threat-escape pattern to the whole of Genesis

---

103. For the sake of convenience, I will consider the author/narrator/editor/redactor as a male individual.

104. Writing in 1972, Westermann succinctly sums up the state of scholarship by stating that PH is "regarded as a separate element of the Pentateuch, that is, as a relatively self-contained unity, and not primarily as a part of 'Genesis'" (Westermann, *Genesis 1–11*, 2).

105. Sasson, "Tower of Babel," 213.

106. Kikawada, "Literary Convention," 3–21.

and observes recurring themes in the Torah.[107] In his 1985 book (coauthored with Arthur Quinn), Kikawada challenges the documentary hypothesis by providing alternative, literary-theological explanations of discrepancies to sources.[108] It is meant to be a "provocative challenge," as the front-page claims. However, without an exhaustive treatment of how PH came about, it falls short of providing a satisfactory alternative to the documentary hypothesis.

Although Kikawada has provided a frame, owing to his synchronic approach, he cannot, for instance, accommodate the genealogies in his scheme. Also, the historical context remains vague throughout. As a result, he fails to realize that PH is not just a nicely structured narrative modeled on ANE literature but has theological and political intentions. He also fails to attend to the aspect of how PH introduces Genesis and the Pentateuch. Still, this is an exceptional early attempt to accommodate the Atrahasis framework into PH and beyond.

In a 1976 article, devoted to Genesis 1–11, which could be considered the introduction to his 1978 book on the theme of the Pentateuch, David Clines raises the question, "What is the theme of Genesis 1–11 as it stands?" What is "theme"?[109] It is the statement of the content, structure, and development of a work. There are four questions Clines considers. (1) Can literary works have more than one theme? Theme might be sought, identified, and articulated on different levels in a literary work but it has only one theme. (2) How can theme be demonstrated? There is no way of demonstrating it for everyone's satisfaction.

> The only formal criterion for establishing a theme is: the best statement of the theme of a work is the statement that most adequately accounts for the content, structure and development of the work. To state the theme of a work is to say what it means that the work is as it is.[110]

---

107. Kikawada, "Genesis on Three Levels," 3–15.
108. Kikawada and Quinn, *Before Abraham Was*.
109. Clines, "Theme in Genesis 1–11," 483.
110. Clines, 486.

(3) How can one discover the theme? Clines' response is: through trial and error.[111] (4) Does the theme need to have been in the author's mind? Not necessarily. Authors do not always conceptualize their work. It is the critic or reader who may find the theme.

After this methodological survey and discussing three suggestions,[112] Clines proposes two themes for PH. First,

> Mankind tends to destroy what God has made good. Even when God forgives human sin and mitigates the punishment sin continues to spread, to the point where the world suffers uncreation. And even when God makes a fresh start, turning his back on uncreation forever, man's tendency to sin immediately becomes manifest.[113]

And second,

> No matter how drastic man's sin becomes, destroying what God has made good and bringing the world to the brink of uncreation, God's grace never fails to deliver man from the consequences of his sin. Even when man responds to a fresh start with the old pattern of sin, God's commitment to his world stands

---

111. Clines, "Theme in Genesis 1–11," 486. The trial-and-error "method" and phrases like "more subjective considerations" in the quotation above make Clines' inchoate approach apparent, in need of a more refined and rigorous methodology regarding theme. Whether or not independently of Clines, J. H. Sailhamer studied the first creation account as the introduction to the Pentateuch asking what the central concern or theme of "the largest meaningful unit," the Pentateuch is. He comes to a methodological conclusion similar to that of Clines and, at the same time, more practical by delineating an agenda: "The central concern of the large narrative unit is not always immediately apparent but usually becomes clearer with a trial and error effort to relate the parts to the whole." Then, he claims "that the most prominent event and the most far-reaching theme in the Pentateuch, viewed entirely 'on its own [sic], is the covenant between Yahweh and Israel established at Mount Sinai." No doubt, covenant is prominent. (Sailhamer, "Exegetical Notes," 75). But why is it more prominent than, say, land (NB: Sailhamer finds the focus of Genesis 1 on land [77–78]) or progeny; and, second, how does the creation account, given its universal perspective, relate to it? Neither question is answered by Sailhamer in a satisfying way.

112. These are, (1) sin-speech-mitigation-punishment theme; and (2) spread-of-sin, spread-of-grace theme; Clines, "Theme in Genesis 1–11," 487–502 (for both, see von Rad, *Genesis*, 152–53); (3) creation-uncreation-re-creation theme; see Blenkinsopp, "Uncreation"; Clines, "Noah's Flood," 128–42.

113. Clines, "Theme in Genesis 1–11," 502.

firm, and sinful man experiences the favor of God as well as his righteous judgment.[114]

Clines then raises two questions: (1) Where does PH end? (2) How does the theme of PH relate to that of the Pentateuch? Responding to the first question, he sees the conclusion of PH as fuzzy, making it possible for the patriarchal narrative to develop from it. As to the second question, his suggestion is rather preliminary and not as well-founded as that in his 1978 book.

Clines' 1978 book *The Theme of the Pentateuch* is a follow-up to his previous work.[115] He claims the Pentateuch's theme is threefold: the partial fulfillment of the promise of land, progeny, and the relationship of God and Israel. By starting his investigation with the patriarchal narratives, however, he first leaves chapters 1–11 "almost entirely out of account . . . partly for a logical reason: they concern a world in which the divine promise to the patriarchs has not yet been spoken, and so their theme – whatever it may be – can hardly be subsumed under that of the patriarchal promises and their (partial) fulfilments."[116] His chapter on PH, apparently discordant with the rest of the Pentateuch, is virtually identical to his 1976 paper.[117] This may be taken as a tacit acknowledgment of a failure to integrate PH in a search for Pentateuch's theme. As a result, the Pentateuch basically has two themes, one in PH and one in the rest. Clines' failure to include PH in his quest for the Pentateuch's theme may be indicative of the limits of the synchronic approach. Owing to his synchronic approach, he does not paint a detailed historical background either.

A doctoral student of David Clines, Laurence Turner set out on the path trodden by his supervisor and studied announcements of plot in Genesis, refining Clines' methodology and some of his theses.[118] He also includes PH in his study, making amends to Clines' failure. Because of his concern with the final shape, he adopts "an agnostic stance toward such questions as

---

114. Clines, 502.
115. Clines, *Theme of the Pentateuch*.
116. Clines, 66.
117. Clines, 66–68.
118. Turner, *Announcements of Plot*.

authorship, date and composition of the book" and considers source- and traditio-historical questions irrelevant.[119]

Turner is a perceptive reader keen to notice motifs, apparently insignificant details, and connections, as he tries to interpret plot and narrative. He works with no rigid methodological presuppositions.[120] Right in his second sentence, he observes, "Narratives in general have several ways of alerting readers to what is likely to transpire in the story as it unfolds, or how to make sense out of what they have just read, and Genesis itself uses several such conventions."[121] Genesis employs what Turner calls announcements of plot, that is "statements which either explicitly state what will happen, or which suggest to the reader what the major elements of the plot are likely to be."[122] The unfolding of plots, however, does not smoothly develop from the announcements. "In fact, if these truly are *plotted* narratives, we must allow for the possibility of surprise, mystery and complication, which are essential elements in any plot worthy of the name."[123] Turner finds Genesis 1:28 as the announcement of the plot of PH. It contains three imperatives to humankind: (1) be fruitful and fill the earth; (2) subdue the earth; and (3) have dominion over the animals.[124] These divine commands, however, do not prove static. The first, "fill the earth," seems to be less susceptible to change, whereas "two of the imperatives in particular (subjugation of the earth and dominion over the animals) undergo significant modification."[125]

In the final section of his conclusion, he comes closest to addressing the issue of the plot of Genesis. He claims that "the Announcements are misleading indicators of how the plot of Genesis will develop"[126] and "the plot of the Genesis stories is not predetermined by the Announcements, but neither is it completely open-ended."[127] Therefore, announcements of plot in Genesis are not foolproof indicators of what will happen but rather "may be seen

---

119. Turner, 16–17.
120. See Turner, 17–18.
121. Turner, 13.
122. Turner, 13.
123. Turner, 15; emphasis his.
124. Turner, 22–23.
125. Turner, 48–49.
126. Turner, 181.
127. Turner, 182.

as declarations of Yahweh's initial intention – what Yahweh would *like* to happen – but no more than that."[128] They are subject to modification. "The book delights in teasing its readers, forcing us to read the text closely to see what is *actually* happening and not, like many commentators, just taking statements, even divine statements, at face value."[129]

I have two remarks. The first concerns Turner's thesis. Genesis 1:28 may indeed be taken as the announcement of PH's plot. More precisely, in my view, 1:28 announces a set of plots in PH and Genesis. It does so explicitly. This is, however, not the only plot. While a narrative can have one theme only, it usually has several plots. As I argued above in a preliminary fashion, the lack of reference to city, kingship, and cult, significant Babylonian concepts, is a telltale indicator of plot in PH. Clearly, this plot is not announced in an explicit way similar to that in 1:28. Instead, it is implicitly present in PH. Indeed, one can securely argue that it is not announced at all in the way Turner defines announcement.

The second is a criticism that concerns Turner's failure to see the first eleven chapters as in some way introductory to the patriarchal narrative in general, and that of Abraham in particular. It could have been easy for him to demonstrate how the announced plot of PH is picked up by what follows but, unfortunately, he fails to read Genesis in this way. He correctly points out, for instance, the importance of land possession and the promise of nationhood for Abraham without linking them to PH's dominant theme.[130] Answering the question of whether or not there is a plot in Genesis, he postpones the answer "until the whole book has been canvassed."[131] He does not give a definite answer to this at the end but customarily speaks of the plots of Genesis, rarely of its plot, and never of theme. Since he studies four stories in Genesis but never the one and whole, he seems to imply a negative response.[132]

---

128. Turner, 182, emphasis original.
129. Turner, 82, emphasis original.
130. Turner, 58–104.
131. Turner, 15.
132. See especially Turner, 181–83.

The Structure of the Primeval History

Since my concern lies with PH as a self-contained unit, I will survey studies dealing with its structure. On the basis of repeated vocabulary and motifs in Genesis 1–2 and 8–9, apparently being unaware of Kikawada, Gary Smith has observed "striking similarities that the author places in the Adamic and Noahic stories" and divides PH into two main sections.[133] He observes eight parallels between the two stories: (1) humankind cannot live on the earth as it is covered with water, thus separation/subsiding of water is needed (1:9–10; 8:1–13); (2) the animals are brought forth to swarm on the earth (1:20–21, 24–25; 8:17–19); (3) God establishes days and seasons (1:14–18; 8:22); (4) God blesses the animals to multiply (1:22; 8:17); (5) humankind is brought forth and blessed to multiply (1:28; 9:1, 7); (6) humankind is to rule over the animals (1:28; 9:2); (7) God provides food for humankind (1:29–30; 9:3); and (8) the image of God in humankind (1:26–27; 9:6).

God's blessing, the theological emphasis in these passages, to "Be fruitful and multiply and fill the earth," is not just the key to understanding the (Priestly) writer but "the key theological focal point."[134] The genealogies in chapters 5 and 10 are the realization of God's blessing. There is a secondary theological structure subservient to the theme of God's blessing: God's curse. Following Clark,[135] Smith finds the following relationships between chapters 3 and 4: (1) Yahweh's command/decision (2:17; 4:4–5b); (2) temptation by the serpent/sin (3:4–5; 4:7); (3) act of sin (3:6; 4:8); (4) result of sin (3:7, 4:8); (5) legal investigation (3:10; 4:9); (6) excuses and denials (3:12; 4:9); (7) accusations (3:13; 4:10); (8) pronouncement of judgment (3:14–19; 4:12); (9) recognition of the justice of judgment by the guilty (3:20; 4:13–14); (10) mitigation (3:21; 4:15); and (11) execution of judgment (3:23; 4:16). In these episodes, God's curse affects humankind's relationship to God, to life and death, and to the ground.[136] In 8:21–22, the curse is removed. God elects Noah to overcome the power of curse. The curse on sin is not taken away but overcome by God's blessing righteous Noah (6:22, 7:5). Genesis 8:21 is

---

133. Smith, "Structure and Purpose," 310.
134. Smith, 311.
135. Clark, "Flood," 184–211.
136. Smith, "Structure and Purpose," 314–15.

aware of the power of sin, thus, Noah's sin comes as no surprise. Still, God's determination to bless the earth is not affected.

In Genesis 11:1–9, there is no formal curse. But humankind is in rebellion against God. God's judgment scatters humans into every part of the earth. By this action, the danger of creating another society (see 6:1–9) is avoided. The inhabitants of Babel are no longer able to do everything they intend to (11:6). Similarly to Cain, they are ejected from their former home to wander about looking for a new home. Missing in this judgment is the note of grace found after the curse of Adam, Cain, and the flood. It is not, however, that now God has no interest in the nations, for, in chapter 12, he elects another man to take the place of Adam and Noah, and it is through Abraham that God brings his blessings on the families of the earth. All in all, Genesis 1–11 is the theological foundation for the Pentateuch with blessing as a dominant concept determining the rest.

Smith's approach is novel in that it tries to make sense of the whole of PH as the introduction to the Pentateuch. Its overall structure needs, however, more elaboration. This was attempted in a 1980 essay by Jack Sasson. He has observed that, from Adam to Noah, there are ten generations just as there are from Noah to Abram. Sasson thus divides PH into two parts.[137]

i. Creation(s) 1:1–2:14	a. The flood and its aftermath 6:9–9:2
ii. Warning and covenant with man 2:15–24	b. Warning and covenant with man 9:3–17
iii. The fall 3:1–24	No equivalent
iv. Cain and Abel 4:1–16	c. Curse of Canaan 9:18–27
v. Mankind's ancestries 4:17–5:32	d. Nations of the earth 10:1–32
vi. The Nephilim 6:1–8	e. Tower of Babel 11:1–9

Sasson's attempt is to be commended in that it tries to accommodate each section of PH, despite the failure to find a neat structure where each unit has its corresponding part. His structure, however, can be improved as I will try to show. In a short essay in 1992, Anthony Tomasino made some amendments to Sasson's scheme. Pointing out similarities in vocabulary and motifs,

---

137. Sasson, "Tower of Babel."

he suggested that Noah's drunkenness is the counterpart to the fall story.[138] I will build on this observation too.

In an important article, David Carr has studied how and to what effect PH narrows its focus. Elaborating on previous studies, he has observed a parallel structure:[139]

Pre-Flood Scene Sequence	Flood/Post-Flood Scene Sequence
Programmatic creation narrative 1:1–2:3	"Descendants of Noah" 6:9–9:29
"Descendants of Heaven and Earth" 2:4–4:26	
Garden of Eden – creation 2:5–25	Flood story – first family 6:9–9:17
Garden of Eden – parents 3:1–24	
Cain and Abel – children 4:1–16	Noah and sons' story – parent and children, 9:18–29
Descendants in 4:17–26	
"Descendants of Adam" 5:1–6:8	"Descendants of Noah's sons" 10:1–11:9
Genealogy 5:1–32	Genealogy 10:1–32
Story of human community as a whole 6:1–8	Story of human community as a whole 11:1–9

This is a creation-uncreation-new creation story line, partly structured by the *toledot* headings. Both sequences conclude with a section of genealogy (5:1; 10:1). There is, however, no total correspondence between the two storylines. Carr then sets out to account for the parallels of the two sequences of creation and uncreation/re-creation to demonstrate the creation-uncreation/recreation sequence and correspondence. He finds similar correspondences between the pre-flood and post-flood scene sequences.[140] The focus on theme and correspondence in PH has become sharper since Gary Smith's first paper. I will draw and try to improve on them.[141]

---

138. Tomasino, "History Repeats," 128–30.
139. Carr, "Βίβλος γενέσεως Revisited (Part Two)," 329.
140. Carr, 330–34.
141. In a recent essay, Spoelstra, "Literary Shapes," 43–60, has suggested an additional chiastic structure of PH. I cannot give here a thoroughgoing critique of his study but he himself has spotted its weakness saying that "various elements of this detailed panelling contain

One final comment on PH's structure. To the best of my knowledge, it was Rolf Rendtorff who first proposed that PH does not consist of chapters 1–11 but ends with the flood. Humankind's history after Noah is then the introduction to the patriarchal narrative preparing Abraham's election, the story with which salvation history and Israel's story starts. J has adopted the Sumerian way of structuring history but significantly changed the concept.[142] In Sumer, for Rendtorff, the golden era was the period before the flood, later times saw only deterioration.[143] Abraham's election is not the restoration of golden times, still, salvation history starts with Israel/Abraham.[144]

Next to follow suit was Fretheim in 1969. He argued that in chapters 1–8 blessing is not mentioned and curse is decisive as opposed to chapters 9–11; the basic subject is humankind in 1–8, in 9–11 it is the nations; geographical references are vague in 1–8, while in 9–11 they are specific; in 1–8 there is no reference to Israel, while in Shem's genealogy, there is; the subject matter is universal in 1–8, while in 9–11 it is historical in character; material is drawn on ANE myths in 1–8, while 9–11 show no relation to ANE material.[145]

Similarly to Rendtorff and Fretheim, Batto, Baumgart, and Ska draw the line between PH and the rest after the flood (9:17, 9:29, and 9:19 respectively), which is not very different from my suggestion below.[146] Genesis 11:1–9 is the first story to be set in a real location,[147] with chapters 10–11 leading up to the Abraham story. Thus, they do not strictly belong to PH. I will still discuss the whole of chapters 1–11 as PH for two reasons. First, the next big section, the patriarchal narrative starts only in 11:27. Second, chapters 10–11 serve as a bridge between PH and the patriarchal narrative and as such provide essential material to round off the preceding material and prepare the

---

asymmetrical aspects, that is, details in one panel which are out of sequence with its counterpart in another panel" (46).

142. Similarly Gese, "Geschichtliches," 134–35, 142–43.

143. See also Kramer, "Man's Golden Age," 191–94.

144. Rendtorff, "Gen 8,21," 75–76. See that Alster, "Aspect of 'Enmerkar,'" 101–9; Alster, "Dilmun," 39–74; and Batto, "Paradise Reexamined," 33–66, however, contend that there was a golden era concept in Mesopotamia.

145. Fretheim, *Creation, Fall*, 21–22. Fretheim makes these observations of chs. 2–8 of J only.

146. Batto, *Slaying the Dragon*, 69, 73, 87–88; Baumgart, *Umkehr des Schöpfergottes*, 34–37; Ska, *Introduction*, 22.

147. Baumgart, *Umkehr des Schöpfergottes*, 16; cf. Uehlinger, *Weltreich*, 559.

succeeding chapters. This bridging function is visible in structural-thematic correspondences, like those between chapters 2–3 and 9:20–29 or 6:1–4 and 11:1–9 discussed below.

Synchronic approaches are keen to point out recurring motifs, themes, and key words as well as to read the text in the light of these as a unitary narrative. On the other hand, as a reaction to the preoccupation of the diachronic approach's putative settings, synchronic studies have not really dealt with the date and setting of PH. Comparative approaches make an important contribution to this aspect as well as shed light on possible parallels.

Comparative Approaches

"Perhaps the single greatest contribution to the study of Genesis 1 in the twentieth century came from comparative study with ancient Near Eastern creation texts," Mark Smith remarks, and his observation seems to hold true of PH in particular.[148] In his comprehensive 1990 study, Christoph Uehlinger investigates Genesis 11:1–9 from this perspective. He gathers massive comparative historical and linguistic evidence in support of his argument. In his view, "city and tower" is a well-attested terminology for a city with a citadel.[149] He traces and critiques the theological interpretation of human hybris in the tower project.[150] The Akkadian equivalent to the term "one mouth/one speech" (11:1, 6) stands for "being of one mind" – that is united under one ruler, either in acknowledgement of the supremacy of the ruler or in opposition to it. As such, it is often related to world dominion. "Making a name" (11:4) is likewise a political term found in the context of founding cities subsequent to military conquests. "One nation" (11:6), as a propaganda term, connotes (Israelite) deportees in construction work of the Assyrian empire. These terms are frequently used in inscriptions directly related to construction work and indirectly to world dominion.[151]

Uehlinger posits to the first layer of the story an anti-Assyrian or anti-Sargonide political motive as a reflection on the failure of the building of

---

148. Smith, *Priestly Vision of Genesis*, 293–94.
149. Uehlinger, *Weltreich*, 201–53.
150. Uehlinger, 254–90.
151. Uehlinger, 344–513.

Dur-Sharrukin by Sargon II.[152] The second level is anti-Babylonian, composed in Babylon during Nebuchadnezzar's reign or in the turmoil following his death, subsequently reworked by a pre-P author[153] until, in the Persian era, it attained its final shape and import as a failed attempt at world dominion.[154] God's intervention is not to create a multitude of languages but only to terminate the common language of the people involved in the building project. The sin of the builders is not named, like that of Sargon (consisting of or related to the profanation of Babylonian holy places), thus may not be pointed out *in concreto*, only theologically, *in abstracto*.[155]

It is hard to ignore and even harder to refute Uehlinger's linguistic and historical arguments. They are judicious as he interacts with both the comparative material and various interpretations. He is to be commended for his propensity for seeing the political dimension of the text. Less convincing are his redaction critical reconstructions. He claims, for example, that 11:4b, 8a, 9b are post-exilic additions to the story. In this way, however, he makes things unnecessarily complicated. The sentences with the verb *pûṣ* make good sense "syntactically, structurally and as regards contents, because it is part of the contrast between 'being spread' all over the earth and living as 'one people' with 'one speech' on one spot."[156] Uehlinger also suggests that the story was originally about an unnamed city that was later identified with Babylon. Kooij correctly critiques Uehlinger's position that "is based on literary-critical arguments which are too subtle or too rigid to be convincing."[157] All in all, whereas Uehlinger's strength is his work with the comparative linguistic and historical evidence, his weakness lies with the interpretation of the canonical story.[158]

Bernard Batto is one of those scholars who consistently read OT texts with ANE texts, iconography, and concepts as background. Through his interpretation, OT texts are seen as being organically related to the ANE world, while at the same time taking on novel meanings. His studies are fruits of this endeavor. His 1992 study (and particularly some aspects of it) has received

---

152. Uehlinger, 514–46.
153. Uehlinger, 546–72.
154. Uehlinger, 572–83.
155. Uehlinger, 535–36.
156. Kooij, "Story of Genesis," 34.
157. Kooij, 35.
158. Cf. Kooij, 37.

insufficient scholarly attention, in my view.[159] In chapter 1, Batto discusses myth. In chapters 2–3, he interprets the Yahwist and Priestly creation stories against a Mesopotamian background. By reading chapter 2 of Genesis against Atrahasis and chapter 1 against the BCS, Batto presents a compelling case of how the early chapters of Genesis might have been composed and what their theological intent is. He takes Atrahasis as the literary model to PH and hence draws the boundary of PH after the flood.

Batto makes important observations about the description of creation. In the first creation account, the formula *kî ṭôb* is not used in relation to the firmament (day 2) and to humankind (day 6). The first omission of the formula can be explained if we realize that the work of day 2 is completed only with the definition of the seas on day 3. But seeing creation's, and, within it, humankind's, completion on day 6 this cannot be a comprehensive explanation. A simpler explanation is that these two works were not perfect. The firmament and the abyss proved later (7:11) defective causing the flood. Humankind proved similarly defective starting in the very next episode (Gen 2–3) and resulting in the violence that effected the flood (6:11–12). Humankind's flaw, Batto goes on, was one within the humans themselves; it was not one caused by the Creator. By placing the creation story in chapter 1 before the second, the later Priestly story before the Yahwist, the author radically reshaped the message of the primeval myth. By this juxtaposition, the Yahwist's story of a humankind gradually being perfected was transformed into one of an originally perfect humankind becoming imperfect.[160]

Batto reads motifs, like the nakedness of the first couple, against their ANE background and comes to novel interpretations. Also, he interprets sections with the whole of PH in mind, thus without losing sight of the trajectory of the narrative in PH. Because of their grounded nature in ANE mythology, I will follow Batto's interpretations at several points. To be sure, the risk of using the comparative approach is to see everything in the light of comparative material. Thus, J. J. M. Roberts criticizes Batto for reading Mesopotamian concepts or ideas into the biblical text when, for example,

---

159. Batto, *Slaying the Dragon*. He is not referred to by Witte, *Die biblische Urgeschichte*; Blenkinsopp, "Post-exilic Lay Source," 49–61; Walton, *Genesis 1*; McDowell, *Image of God*. The other side of the coin is that there is no interaction by him with newer approaches to the Pentateuch.

160. Batto, *Slaying the Dragon*, 90–91.

he sees humankind's function in the J creation account as providing for the deity, a motif imported from Atrahasis.¹⁶¹

There is one aspect I am dissatisfied with. About P, Batto writes: "I will examine how the priestly additions within Genesis 1–11 changed both the storyline and the meaning of the primeval myth first penned by the Yahwist in order to meet the new existential faith needs of his community."¹⁶² This is an important aspect. Apart from a few observations, like that quoted above, however, Batto attends to this aspect indirectly only. In a characteristic way, he short-circuits this question in his last footnote of his 2000 paper, "Whether and how the Yahwist's view in this matter may be reconciled with the priestly theology of humankind's obligation to 'be fruitful and multiply and fill the earth' (Gen 1:28) are questions best left to another forum."¹⁶³ His reluctance to interpret the canonical text might be due to his methodology as he proceeds diachronically, that is, he first studies the Yahwist account and then the Priestly source. He does not concern himself with the question How did PH address the problems of the first audience? Nor What is the theological import of the final shape?

In his 1999 study on the flood narrative, Norbert Clemens Baumgart examines the final form of the text, thus preferring a synchronic approach. In his view PH concludes with the death of Noah (9:29). Both terminology and themes make PH a self-contained unit. PH takes place either everywhere or in no concrete historical location.¹⁶⁴ He elaborates on the links between chapters 10–11 and the Abraham story.¹⁶⁵ He provides a detailed analysis of the Mesopotamian background, the flood accounts in Gilgamesh and Atrahasis and relates them to Genesis.¹⁶⁶ Baumgart also discusses flood accounts and motifs in different Mesopotamian traditions like the SFS, the Erra myth, and Berossus.¹⁶⁷ He observes that Yahweh demonstrates three clearly different

---

161. Roberts, Review of *Slaying the Dragon*, 102.
162. Batto, *Slaying the Dragon*, 74.
163. Batto, "Institution of Marriage," 631n30.
164. Baumgart, *Die Umkehr des Schöpfergottes*, 5–8, 14–16. He lists 2:10–14 as an exception but I think, disregarding the Tiger and Euphrates, it is no exception either; see my discussion of the passage.
165. Baumgart, 18–28.
166. Baumgart, 419–559.
167. Baumgart, 480–90.

attitudes in the flood: punishing-attacking; benevolently turning to humankind in the punishment; and a readiness to convert to his previous behavior and revaluation of human life.[168]

Baumgart further notices that Yahweh unites in his person aspects of the three Mesopotamian deities known from Gilgamesh: Enlil, Ea, and the Mother Goddess, Ishtar/Mah/Mami/Nintu.[169] His conclusion is twofold: first, Yahweh (Enlil) seeks to destroy all creatures (6:7), on the other hand Yahweh (Ea) wants to save all life (7:1–3); and second, Yahweh's turning to Noah is his getting involved in the story to start a rescue operation for all creation. Finally, he discusses the link between ark and sanctuary from a comparative religion point of view and relates the ark with the tabernacle and the Jerusalem Temple, and provides a helpful treatment of the concepts of ark and sanctuary in Mesopotamia and Israel.[170]

There had been others first to draw attention to the connection of the *mīs pî* ritual and Genesis 2.[171] But it was Andreas Schüle who first interpreted Genesis 2 in the light of the *mīs pî* comprehensively. Schüle sees the P material as temporally preceding J in Genesis 1–3 – where chapters 2–3 are a corrective of the high and general view of humankind created in the image of God. Based on the similarity with the *mīs pî* ritual, his argument is that the creation of humankind in Genesis 2 proceeds in a way where

> God *reacts* and *corresponds* to Adam's needs and desires which he did not anticipate. From a certain point on the *creation* of man becomes more than his *making*. This is to say that *within the space of God's creating* humans start to respond to *their being created*. Adam's longing for a "corresponding other" and his desire for what the tree of wisdom has to offer are such instances of human response that make God change the course of his working on Adam.[172]

---

168. Baumgart, 135–52.

169. Baumgart, 422–27.

170. Baumgart, 496–559.

171. McDowell, *Image of God*, 15–16, finds the first studies relating the ritual and Genesis 2 in Müller, "Neue Parallelen," 195–204; Niehr, "In Search of Yhwh's Cult," 73–95; Berlejung, *Theologie der Bilder*.

172. Schüle, "Made in the 'Image of God,'" 18–19, his italics.

Thus, human responsiveness is crucial for the understanding of the story.

The mouth washing ritual was performed not just on idols but on several other objects and living beings as well.[173] This ritual thus seems to have played a significant role in ancient Mesopotamia. Still, by alluding to both Atrahasis and the *mīs pî* ritual, the narrator shrewdly attacked Babylonian religion and worldview.

After discussing Uehlinger, Schüle attributes universal significance to 11:1–9.[174] The city with its tower stands for empire, the endeavor of humankind is to build empires. Assyria, Babylonia, Persia are but the historical expressions of this endeavor. The story is neither polemical nor political. Rather, the main intention of humankind is to avoid being scattered. Genesis 11:1–9 reflects an attempt at coming to terms with the political situation of the Persian era. Its idiosyncrasy is that it does not expect the fate of post-exilic Jewry to change in the present or future, still is convinced that history is in the hand of the Creator God.

Schüle sees PH as a prologue to both the Pentateuch and the OT in that in its way it reflects the threefold division of the canon.[175] To achieve this interpretation, historical background is sketched in rather vague terms and a more universal message is conveyed, usually of the Persian period.

The Narrator's Literary Strategy

How could Jewish exiles living in Babylonia express their religious conviction? How could they formulate their criticism of the dominant culture? How could they address fellow exiles in an attempt to persuade them not to give up? How would they present an alternative worldview to that held and celebrated by the dominant culture of the captors?

The response to these questions significantly depends on the political and social situation as well as the objectives of what the exiles want to achieve. If they aim at ridiculing the other, they may take a rather sarcastic and deprecating approach (like, say, Deutero-Isaiah does every now and then). If they are, however, determined to present their worldview not just to encourage the

---

173. See Berlejung, *Theologie der Bilder*, 182–83.
174. Schüle, *Prolog*, 410–16.
175. Schüle, 428.

like-minded but possibly to persuade those who surrendered to the claims of the winning party, too sharp a polemic will only alienate them. Therefore, a more delicate and subtle strategy is needed, one that is more positive toward the gentile heritage.

PH's author adopted a strategy by which he presented an alternative view to Babylon's imperialistic religion and politics. By referring and alluding to Mesopotamian myths, rites, and heroes, he showed a sympathetic approach to the Mesopotamian cultural and religious heritage. On occasions, however, he leveled criticism at Babylon. Often, it is a tongue-in-cheek polemic critiquing Babylon's treasured rites, heroes, values, and worldview. If one understands polemic as "a speech or a piece of writing that argues very strongly for or against sth/sb,"[176] then, in this narrower sense, PH is not polemical. This is how the word is generally understood and used.[177] My use can, for lack of a better term, be called a "soft polemic."

In his soft polemic, the narrator used genres like creation myth and genealogy well-known to Babylonians, alluded to and drew on their beloved epics, and elaborated on popular themes such as creation, multiplication of humankind, and the flood. Indeed, he structured his work (or, from the viewpoint of Pentateuch, the introduction of his work) as one of those epics, such as Atrahasis is structured. Even vague allusions to themes, persons, or works came in handy on occasions. It seems that PH's author was well-versed in the contemporary issues of sixth-century Mesopotamian culture, mythology, religion, and politics. Had it been different, had he retreated into the confines of his own religion and (sub)culture, I am sure PH/Genesis (and much of the OT, for that reason) would not have been written.

It is sometimes argued that allusions or references to Mesopotamian sources are too indirect to constitute evidence of dependence.[178] In this vein, Walton claims,

> When literary pieces are being compared to consider the question of dependency among them, the burden of proof has been on the researcher to consider the issues of propinquity and transmission. After all, if Israelite literature were to be suspected

---

176. Turnbull, *Oxford Advanced Learner's Dictionary*, 1171.
177. See, e.g. Schüle, *Prolog*, 63.
178. E.g. Routledge, "Did God Create Chaos," 73.

of borrowing an Akkadian text, the claim of borrowing would need to be substantiated by evidence that the Israelite writers were aware of the Akkadian text and could plausibly have had access to it.[179]

This is a helpful observation commending caution. Of course, until an ancient Genesis manuscript with footnote references to the secondary Akkadian sources emerges, seeing references to ANE sources remains a working hypothesis and nothing more. Arguments from silence are suspect. On the other hand, there are too many similarities and parallels with Atrahasis, BCS, Gilgamesh, and the *mīs pî* ritual, to mention just the most important ones, to ignore them as points of reference.[180] Indeed, McDowell contends that the connections of the *mīs pî* ritual and Genesis 2:5–3:24 "indicate a historical relationship. They suggest that the Eden author not only knew how divine statues were made but understood the ritual means by which they were activated."[181]

By laying out his understanding of how P used Mesopotamian literary traditions, Sparks similarly claims that the Pentateuch imitated certain Mesopotamian textual traditions.

> Whether the evidence for this in certain cases is best described as an "allusion" by P, or "influence" on P, or an "echo" in P is not something that matters so much. But the overall case will depend on P's true allusions to other literature, in which the author utilizes "the marked material for some rhetorical or strategic end."[182]

---

179. Walton, *Genesis 1*, 3.

180. Drawing on Alter, *Pleasures of Reading*, 111–40, Kvanvig discusses allusion at some length and posits a tradition, oral or written, of "strange primeval beings" and "a specific incident, taking place at a specific time before the flood" (Kvanvig, "Gen 6,1–4," 91–92). One has the impression that the underlying motive to deny references to ANE material sometimes is a reluctance to pinpoint the historical background. For example, Walton, *Genesis 1*, fails to account for a *Sitz im Leben* of Genesis 1.

181. McDowell, *Image of God*, 175–76.

182. Sparks quotes Sommer, *Prophet Reads Scripture*, 15.

> Any unconscious "echoes" of Mesopotamia in P would only reinforce (but not detract from at all) the argument that P has intentionally imitated Mesopotamian traditions.[183]

Briefly, each case needs to be judged on its own terms.

My interpretation takes the socio-cultural background of the Babylonian context into account by assuming that the exiles, intent on taking on exploitative imperial ideology and, at the same time, putting forward their alternative worldview, must have formulated their criticism and the tenets of their faith (i.e. the narrative of Genesis) with extreme caution unless they wanted to face the authorities' wrath.

Since, at the New Year festival, BCS was recited and re-enacted in Babylon in the Neo-Babylonian period,[184] Jewish exiles were regularly confronted with Marduk's supremacy and the Babylonian version of what the world looks like. Even if the BCS was not a standard Mesopotamian creation myth,[185] in sixth-century Babylonia, it was definitely normative and a concept Jewish exiles regularly came across.[186] Certainly, it would not take much for exiled Jews to feel the urge to take up the challenge of giving their own account of how the world should look under the reign of their God.

Methodology

Even though this study is not concerned with genetic questions, a brief discussion of some genetic aspects seems helpful. I read Genesis assuming two main sources, which I call P and J (non-P) for the sake of convenience. I posit a J dating in the early Israelite monarchy[187] and can imagine that the original J creation account drew on Atrahasis and as such was more reminiscent of

---

183. Sparks, "*Enūma elish*," 628–29.
184. See Lambert, "Great Battle," 189–90; Lambert, "Another Look," 1–2.
185. See Lambert, "New Look," 291; Millard, "New Babylonian 'Genesis,'" 4.
186. Note, however, that Speiser, *Genesis*, 9, calls it "Mesopotamia's canonical version of cosmic origins."
187. J's existence has recently been questioned. See, e.g. Gertz, Schmid, and Witte, eds., *Abschied vom Jahwisten*; Wenham, "Priority of P," 240–58; and LaCocque, *Trial of Innocence*, among others, have argued for J's priority over P. Hendel, "'Begetting,'" 38–46, arrives, on linguistic grounds, at an early monarchic dating of J. My argument is not affected by an exilic date suggested, for example by LaCocque, *Trial of Innocence*, 17–21, assuming J is prior to P.

it, as discussed by Batto,[188] than the present text suggests. I can also imagine an original source written in ninth-century Judah telling a story from the creation of humankind in Genesis to Solomon's ascension to the throne in 1 Kings.[189] My thesis, however, does not depend on the date of J. This is different with P which, in my view, is mainly post-exilic with PH as good as complete in the exile.

As for P, David Carr, among others, has argued that P is subsequent to "non-P."[190] He asserts: "With the priestly document, we come to a comprehensive counter presentation of the Genesis story, indeed one designed to replace the account on which it is dependent."[191] Whether or not P replaces J is a matter of how one defines their respective theologies and the redaction process. Also, it is possible in my view that Genesis 11:1–9 and the Moses/Exodus narrative (or part of it) originally were polemics against Neo-Assyrian cultural and political claims.[192] They have, however, been incorporated in PH as anti-Babylonian polemics first and foremost.

Since my concern is not with the coming about of the text, I will not deal with what David Carr calls "transmission history"[193] but with the final work as a literary and theological composition. This is not only because "conventional criteria for determining textual incoherence are hardly convincing."[194] My main reason for this is that the quest for sources/traditions has contributed little to a theological interpretation of the present literary work.[195] Scholarship now is in favor of literary integrity in general.[196]

---

188. Batto, *Slaying the Dragon*, 41–72; cf. Carr, *Reading the Fractures*, 240–46.

189. See Friedman, *Hidden Book*; cf. Carr, *Formation*, 456–69.

190. Carr, *Reading the Fractures*, 67–68. See also his criticism of the J material's different putative contexts and dates as well as his proposal (220–32).

191. Carr, 312.

192. See Uehlinger, *Weltreich*; Otto, "Geburt des Mose," 43–83.

193. Carr, *Reading the Fractures*, 23–40.

194. Stordalen, *Echoes of Eden*, 194.

195. Some studies, like Batto, *Slaying the Dragon*, 15–101, and Carr, *Reading the Fractures*, have definitely had a positive contribution. But see Stordalen's discussion of how little knowledge of the evolution of Gilgamesh or Atrahasis is needed to understand and appreciate them (*Echoes of Eden*, 201–5; cf. Baden, "Tower of Babel"). Also, scholarship, particularly when source hypotheses and redaction criticism are concerned, too often resorts to arguments from silence. Waschke, *Untersuchungen*, 16, has called attention to this fallacy by reference to W. H. Schmidt's thesis ("Anthropologische Begriffe im AT. Anmerkungen zum Hebräischen Denken") that Israel's credos never speak of creation.

196. See Stordalen, *Echoes of Eden*, 197–98.

Even though I see various approaches to PH as helpful and legitimate, I have opted to read it synchronically, comparatively, and theologically. For instance, I sympathize with the shame interpretation of the nakedness motif in 2:25, but view the animal-like explanation, a comparative interpretation, as doing justice to the Babylonian context and fitting PH better than the shame-and-gender or coming-of-age explanation.[197]

It is theological interpretation that interpreters often are after. So, I am first interested in the particular: what the text might mean to sixth-century exilic Jews. Whereas theological interpretations often ignore the specifics of historical background and comparative material, I will try to do justice to the particularities while, as step two, aiming at a theological interpretation that is significant for us today. This study basically is a theological commentary on PH.

PH/Genesis was intended as theological literature. This does not mean that it is concerned with "spiritual" things only. To risk a platitude, theological concern for PH means a rather holistic approach to every phenomenon encountered from politics to society, ethics, values, culture, and religion – all seen from a theological vantage point. Bearing that in mind the evaluation of political, social, or other aspects are a must.[198]

The concern of this study is the theme of PH. However, it seems desirable to read PH in its wider context. That is to say, the theme of PH cannot be studied in isolation from Genesis and the Pentateuch. The literary context of PH is, first, that of Genesis and then of the Pentateuch. I will thus read PH's sections in their immediate and wider contexts and not as isolated literary units. Whatever its literary provenance, the introduction to the flood narrative (6:1–6), for instance, is not to be interpreted as a disjointed fragment of previous literary sources but in its narrower context of chapters 5–8. At the same time, it is an imperative for me to read PH against the cultural-historical background of sixth-century Babylonia. Having "bifocal lenses" on will prove profitable for this, I hope.

The attempts by Kikawada to read PH in the light of ANE material as well as a self-contained literary work will be appreciated and improved upon. The

---

197. For this, see, e.g. Schüle, *Prolog*, 175.

198. Needless to say, in ANE, there was no dichotomy between religion and society or politics – theology concerned itself with every aspect of human life.

approach by David Clines will be appropriated by asking similar questions as to the theme of PH and, to a limited extent, how it relates to the rest of Genesis and the Pentateuch.[199] What associations would it evoke in the minds of exilic Israel as they listened to the story? I will try to read PH as one literary work, indeed, as an introduction to a major literary opus. It is also clear that PH is both a self-contained and structured unit. Each section must be integrated in the whole of PH, even those that resist most violently, like 6:1–4 and 11:1–9.

Comparative studies read sections of PH against their cultural, political, social, ideological, and linguistic ANE background. This is necessary if we are to understand what they tried to communicate to the first audience. I will do my best to emulate Uehlinger's political awareness as well as Batto's and Baumgart's comparative approaches – while reading the canonical text.[200] I will try to detect both similarities between the biblical and ANE material as well as differences. To this end, I will adopt what Hallo calls the contextual approach:

> It is, then, the balance between comparison and contrast, or their combinations in the appropriate proportions, which first provides overall context for the biblical text. . . . The goal of the contextual approach is fairly modest. It is not to find the key to every biblical phenomenon in some ancient Near Eastern precedent, but rather to silhouette the biblical text against its wider literary and cultural environment and thus to arrive at a proper assessment of the extent to which the biblical evidence reflects that environment or, on the contrary, is distinctive and innovative over against it.[201]

In other words, it is important to give "consideration not only to the parallels between Israel and the other peoples, but also to the divergences between them; for the differences are likewise instructive, perhaps even more so than the similarities."[202] Recognizing an important methodological principle,

---

199. Clines, "Theme in Genesis 1–11" and *Theme of the Pentateuch*.
200. Uehlinger, *Weltreich*; Batto, *Slaying the Dragon*; Baumgart, *Umkehr des Schöpfergottes*.
201. Hallo, "Compare and Contrast," 3; cf. Hanson, "Jewish Apocalyptic," 33.
202. Cassuto, *Genesis*, 1.

Cassuto stated this in the preface of his Genesis commentary as long ago as 1944.[203]

One caveat seems necessary, however. The staggering number of parallels in comparative religion and literature makes one's head dizzy. Sandmel therefore warns of "parallelomania," a zealous search for parallels in comparative religion that tempts the scholar.[204] In this respect, John Walton's "cosmological cognitive environment" seems helpful.[205] It is constituted by wide-spread cognitive concepts in ANE worldview.[206] Sumerian parallels, for instance, beg the question: how many Hebrews living in the sixth century would get the literary allusions? On the other hand, Bosserman argues that there must have been iconographically "illiterate texts," that is, texts unaware of the iconography's original meaning still using its symbols, Genesis 2–3 being one of them.[207]

I will interpret PH with its Babylonian setting in mind. My thesis is that, meant for exilic Jews, PH was an alternative to the Babylonian narrative. It addressed the particular situation of the exiles, more so than perceived by most modern readers, alluding to different Mesopotamian myths, epics, and rites thus trying to challenge the rather particular Mesopotamian narrative by a universal one.[208]

This study will read the text in its putative historical setting as well as "in its integrity and interconnectedness"; it will draw attention to the "alternative view of power and order in the world" presented by PH.[209] I will use McConville's idea that Yahwist monotheism was liberating, creating a counter-culture.

Last but not least, I will occasionally use, as a method, imagination. Perdue states that

---

203. Cassuto, 1; cf. Hasel, "Significance of the Cosmology," 1–20.

204. Sandmel, "Parallelomania," 1–13; cf. Van Seters, *Prologue to History*, 109.

205. Walton, *Genesis 1*; cf. Lowery, *Toward a Poetics*.

206. Westermann, for instance, sees Gen 1 "in the context of a number of creation stories" (Westermann, *Genesis 1–11*, 81).

207. Bosserman, "Seeing Double," 39–61.

208. To be sure, because of its universal substance and subject matter, it allows for a more general interpretation; see Stordalen, *Echoes of Eden*, 25–26.

209. See McConville, *God and Earthly Power*, 11.

> It is the power of human psyche (conscious and unconscious) to form mental images, either immediately or indirectly derived from perception or sensation, that lead to the attainment of meaning. In relationship to epistemology (experience, perception, and intuition) and cosmology (especially the construction and authentication of worldviews), imagination may range from a rather common ability to arrange and categorize experiences of sense perception to a more creative power to re-describe reality in highly unusual and provocative ways.[210]

More specifically, my method may be reminiscent of what Perdue calls "common imagination."

> [This] operates when the senses perceive an object, say, for example, the front of a house, and the mind projects that the house has rooms that are not immediately experienced. This projection may be based either on past experience (i.e., the person has been in the house before), or by the more general mental activity of classifying the object in the general category of "house," which ordinarily has rooms, and interpreting it as such. Thus, common or ordinary imagination completes the fragmentary data of the sense, since we cannot perceive the whole of an object at once.[211]

I will employ my very common imagination to complete, for instance, the fragmentary data of the tower of Babylon story, since we cannot perceive the whole of it. To be sure, in the story there are, instead of an object, a whole network of overt or covert references to Babylonian ideology and power claims based on the city-temple-king triad. But the gaps need to be filled in by imagination.

Albright, reviewing Sigmund Mowinckel's *The Two Sources of the Predeuteronomic History (JE) in Gen. 1–11*, remarks that "truth is generally found on the side of moderation."[212] It is not up to me to decide how moderate

---

210. Perdue, *Collapse of History*, 263–64; drawing on Warnock, *Imagination*, 10; Crites, "Unfinished Figure," 155–84; Scharlemann, "Transcendental," 109–22.

211. Perdue, *Collapse of History*, 265.

212. Albright, Review of *The Two Sources*, 230; Mowinckel, *Two Sources*.

the views presented here are. But, even though not being an Assyriologist myself, I have made every effort to meet Albright's second principle that "these days the Biblical scholar must also be a master of the extra-biblical sources from which we must reconstruct the world of the Bible."[213]

---

213. Albright, Review of *The Two Sources*, 230.

CHAPTER 2

The Primeval History: An Alternative to Babylon's Metanarrative

There is a general consensus that Genesis 1–11 is unique in the OT by virtue of its foundational position and content. Yet, the "Primeval History is almost always treated in isolation," as Fox states.[1] Even though much has changed since Fox's assertion, the relationship of PH and what follows is not clear. PH is without a doubt very different from the successive material. At the same time, however, it is the introduction to Genesis and the Pentateuch.[2] What I am interested in, then, is What does PH want to communicate? What is its purpose by its use of Mesopotamian material? And in what way is PH, to follow on Rogerson's observation, foundational for Genesis/Pentateuch?

Dethroning Marduk: The Beginnings (1:1–3:24)

The Babylonian creation story (BCS) is an epic statement of Marduk's supremacy among Babylonian gods. Like other ANE myths, the BCS does not discuss the creation of the world per se. In it, creation is clearly as much a political statement as a theological one. The parallels with Genesis have been extensively demonstrated. The Genesis narrator is well aware of the world BCS has created and, sometimes overtly other times obliquely, articulates his view when in disagreement with BCS. At the same time, Genesis makes a strong

---

1. Fox, "Can Genesis Be," 32.
2. For an elaboration of PH themes in Genesis/Pentateuch, see Fox, "Can Genesis Be"; Carr, "Βίβλος γενέσεως Revisited (Part One)" and "Βίβλος γενέσεως Revisited (Part Two)."

case for the end of Marduk's kingship and Yahweh's supremacy. By redefining creation, Genesis launches its first line of attack on Babylon.

Genesis 1 is cosmogony drawing on BCS. In chapter 2, humankind's creation is related in more detail. The intertextual backdrop is Atrahasis and the *mīs pî* ritual that time – it is anthropogony. Despite the dissimilarities, the Genesis account is likewise concerned with politics.

Cosmogony (1:1–2:3)

The BCS tells the story of how the generations of gods came to be starting with the well-known words:

> When skies above were not yet named
> Nor earth below pronounced by name,
> Apsu, the first one, their begetter,
> And maker Tiamat, who bore them all,
> Had mixed their waters together,
> But had not formed pastures, nor discovered reed-beds;
> When yet no gods were manifest,
> Nor names pronounced, nor destinies decreed,
> Then gods were born within them.[3]

With the gods around, Tiamat feels threatened and plans to destroy them. On realizing this, they call on Marduk who accepts the challenge on the condition that he will be head of the gods. Marduk addresses his father Ea expressing his demand to become, in case he wins, head of the gods.

The deal is struck, a token of which is the "princely shrine" erected for Marduk after his victory. Here, he takes up residence as proclaimed king. In the ensuing fight with Tiamat, Marduk defeats the monster. With Tiamat and her evil allies annihilated, triumphant Marduk sets out to create or organize the world. To this end, he uses Tiamat's corpse. Next, Marduk makes a new order in the sky. Finally enthroned, Marduk makes himself in Babylon a house, a cult center to confirm his kingship.

The first verses of Genesis are notorious as far as translation is concerned. Some nine hundred years ago, and without being familiar with comparative material, it was Rashi who was first to consider the introductory Genesis 1:1

---

3. Dalley, "The Epic of Creation," in *Myths from Mesopotamia*, 233.

being in construct to 1:3, with 1:2 constituting a circumstantial clause.[4] The similar syntax of the starting lines of Genesis and BCS, parallel motifs, and the order of events have long been noticed.[5] With its incipit, a bridge between this composition and exilic Jews has been constructed.[6] In addition, both creation accounts refer to a watery chaos that is then split by the principal god into heaven and earth; both know of light as existing prior to the creation of the heavenly bodies; both have a very similar sequence of creation; and in both the number seven plays a significant role.[7] Whereas, however, BCS is concerned with theogony, Genesis is not at all, it starts *in medias res*.[8]

In PH, the day-by-day creation process, the filling-in of spaces, prepared to this end, with creatures, the leisurely progress make it all appear as a well-planned job with God as an organized and sovereign chief executive – God's creating activity is masterly.[9] Flora and fauna in Genesis are assigned significance in their own right, whereas, in BCS, they do not figure at all.[10] The world itself and humankind as its crown are the purpose of creation. Creation is seen from the perspective of humankind, not like in Mesopotamia. A rather cosmocentric and anthropocentric approach emerges in the first sentences of PH instead of the theocentric view of BCS – creation matters.

The creational acts of days 1–3 prepare the acts of days 4–6, as suggested first by Herder, thus lending creation structure.[11] The absence of

---

4. Rashi, *Kommentar zum Pentateuch*, 1–2; see Orlinsky, "Enigmatic Bible Passages," 208.
5. E.g. Speiser, *Genesis*, 9–10.
6. Contra Lim, *Grace in the Midst*, 107.
7. Heidel, *Babylonian Genesis*, 82.
8. See Miller, "Old Testament," 32. Jacobsen has argued that "Marduk," ᵈAMAR-UD in cuneiform, etymologically goes back to the Sumerian MAR-UTU, meaning "son of Wind" which fits the combat scene in BCS where Marduk triumphs by using as weapons various winds (Jacobsen, "Battle," 104–8). What concerns us in this context is that, at the beginning of the first creation account, we see God's *ruaḥ*, sometimes translated as "God's wind" (e.g. Smith, *Priestly Vision*, 85), hover over the waters of the deep (1:2). To be sure, in Genesis, there is no battle, no violence. As a consequence of "the Israelite purging of the *Chaoskampf* of its cosmogonic associations" (Levenson, *Creation*, 11; cf. Day, *From Creation to Abraham*, 15), God sovereignly rules and creates with mere words. The muffled echo of Marduk's triumph over the watery monster may still be heard reverberating from the distant Akkadian epic. For a potential Phoenician background, see Darshan, "Ruaḥ 'Elohim," 51–78.
9. Levenson, *Creation*, 3; cf. Goldingay, *Old Testament Theology*, 94–96.
10. See, Heidel, *Babylonian Genesis*, 117–18.
11. Day, "Meaning and Background," 1.

the *Chaoskampf* motif and the way he creates make God appear in control.[12] Structure, a prerequisite of order and the ensuing work, is always given to things that matter. Thus, structure is being given to the world to be populated. Though there is a similar structuring of creation in BCS, the structuring in Genesis, through its day-by-day design and sovereign Creator, seems an organized and well-executed creation.[13] In Genesis, the world is not created by God at the end of a long sequence of reactions to evil forces but due to proactive decisions.

This sense of a well-ordered and good world is not disturbed by the muted references to Tiamat (1:2) and the *tannînim* (1:21) – nothing and nobody threatens God's good creation.[14] The plural in 1:26 may be an allusion to other divine beings in the heavenly court.[15] Even when Marduk creates with peaceful means, there are obvious contrasts to Genesis. Right after his defeat of Tiamat, Marduk's creation of the sky is told at some length. This is more than understandable, since, for Babylonian religion, astrology was significant. In Genesis 1, creating heavenly bodies is just a day's work, no more, and they are accorded no astrological significance.

Related to this is naming, a frequent motif in Mesopotamian mythology. It is always gods who name cultural or technological innovations (see, e.g. The Disputation between Ewe and Wheat, lines 10–11). Usually, it is gods who name humankind, just as in BCS.[16] In Genesis, God names things deemed gods in Mesopotamia (Anu, Enlil): the sky (1:8) and land (1:10). They are relegated to a calendar function. God's naming activity comes to an end with day three, however. Startlingly, neither God nor the narrator bothers to

---

12. Indeed, Kenneth Gros Louis wonders if the account makes one "somewhat uncomfortable with a God who is so distant, so transcendent . . . The God who emerges is majestic, but distant; omnipotent and transcendent, a God of order and of pattern and of hierarchy" (Gros Louis, "Genesis I–II," 44–45). Gen 2 will rectify this impression.

13. See Heidel, *Babylonian Genesis*, 129; Robinson, "Literary Functions," 598–99.

14. Like the dependence of Genesis on BCS, the relationship between Tiamat and *tĕhôm* is not settled. Gertz, "Antibabylonische Polemik," 141, misses the hints at a *Chaoskampf*. Given Genesis' strategy outlined above, the non-naming may well be an element of this strategy along with the anarthrous *tǝhôm* (but see Day, *From Creation to Abraham*, 17–18), unaccounted for by Gertz.

15. See Garr, *In His Own Image*, 87–92.

16. Naming in the first creation narrative is not just an act and exercise of dominion but provides the named one its destiny. God names not only light which he created but also darkness of which it is not stated that he created so demonstrating his lordship; Westermann, *Genesis 1–11*, 114–15.

name the two most important heavenly bodies of creation, the sun and the moon, worshipped as Shamash and Sin in Babylonia, even though God had named entities previously created or separated.[17] They are ordered by God to govern the day and the night (1:16) but "differ from God in that they have a limited function within creation. It is this function of service that distinguishes them from God" – they serve the Creator's purpose and creation.[18] As an afterthought, God is reported to have made the stars (1:16), among them, presumably, Ishtar-Venus, Marduk-Jupiter, Nebo-Mercury, Nergal-Mars.[19] Importantly, heavenly bodies seem to have no light, hence no significance, of their own as light was created on day one.

However, Gertz argues that referring to the sun and moon as "great lights" in Mesopotamian literature was quite common. Moreover, disregarding humankind's creation, that of the planets is the most detailed and complex, with day 4 being the center of the creation week. These all suggest not a marginalization but rather the central significance for P's creation account, that is, the sovereignty and universality of the one Creator who is superior to all other powers including Marduk (see BCS IV–VII).[20]

God's unrivaled might and authority are underlined in another way as well. Mark Smith has compared Genesis 1 and Psalm 74 and observed that the Genesis account plays down the conflict aspect by stressing God's creating speech and omitting references to the primordial *Chaoskampf*, indeed, to

---

17. Cf. Hasel, "Significance of the Cosmology," 13–14.

18. Westermann, *Genesis 1–11*, 127. Westermann also points out two further differences between BCS and Gen 1. First, in BCS, the position of the star Nibiru/Jupiter, Marduk's star, is stressed; in Genesis, it is one amongst the stars with only the two large heavenly bodies mentioned. Second, in Genesis 1:14 and 18, at the start and end of the day's work, God's separating actions go further than Marduk's creating actions. The separation of light and darkness on day 1 "introduces and provides the foundation of the work of creation", which is then further developed on day 4 (Westermann, *Genesis 1–11*, 133–34).

19. In the subsequent narrative, naming becomes a human privilege (e.g. 2:19–20; 3:20; 4:1, 26), with God occasionally naming human characters (see 5:2; 17:5, 15). Thus, while naming in Mesopotamia is a divine prerogative, in Genesis it is shared between God and humankind and related to plot and characterization. The reason is not spelled out and I wonder whether it is humankind's being created in the image of God.

20. Gertz, "Antibabylonische Polemik," 144–49. As far as the import of Gen 1:14–19 in comparison with BCS is concerned, Gertz is correct except that he ignores the literary effect of the non-naming of sun and moon which seems to be in line with the non-naming of other important Babylonian entities. After all, the moon and sun are named in BCS (Tablet V) and P could have easily named those two heavenly bodies too.

the deep, the sea, and monsters as God's primordial enemies in the psalm.[21] What does Genesis want to achieve by so doing?

> The aim would appear to be to substitute divine speech for divine conflict and thus read conflict out of creation. In this way, God can be viewed as a power beyond conflict, indeed the unchallenged and unchallengeable power beyond any powers. Creation does not occur in the aftermath of divine powers in opposition. It is not the result of two wills in opposition, but it evinces a God unopposed, bringing about creation simply by expressing good words.[22]

Smith has also compared light in Genesis and in BCS I.101–104 where Marduk appears clothed in light. Though this vocabulary is more comparable with Psalm 104:2, God can in Genesis 1 be seen as compared to Marduk. If so, this feature along with the omission of the conflict element, powerful in BCS, makes God, who creates by speech, superior to Marduk.[23] If BCS is an epic statement of Marduk's supremacy, Genesis 1 is one of Yahweh's unrivaled sovereignty.

Walton has drawn attention to the Akkadian phrases *šimtu*, represented by the gods' Tablet of Destinies, and *parṣu*, a concept denoting "control attributes." Though there is no corresponding Hebrew equivalent, these phrases in Akkadian literature denote the world's good order – something similar we see in Genesis 1. Days 1–3 can thus be seen as establishing the cosmos's *parṣi*, while days 4–6 as determining the destinies of the cosmos's functionaries. With the gods' destinies determined in ANE, powers and responsibilities could be delegated, which resulted in other gods' taking up the responsibilities of work. This is reminiscent of humankind being created in God's image and having power delegated to them. Significantly, God in Genesis 1 is portrayed as solely responsible for cosmic order.[24] In Atrahasis as well as in BCS, work is seen as troublesome, unworthy of gods. Therefore, humankind is not the

---

21. Smith, *Priestly Vision of Genesis*, 115–27.
22. Smith, 124.
23. Smith, 127–39. Beginning with the ת of בראשית in Genesis 1 and שמות in Exodus 1 respectively, every fiftieth letter added produces "Torah." This might be seen as an alternative to Marduk's fifty names to provide a rationale for the world's structure.
24. Walton, *Genesis*, 14.

crown of creation but a solution to a problem. Creating for God, where he gets his hands dirty, is enjoyable and effortless.

As for the cause of creation in Genesis, one is perplexed to find none. As I have stated, there is no noise challenging God and leading to a bloody theomachy. God states that the created world, with the creatures in it, is good – good for creation itself and not necessarily because it is useful to God. This impression is reinforced by God's very first command to creation that both animals and humankind multiply (1:22, 28). God is not concerned about overpopulation as his colleagues in Atrahasis are. Seeing this, one is forced to conclude that God created the world for no particular reason – he just felt like creating it. The created things serve their purpose; creation, good and beautiful, does its job.[25]

This might be underlined by the creation of plants. Whereas in BCS there is no reference to the plants' creation when listing Marduk's creating acts (Tablets V–VI), and only an incidental note mentions plants being created by Marduk (VII.2), in Genesis 1, day 3 is devoted to, after the waters are separated, creating plants.[26] Apparently, plants contribute to the world's goodness and beauty.

In the BCS, the apex is reached with the creation of Babylon. It is emphatic, whereas the "creation of mankind is in fact little more than a subsidiary theme in the middle of the story of the building of Babylon."[27] Humankind is created for the service of the gods. The alternative to the Babylonian worldview is set forth by P in the account of the creation of humankind. Having created the animals, an aspect missing in BCS,[28] God says: "Let us make man in our image, in our likeness, and let them rule over the fish of the sea and the birds of the air, over the livestock, over all the earth, and over all the creatures that move along the ground" (Gen 1:26). This is the only instance in chapter 1 where God does not create by divine fiat but by "making";[29] he seems to be more involved than on the previous occasions.[30] And this terminology is more in line with that of chapter 2.

---

25. Cf. Westermann, *Genesis 1–11*, 166–67.
26. *Pace* Westermann, 123–24.
27. Hallo, "Urban Origins," 559.
28. Hasel, "Significance of the Cosmology," 18
29. Sarna, *Understanding Genesis*, 216.
30. Firmage, "Genesis 1," 101.

McDowell has pointed out that the term "according to its/their kind," occurring ten times in seven verses (1:11–12, 21–25), stresses "the creation and reproduction of each species *according to its own distinctive type or class*."[31] Contrary to expectations, the creation of humankind is not described by this term but by "in our image, in our likeness" (1:26–27). In this way, the narrator draws "a sharp distinction between humans and the other created beings."[32] Humankind is thus distinct from animals and plants and more God-like, though distinct from God.

> In other words, humans are not divine, nor are they members of the heavenly host. They are their own category, type, or species, which is defined by being created in the image and likeness of God. However, at some level, humans belong to the divine class or species, that is, humanity's *kind or type is God*.[33]

Humankind is created in the image of God with a mandate of ruling over the world.[34] As argued compellingly by Batto, the two seem to be correlated: being the image of God means rule over creation.[35] This reflects the Mesopotamian (and Egyptian) view where the king was seen as the image of the deity and as such their representative and ruler of creation.[36] God's statement is a theological move where P "does not push the image of the king off its base to make it equal to the people but lifts humankind out of the dust."[37] Put differently, in the image concept, the king's status and function are transferred onto the whole of humanity.[38] Embodying God's qualities, humankind

---

31. McDowell, *Image of God*, 132, her emphasis.
32. McDowell, 132.
33. McDowell, 133, her emphasis.
34. See Niskanen, "Poetics of Adam," 429–30.
35. Batto, "Divine Sovereign," 143–86.
36. See Walton, *Genesis*, 20–21. Day, *From Creation to Abraham*, 27, finds "no evidence that the Israelite kings themselves were ever spoken of as being in the image of a god." That is very true. Indeed, it would be surprising to find any such evidence given the Old Testament's theological stance toward Yahweh and kings. That does not mean, however, that the idea of kings bearing the divine image was unknown to exilic Israel.
37. Waschke, "Der Mensch," 503.
38. Waschke, *Untersuchungen*, 22; cf. Sarna, *Genesis*, 12; McConville, *God and Earthly Power*, 26. On the other hand, being aware of PH's anti-royal attitude and kings as a tough species, why not give a push as PH often does?

is supposed to do the deity's work on earth.[39] Being created in God's image concerns each individual, the human person and the human family.[40]

Hermann Gunkel, back in 1895 with Assyriology and comparative religion in their infancy, claimed, "we do not directly discern what this image might be."[41] It is not the rule of humankind over the animals, he goes on, that is meant.[42] Even if direct interpretive hints are in short supply comparative material has established itself as a solid starting point. We will also see in what way the concept is linked to human rule over the animals.

The representational or royal interpretation of the image of God concept has become virtually a consensus among OT scholars and has significantly contributed to our understanding thereof in the last one-hundred years or so.[43] It can be summarized in the following way. Neo-Assyrian and Neo-Babylonian texts speak of the king as being the image of the deity. "In these texts the designation of the king as 'image of the god' serves to emphasize the godlike nature of the king in his ruling function and power."[44] The Akkadian phrase *muššulu*, "image," occurs "in a proverb quoted by Adad-shum-uṣur in a letter to Esarhaddon, in which he refers to the king as *muššuli ša* DINGIR(*ili*), 'the likeness of god.'"[45] The primary Akkadian word, however, is *ṣalmu* to which the earliest reference is in a victory hymn of Tukulti-Ninurta I in the thirteenth century BCE. Here, the king is a permanent *ṣalmu* of Enlil. But most evidences are found in Neo-Assyrian letters of the court astrologers-magicians of Esarhaddon and Ashurbanipal. Here, the king is *ṣalmu* of Shamash/Bel/Marduk. The image of god concept in Genesis thus probably originates in ANE king ideology. It is not the result of an inner-Israelite democratization of the royal concept though, but, after the collapse

---

39. Walton, *Genesis*, 21.
40. Niskanen, "Poetics of Adam," 426, 434–35. Jacob comments that what 1:27 teaches "is the opposite of racism and emphasizes the unity of mankind" (*First Book of the Bible*, 10).
41. Gunkel, "Influence of Babylonian Mythology," 29.
42. Gunkel, 29.
43. See Jónsson, *Image of God*, 219–23.
44. Bird, "Male and Female," 141–43.
45. Curtis, "Images in Mesopotamia," 33.

of the Judahite monarchy, the result of a universalizing of the lordship concept in which metaphors of the royal ideology are intentionally integrated by P.[46]

Studying the Tell Fecheriyeh inscription, Dohmen has further clarified the functional aspect of *ṣelem* as opposed to the representational concept inherent in *dəmût*. The identity of the picture (humankind) and the one depicted (God) is stressed in this way.[47] Bray sums it up succinctly, "The former refers primarily to a concrete image, a definite shape; the latter is more abstract – a resemblance, or a likeness."[48] Janowski claims that humankind is not God's image by virtue of an unknown quality through which he is supposed to rule over the animals but he is God's image in that he is empowered to rule the animal world. Thus, a double responsibility of humankind is formulated: one toward the Creator and one toward creation.[49] Smith concurs with this:

> The statue, this image and likeness, in this case represents the image of the vassal of an overlord. We may read the terms in Genesis 1:26–28 in a similar manner. As the image and likeness of the god, the human person is to be the devoted worshipper of the god who also serves God the sovereign as servant and agent on earth.[50]

Thus, the application of *ṣelem* to humankind in Genesis 1 is "an example of both positive and negative influence."[51] The application is positive in that the *mīs pî* ritual seems to have influenced the image concept in Genesis 1. It is negative in that Genesis 1 reacted to the original concept with a democratization of the royal ideology.[52]

For today's reader "subduing" and "ruling" may be reprehensible; in a culture where both rule and the image of god concept were predicated only

---

46. Waschke in communication with the author; contra Bray, "Significance of God's Image," 197. The difference between the democratization and universalization of the concept may seem trivial though.

47. Dohmen, "Die Statue von Tell Fecherīje," 91–106; cf. Janowski, "Die lebendige Statue Gottes," 149–53.

48. Bray, "Significance of God's Image," 196.

49. Janowski, "Die lebendige Statue Gottes," 153; referring to Gross, "Die Gottebenbildlichkeit," 260.

50. Smith, *Priestly Vision of Genesis*, 170.

51. Smith, 170.

52. McDowell, *Image of God*, 181.

on kings, it is rather democratic. Pictures depicting the Mesopotamian king as killing bulls and lions portray him as master of the animals and thus protector of the land from any threat posed by wild animals. "When kings killed wild beasts, symbolically they were acting in place of the divine sovereign, divinely appointed shepherds ridding the earth of threats to the divinely willed peace."[53] Indeed, Schüle claims that humankind's rule is meant to forestall violence and destruction.[54] Humankind is given the responsibility to rule, to bring order in creation.[55] This aspect too is democratized in Genesis.[56] As Clifford presents it, "The human race rules (*rādâ*, 1:26) the life of each of the three domains, as the sun and moon govern (*māšal*) day and night. And only the human race, by virtue of its climactic sixth-day position and its freedom to respond to the divine word, directly encounters God."[57] The concept thus connotes the representation of the divine by humankind in the created world.[58] This is specified to mean rule over the animal world (1:26, 28), further qualified by Goldingay who takes *kābaš*, the "rarer and more forceful verb," to refer to the earth's subjugation only and not to that of the animal world.[59] "More explicitly," he goes on, "it implies that the way humanity is to go about subjugating the world is by procreation, not by violence – which Genesis abhors (Gen 6:11, 13)."[60] Being created in God's image and given the mandate to rule demarcate humankind's place in creation.[61] Along with other aspects, this will be affected by humankind's disobedience and God's curse in chapter 3.[62]

The ordered creation also provides for humankind's physical needs: they can eat every plant and fruit (1:29–30). In contrast to Mesopotamia's standard

---

53. Batto, "Divine Soveriegn," 182.
54. Schüle, "Reluctant Image," 34–36.
55. Walton, *Genesis*, 21.
56. Batto, "Divine Sovereign," 180–82.
57. Clifford, *Creation Accounts*, 144.
58. See Miller, "Old Testament," 35. Though, in Mesopotamia and Egypt, the image concept and the representative function are related to each other with reference to the king (Schüle, *Prolog*, 107), Smith, *Priestly Vision of Genesis*, 173–74, notes that in P's agenda the verb *kābaš* "denotes God's gift to humanity."
59. Goldingay, *Old Testament Theology*, 113.
60. Goldingay, 113.
61. Goldingay, 113. I cannot see why P would not have cared to confront the pagan view as Firmage, "Genesis 1," 100, claims positing a solely ritual concern to P.
62. So much so that in 8:15–19 God refrains from commanding this; cf. Gros Louis, "Genesis 3–11," 47.

view where humankind was created to provide for gods, God in Genesis provides for his creatures.[63]

As on the previous five days of creation, God's word proves powerful – "And it was so" (1:30; cf. 1:7, 9, 11, 15, 24). The verbs associated with God "connote a being who operates by immediate command and with complete foreknowledge."[64] But it is not creation through the word that is emphasized in this account. Rather, the narrator's "purpose is to arrange God's work of creation into a network of sentences whose succession follows the pattern of a fulfillment of a command."[65]

God views the work done with gratification, summing up the quality of the created world: it is good, indeed, very good (1:31; cf. 1:4, 10, 12, 18, 21, 25; seven times in total). This is in sharp contrast with the quality of creation in Mesopotamian accounts. Marduk's act of creating the first man in the BCS comes close to a showing off and an afterthought; it is meant to release the gods from labor. In this way, the social hierarchy of Babylon was "vigorously legitimated. If the purpose of the mass of humanity is to serve the gods, and the king represents those gods as their son and image, then, the gods are served precisely by serving the king, who wills the present social order."[66] The concluding, climactic work of humankind's creation in Genesis serves humanity *en bloc*, who takes the place of kings.

In BCS, the purpose of creation is unmistakably the divine world, more particularly Marduk's kingship and worship as the organizing principle of the world. That is why both the senior and junior gods give their consent to build a shrine and joyfully accept Babylon as their cult center. Marduk's kingship is the rationale of Babylon's supremacy. It is noteworthy that any overt reference to a king or shrine in Genesis' creation account is missing. Genesis 1–2 do not know of kingship based on creation, nor of primeval shrines. As a matter of fact, PH does not mention either. This is the first but not the last instance in Genesis where the lack of such references has the effect of a deafening silence. Here, it is not a temple that is declared holy but a day.

---

63. Walton, *Genesis*, 21.
64. Gros Louis, "Genesis I–II," 45.
65. Westermann, *Genesis 1–11*, 85.
66. Middleton, "Liberating Image," 8–25.

> There is no reference in the record of creation to any object in space that would be endowed with the quality of holiness. . . . This is a radical departure from accustomed religious thinking. The mythical mind would expect that after heaven and earth have been established, God would create a holy place – a holy mountain or a holy spring[67] – whereupon a sanctuary is to be established. Yet it seems as if to the Bible it is *holiness in time*, the Sabbath, which comes first.[68]

That God brings about creation without a temple needs qualification though. Even if there is no reference to a sanctuary in the creation account, Levenson has shown the similarity between the accounts on tabernacle building (Exod 25–31) and creation in Genesis 1.[69] Correspondence in structuring features, motifs, and terminology of the two accounts "underscore the depiction of the sanctuary as a world, that is, an ordered, supportive, and obedient environment, and the depiction of the world as a sanctuary, that is, a place in which the reign of God is visible and unchallenged, and his holiness palpable, unthreatened, and pervasive."[70] The potential effect is that "the Temple within the world is absurd because the world is itself a temple."[71]

Having brought order into and thus completed creation, God lays back (2:2) – a sign of divine sovereignty.[72] There is no-one posing threat to the created order or the Creator. Rest also connotes disengagement from order bringing activities (order has been created) and engagement of maintaining order.[73] Mesopotamian gods first needed their temples built so that they

---

67. Or, in Babylonia, a holy city, note added by this author.
68. Heschel, *Sabbath*, 9 (italics his). Cf. Heschel's apt remark, "'The day of the Lord' is more important to the prophets than 'the house of the Lord'" (Heschel, 79).
69. Levenson, *Creation*, 82–90. Schüle, *Prolog*, 81–83, (cf. Smith, *Priestly Vision in Genesis*, 133–35, 182–84; Enns, *Evolution of Adam*, 70–73) has also drawn attention to the correspondence between the creation in Gen 1 and the furnishing of the tent in Exodus and concluded that just as creation is completed as a perfect handiwork of God so is the tent by Moses. Still, and as opposed to Mesopotamian texts, the tabernacle is "no integral part of the cosmos" (83).
70. Levenson, *Creation*, 86. Cf. Brown's discussion of the structure of the seven days as a cosmic temple and of God depicted as a royal priest (Brown, *Seven Pillars of Creation*, 37–41, 46–47).
71. Levenson, *Creation*, 89; cf. Goldingay, *Old Testament Theology*, 124.
72. Batto, "Sleeping God," 159.
73. Walton, *Genesis*, 23.

could rest. In contrast and as a sign of work well done, God works for six days and rests on the seventh (2:2–3) – without a temple. "While in Genesis God could rest because creation was set in right order, the gods could not rest in Atrahasis, because there were serious mistakes in the creation."[74]

The Akkadian word for the fifteenth day, *šabattu*, is cognate with Hebrew *šabbāt*.[75] The Hebrew narrator is utilizing an Akkadian concept while investing it with new content. Israel commemorated God's order bringing creation weekly not annually as in Mesopotamia.[76] Work is seen as something good and rest as necessary after a week's well-done job. This motif only reinforces the picture we have had so far of a majestic, omnipotent Sovereign with no rival or opponent – a startling difference from the violent theomachy of BCS.

Mark Smith compares divine rest in Genesis and in Mesopotamian accounts.

> In *Enuma Elish* and *Atrahasis*, the creation of humanity allows the gods to rest from their work. These Mesopotamian texts understand that divine rest comes at the expense of human rest. Yet unlike the Mesopotamian perspective, for Genesis 1 rest is designed not only for the deity, but also for humanity as an imitation of the deity. The human person is made for work, but not on the seventh day. On that day, humanity is to participate in the divine rest.[77]

After an effortless creation, God rests in his sovereign fashion.[78] Genesis 1 breathes with order and structure, with the sense of a perfect and wonderful world. Jews living in Babylonian exile after the destruction of their national shrine and the loss of their kingdom were definitely given hope by this account. They are ruled by a benevolent, sovereign god and not by whimsical forces, fate, planets, fighting deities, nor by the conquerors' god, Marduk.

> The divine sovereign has delegated his authority to humankind. This is both privilege and duty, it would appear. Every human is anointed to continue the agenda of the divine sovereign by

---

74. Kvanvig, *Primeval History*, 259.
75. Dalley, *Myths from Mesopotamia*, 275n28.
76. Walton, *Genesis*, 23.
77. Smith, *Priestly Vision of Genesis*, 180.
78. See Millard, "New Babylonian 'Genesis,'" 15.

working to eliminate from this world every form of oppression and injustice (chaos) so that peace and universal weal (cosmos) may prevail throughout this universe that God created "perfect" (טוב מאד).[79]

God commissions humankind to act as his representative on earth, to rule and manage the affairs of the world. Animals can be ruled by one who is superior to them. To what extent humankind is superior to the animal world will be touched upon in what follows.

Anthropogony (2:4–25)

After this bird's eye view of creation, the narrator takes a closer look at how humankind was made in order to clarify some aspects.[80] From cosmogony, he turns to anthropogony.

In the creation story Marduk, Creator of the World does the creating (lines 1–40).[81] The myth enumerates entities without which creation does not work. This cosmogony does "not express nonexistence abstractly as nothingness, but as a period when essential institutions did not yet exist."[82] The ones most stressed are temples, ziggurats, and cities, unknown in the biblical account. To be sure, there are parallels as well. The way humankind is created in Genesis 2 resembles the way Marduk creates as in both cases soil is used. Genesis tells a detailed story of humankind's creation – in Marduk, Creator of the World, it is but an aside, which is standard in Mesopotamian literature. The reason is clear enough:

---

79. Batto, "Divine Sovereign," 185.
80. Kikawada, "Double Creation," 43–45, has compared humankind's creation in the Sumerian Enki and Ninmaḫ myth, the Akkadian Atrahasis, and Genesis, stories similarly structured. He found that all three first told creation in more general and then in more specific terms, i.e. a general account of humankind's creation followed by a second creation account in some detail. Regarding this, Kvanvig claims, "They are not to be read as two actions in succession, but rather like a bicolon in poetry where the second member elaborates the first" (Kvanvig, "Gen 6,1–4," 99, cf. Kvanvig, *Primeval History*, 237). McDowell, *Image of God*, 178–202 (cf. also Brodie, *Genesis as Dialogue*, 125–28), too argues for a close relationship between the two creation stories.
81. Foster, *Before the Muses*, 488–89.
82. Clifford, *Creation Accounts*, 64.

> In order to settle the gods in a comfortable dwelling,
> He created humankind . . .[83]

Genesis 1:26–28 is fraught with the concept of the divine image. The second creation account begins as a genealogy, a *tōlǝdōt*,[84] followed by a summary statement of creation (2:4), and is set in a garden, itself described at quite some length (2:8–14), with humankind's formation narrated prior to it (2:7). The setting is prepared by reference to the primitive state of the earth at the dawn of creation. This is reminiscent of Atrahasis where humankind's origin in the soil and their being created to provide for the gods are emphatic.[85] Additional similarities have been observed in chapters 2–3 by Batto: the similar setting of wasteland/steppe implying a Mesopotamian background; proto-humans/primeval human created to provide for the gods/God; they are modeled from clay; are implicitly immortal; revolt against the divine sovereign/aspire to divine status.[86]

The "stream" in 2:6 may correspond to the stream in relation to Abzu, the subterranean waters in Akkadian texts bringing fertility.[87] The problem here is not lack of water but rather lack of adequate water.[88] In Genesis 2:5–9, God "gives rain," "forms," "breathes," "plants;" in 2:15, he "takes" and "puts" humankind into Eden; in 2:19, he "forms," "takes," and "leads" animals; in 2:21–22, he "takes," "closes," "builds," and "brings." As opposed to Atrahasis' gods, Yahweh appears as a (pro)active deity, keen to work. Indeed, he provides for humankind a garden well-watered by a river (no need to dig canals) as well as fruit trees.[89] The verbs in chapter 2, as opposed to those of chapter 1,

---

83. Foster, *Before the Muses*, 489.

84. For the first creation account concluding at 2:3, see Levenson, *Creation*, 66–68. For 2:4 being both a summary of the preceding and an introduction to what follows, see McDowell, *Image of God*, 26–28. Because of the word's basic meaning "begetting" *tōlǝdōt* must refer to Sumerian-Babylonian mythology, BCS in particular, where the world originates from the genealogy of gods; Westermann, *Genesis 1–11*, 16.

85. Miscall, "Jacques Derrida," 4, has noticed that "negativity infects the narrative," as opposed to the first account, in the form of negative particles and references to something not good, evil, death, lack, and dissymmetry (4–5). This is also reminiscent of Atrahasis's less than perfect world.

86. Batto, *Slaying the Dragon*, 51–52; cf. Millard, "New Babylonian 'Genesis,'" 9–10.

87. Walton, *Genesis*, 25.

88. Tsumura, *Earth and the Waters*, 119.

89. Batto, *Slaying the Dragon*, 50–51, reads Gen 2 against the backdrop of Atrahasis and sees humankind as created to relieve God from labor. This may be correct as far as J is concerned

connote a "God who is working with his hands and with his breath to create man and other living creatures."[90] We see here a more immanent and error-prone God, not unlike Enlil and Ea.[91] God is more involved, both physically and mentally, in the second account. God's presence is highlighted by the term "Yahweh God," occurring twenty times in chapters 2–3 and thus granting God a nearly overbearing presence.

The reader has the impression in 2:8–9 that God plants the garden for humankind. Fauth has amassed massive evidence of ANE kings planting gardens with beautiful and exotic plants and animals for their own pleasure.[92] Here, it is God who plants for humankind. Indeed, Walton sees creation as God's palace, "a sacred spot featuring a spring with an adjoining well-watered park, stocked with specimens of trees and animals."[93]

Transferring humankind from the "scanty land" to the garden of Eden, probably meaning "abundance,"[94] and having them cultivate it is a horticultural rather than an agricultural task. Humankind is made to till and guard the garden, not the land.[95]

Genesis 2:10–14 describes the four primeval rivers at some length. Stordalen has studied Eden against the background of ANE topographical concepts with the following agenda:

> The present study is conducted under the impression that historical etymologies and foreign homonyms are only remotely relevant when it comes to perceiving the sense of the passage to the implied reader. The object is to identify topographic convention rather than historical geography, to study the world as it was

---

but Batto fails to sufficiently deal with the import of the final text; cf. Levenson, *Creation*, 117. The basic difference between Genesis and Atrahasis is that the former stresses that humankind serves the Creator "in a priestly role in a sacred space;" Walton, *Genesis*, 27.

90. Gros Louis, "Genesis I–II," 47.

91. Cf. Carr, *Reading the Fractures*, 64. I can well imagine P/the redactor drawing on older traditions as well as resorting to his own theological concepts, as having both a high view of God and creation (ch. 1) and approaching creation and the Creator more critically. After all, good theologians seek to balance transcendence and immanence and P was a good theologian.

92. Fauth, "Der königliche Gärtner"; cf. Stordalen, *Echoes of Eden*, 94–98.

93. Walton, *Genesis*, 28.

94. See Tsumura, *Earth and the Waters*, 123–37; Tsumura, *Creation and Destruction*, 112–25; Walton, *Genesis*, 27.

95. Stordalen, "Man, Soil, Garden," 16, 21.

> conceived to be, not as it was. Of course, there would expectedly be some correspondence between the two. Still, the primary task is lexicographic rather than geographic.[96]

Ancient people were more concerned with theology and politics than with geography or topography when describing spatial quantities or conceptualizing a geographic area. Referring to a sixth-century copy of an original world map (BM 92687), with Babylon in the center and the uncharted regions on the edges, Stordalen states that it "presents a mixture of topography and cosmology," which he labels "cosmography".[97] He reads Genesis 2:10–14 in these terms. The chapter decreases in describing details which

> is marked by a specific reduction in the number of words employed. The Pishon takes 20 words for its description; the Gihon, 10; the Tigris, 8; and the Euphrates, 4. One river becomes four and twenty words become four. The number of words are halved in two sets; the sets correspond to the unknown and the known.[98]

Since, in ANE, "the number four is symbolic, indicating spatial and geographical completeness" the four rivers imply the four corners of the world, hence the whole.[99] The first river, Pishon,[100] unknown to us from elsewhere in the OT, encircles Havilah on the furthest southeast, famous for its gold, resin, and onyx. The second, Gihon, another mysterious river, encircles Cush, "a region on the borders of the world" on the southwest.[101] The third, the Tigris, is the river of Ashur in the northeast, while the fourth is the Euphrates in

---

96. Stordalen, *Echoes of Eden*, 271.
97. Stordalen, 272.
98. Miscall, "Jacques Derrida," 7–8; cf. Stordalen, *Echoes of Eden*, 273. In this way, "The passage moves from the unknown to the known or, in other terms, from the mythic to the real. The passage announces its literary status" (Miscall, "Jacques Derrida," 8).
99. Stordalen, *Echoes of Eden*, 275. The rivers do not originate in the primeval river of Eden (2:10), issuing from the divine realm, which, in Stordalen's view, flows, at the rim of the world, into the world ocean from which the four rivers, from the four terrestrial corners, send Eden water to the regions of Genesis' world (284–86).
100. The uncorroborated suggestion of Ottosson, "Eden and the Land," 179, that Pishon is identical with the Nile is to be rejected for the latter had a well-established Hebrew name.
101. Stordalen, *Echoes of Eden*, 280. By "Gihon," the brook at the temple mountain may be alluded to and the garden of Eden as a symbolic temple is presented; Witte, *Die biblische Urgeschichte*, 266; Stordalen, *Echoes of Eden*, 286; cf. also Smith, *Genesis of Good and Evil*, 131n11.

the northwest. As the most essential for Mesopotamian life, the Tigris and Euphrates are mentioned by name, but only as third and fourth among the rivers. Even Ashur deserves being mentioned but not Babylon in relation to its river. It is not just the two Mesopotamian rivers that matter. Rather, it is four rivers that are the cradles of human civilization.[102] "The picture here is of a mighty spring that gushes out from Eden and is channeled through the garden for irrigation purposes. All of these channels then serve as headwaters, for the four rivers flow out in various directions as the waters exit the garden."[103]

To Stordalen, the ancient topographic design is of paramount concern. He concludes that "being forced by topographical realities to include both Mesopotamian rivers in Genesis 2:10–14, the overall scheme threatens to collapse."[104] In my view, the main intent of this topography is to caricature Babylonian worldview and ideology by emphasizing the border areas and de-emphasizing the center. Second, there is no geographical place on this globe corresponding to this description – Eden is a non-place,[105] or, in Brown's terms, it is "half real and half imaginative."[106] As opposed to the local interest of BCS, Genesis does not serve the national agenda, it is universal in outlook right from the beginning.[107] And third, their origin and water, essential for Mesopotamian society and culture, are not related to any divine being like Ea. The river only provides the garden with the water needed. Genesis' universalism is making a brief appearance.

We have seen how the similarities in the first creation account and the building of the Tabernacle at the end of Exodus yield a "homology" of temple and created world. Even though no reference to altar, sanctuary, and the like can be found in the Eden story, sanctuary symbolism is very much present. Indeed, Gordon Wenham has drawn attention to the highly symbolic nature of the narrative by noticing parallel features with the Tabernacle account. First, God's "walking," *hithallēk*, in the garden (3:8) is reminiscent

---

102. For a detailed discussion of the rivers' location as pointers to the four corners of the world, adopted here, as well as the interpretive problems involved, see Stordalen, *Echoes of Eden*, 273–86.

103. Walton, *Genesis*, 29.

104. Stordalen, *Echoes of Eden*, 284.

105. Amit, *Reading Biblical Narratives*, 43–44; cf. Carmichael, "Paradise Myth," 48; Stordalen, *Echoes of Eden*; contra Hoffmeier, "Genesis 1–11," 32–35.

106. Brown, *Seven Pillars of Creation*, 82.

107. See Schüle, *Prolog*, 65; cf. McConville, *God and Earthly Power*, 34–36.

to his presence in the tabernacle in Leviticus 26:12, Deuteronomy 23:15, and 2 Samuel 7:6–7. Second, the cherubim were stationed east of the garden to guard the way to the tree of life (3:24). Cherubs guarded the entrances to sanctuaries in Mesopotamia.[108] Both the tabernacle and the Jerusalem Temple were entered from the east, and the holy of holies of the Temple was also guarded by cherubim (1 Kgs 6:23–28) as the ark was (Exod 25:18–22; cf. Exod 26:31 and 1 Kgs 6:29). Third, as the tree of life gives eternal life, so does the sanctuary through sacrifices; the tabernacle menorah itself can be seen as a stylized tree of life.[109]

Fourth, Adam's job was to cultivate and keep, *lə'obdâh ûləšomrâh*, the garden (Gen 2:15). The only other occurrence of these verbs in the Pentateuch is in Numbers 3:7–8, 8:26, and 18:5–6, of the Levites guarding and ministering at the tabernacle. Adam is then viewed as an archetypal Levite. Fifth, this priestly role of Adam may be underlined by the note in Genesis 3:21, "The LORD God made garments [*kotnôt*] of skin for Adam and his wife, and clothed them [*wayyalbišēm*]." This vocabulary is applied when Moses dresses the priests (Exod 28:41; 29:8; 40:14; Lev 8:13).

Sixth, the geographical description in 2:10–14 makes several links with the sanctuary. There is the river flowing out of Eden. Water is a powerful symbol of life in the OT (see Ps 46:5; Ezek 47). Gold and the precious stones bdellium and onyx (NASB) suggest associations with the tabernacle and temple (see Exod 16:4, 33; 25:7; 28:9–14, 20; Num 11:7; 1 Chr 29:2). Seventh, the tree of the knowledge of good and evil "was good for food and pleasing to the eye, and also desirable for gaining wisdom" (Gen 3:6) which may be echoed in Psalm 19:8–9 where the law, kept in the holy of holies, is described in similar terms. Also, touching or even seeing the ark uncovered brought death (Num 4:20; 2 Sam 6:7) as eating the fruit of the tree of knowledge did. The garden, for Wenham, should be viewed as an archetypal sanctuary, and the context supports this interpretation.[110] Genesis 1 relates the creation of the world in six days. The parallels in phraseology between the conclusions of the creation account and the tabernacle building account (Exod 25–40) have

---

108. Cf. Westermann, *Genesis 1–11*, 274.
109. See Meyers, *Tabernacle Menorah*.
110. Wenham, "Sanctuary Symbolism," 399–404.

been noticed.[111] The six commands in the instructions to build the tabernacle correspond to the six days of creation as does God's dwelling in the tabernacle to his rest on the sabbath.

In Mesopotamian creation stories, humans are normally placed in cities to build shrines and provide for gods.[112] Thus, it is curious to see the human being "put" in a garden. Indeed, it may be more appropriate to translate the verb *wayyanniḥēhû* (Gen 2:15) with install. McDowell does so when he states: "Yahweh installed him there in the office of royal caretaker and watchman, similar to the way a divine statue would have been installed in its own temple, as in the *mīs pî pīt pî*."[113] Whereas Mesopotamian gods had images in their respective sanctuaries to represent them, in Genesis 1–2, God installs his image in his garden-temple so that creation may worship him through the image. Humankind ought to represent the Creator by subduing (1:27) and taking care of the earth (2:15).

God puts Adam to the test and gives him the task of naming animals. As in Mesopotamian myths, in chapter 1, it was God who named his handiworks (1:5, 8, 10). Now, however, it is up to his image to perform a similar job. God brings the animals to them to see what they would name them; and whatever the human being called each living creature, that was its name (2:19–20). Walton highlights that "A name may identify the essential nature of the creature, so that giving a name may be an act of assigning the function that creature will have."[114] Humanity has further, according to Chapman, "learned to exercise his capacity for authoritative, divinely sourced, generative speech."[115] Moreover, names establish relationships.[116]

Thus, part of creation was nameless until humankind came along to fill this hiatus. God entrusts the garden of Eden to humankind, planted for them to keep and work (2:15). Whereas in Mesopotamia work is meant to deliver the

---

111. Kearney, "Creation and Liturgy," 375–87; Weinfeld, "Sabbath, Temple," 501–12.
112. McDowell, *Image of God*, 151.
113. McDowell, 158. I have found McDowell's argument about humankind being clothed with divine glory unconvincing; see *Image of God*, 158–68.
114. Walton, *Genesis*, 31.
115. Chapman, "Breath of Life," 248.
116. O'Connor, *Genesis 1–25A*, 53.

gods from drudgery, Genesis deprives work of any relation to the world of the gods.[117] This task of humankind is part of the mandate to subdue the earth.

> By tilling the earth, humans subject it to their will, making it produce what humans subject it to their will, making it produce what humans desire rather than what it would produce if left to its own devices. They relate to the earth as a suzerain would to a vassal.[118]

Moye notes that "Just as God names his creation as he made it, so the man, in the likeness of God, names God's creatures."[119] Giving names to the animals creates the world of humankind.[120] The created world receives a more and more ordered form. By naming the animals, the human being also proves their superior mental qualities, their ability to rule and, by Mesopotamian standards, humankind's "divine" capacities. From now on, naming will predominantly be a human job in Genesis.[121]

God realizes that no animal has proven a suitable companion for Adam (see 2:19). After the declaration in chapter 1 that the created world is good, being alone for Adam is "not good" which comes as a surprise.[122] When God fashions the woman, Adam appears little more than an animal.[123] Being formed from the same material, having the same breath of life as the animals (2:7, 19) and unclothed, the human being is closer to the animal world.[124] So, God gets to work by undertaking major surgery on him by refashioning a ṣela', usually translated "rib." This sense seems beyond doubt for Blenkinsopp

---

117. Westermann, *Genesis 1–11*, 222.

118. Turner, *Announcements of Plot*, 34. Note, however, the difference in vocabulary between 1:28 and 2:7, noticed and discussed by Turner (35).

119. Moye, "In the Beginning," 585.

120. Westermann, *Genesis 1–11*, 228.

121. Cf. Blenkinsopp, *Pentateuch*, 62.

122. Galambush, *Reading Genesis*, 27.

123. It is noteworthy that, in 2:22, the verb applied to creating the woman is *bānâ*, cognate with the Akkadian *terminus technicus banû*, used to denote creation. This usage may witness to either dependence on or imitation of Akkadian parallels. McDowell, *Image of God*, 81–82, cites an Akkadian *mīs pî* incantation as representative of the genre, in which the divine image is "created," *banû*. Schüle, *Prolog*, 169, views Eve's creation as a sign of God's readiness to make artifacts. This can be a nice indication of how the ritual is seen and modified in the Genesis narrative.

124. See Batto, *Slaying the Dragon*, 54–56; Mobley, "Wild Man," 220–23, 227; cf. Joines, "Serpent in Gen 3," 7; Good, *Genesis 1–11*, 26.

as "no one has suggested a better alternative."¹²⁵ Batto, however, may have done just that:

> The image here is that of reworking "one of his sides," that is, of reshaping the whole into two complementary halves. With this redefinition of humankind, creation has been advanced tremendously, according to the Yahwist. The tiller of the garden now has a "helpmate ['ēzer] corresponding to himself." The complementarity of the sexes is immediately confirmed in the institution of marriage, which is presented as the natural conclusion of the creation of man and woman. With these advances the distinction between humans and animals is clear; humankind is a species unto itself and subject to an entirely different order.¹²⁶

This aspect is buttressed by a further motif. In 2:7, God formed Adam from the ground, in 2:9, he "made all kinds of trees grow out of the ground," and, again, in 2:19, he formed the animals from the ground, *min-hă'ădāmâ* (all three times). When God decides to create a companion to Adam, one expects her to be formed from the ground. Instead, the woman is formed from *hā'ādām* (2:22), thus making the point of the interdependence of man and woman yet more poignant.¹²⁷ Their interrelatedness is also underlined by the *'îš-'iššâ* wordplay.¹²⁸

It is important, however, that whereas in chapter 1 the issue is the two genders constituting humankind, in chapter 2 it is their interrelatedness – something, as a mythopoeic theme, unheard of in Mesopotamian literature.¹²⁹

---

125. Blenkinsopp, *Creation, Un-Creation*, 70.
126. Batto, *Slaying the Dragon*, 54.
127. Cf. Hauser, "Genesis 2–3," 386.
128. Although the link may seem weak, note that in BCS (Tablet IV), it was Marduk who, after defeating Tiamat, opens up gates in the female monster's ribs. In Gen 2, it is Yahweh who uses the rib or side of Adam in order to separate male and female. LaCocque, *Trial of Innocence*, 117–20, has convincingly argued for Adam being created androgynous (see also Batto, "Institution of Marriage," 628; Cotter, *Genesis*, 9–30; O'Connor, *Genesis 1–25A*, 55–56; Galambush, *Reading Genesis*, 29; for a different view see Chapman, "Breath of Life"). Borgman, *Genesis*, 26, citing the Midrash, also sees *hā'ādām* as a sexually undivided creature before 2:23. Whitt, *Genesis*, 125, sees the union of man and woman in 2:24 as a recreation of their original state.
129. Schüle, *Prolog*, 169–70. Miscall, "Jacques Derrida," 3, notes that whereas, in ch. 1, "Humanity is divided into the biological 'male and female,'" here, it is the human and social aspects that are emphatic.

Indeed, the second creation account of Genesis is unique in ANE in that it appreciates "the meaning of woman, i.e., that human existence is a partnership of man and woman."[130] Their interrelatedness in marriage (2:24) is set on a new foundation that defies social conventions in both Mesopotamia and Israel. What Adam needs is a companion and not a helper,[131] with whom he "can share because there is a unique level of correspondence."[132] The woman's creation is narrated from as much a relational as a functional perspective.

The resumption of the image of God motif by the allusion to the *mīs pî* ritual in its own way stresses humankind's divine consecration, that is their mandate to rule (see 1:26–28) over creation and all creatures. The events in Genesis 2–3 resemble the procedure of the ritual summarized above.[133] (1) God forms Adam, breathes the breath of life into his nostrils, so he becomes a "living being."[134] (2) A river flows from Eden to water it. (3) God takes and puts Adam in this garden of plants and animals. Animals are named by Adam. The woman is made out of a rib of Adam. God comes into the garden in the coolness of the day. (4) Adam and Eve eat from the tree of knowledge and are expelled from Eden. They cultivate the *ʾădāmâ* and Eve becomes the "mother of all living" (3:20 ESV).

The general similitude between the ritual and the second creation narrative cannot be denied. Indeed, there are more points of correspondence. To

---

130. Westermann, *Genesis 1–11*, 232.

131. Schüle, *Prolog*, 172, 168–69.

132. Schüle, "Made in the 'Image of God,'" 15. Whether the creation of man and woman in ch. 2 is to be understood as an elaboration on the first account or a critique of the image concept because ch. 1 "does not account for what human beings aspire to: the unique relationship to a woman/to a man and the knowledge of good and evil as the most fundamental distinction, underlying all human judgment and human action" (Schüle, 14), the difference to me seems trivial. I consider ch. 2 an elaboration of ch. 1, so seeing chs. 1–3 cohere canonically and thematically to a higher degree. Schüle, 15, overstates his case, fundamental to his thesis, by adding that God is not "the kind of companion for whom Adam is really longing, and we might take that as the first indication that Gen 2 is somewhat suspicious that the idea of man as the image of God could possibly cover this special human need." Gen 1:27 hints at the second account and agrees with it that humankind's being created in the image of God is closely related to humankind's being created as male and female as well as the need of a companion. The author did not elaborate on this in ch. 1 but did so in ch. 2.

133. Schüle, 13. See page 19 for an explanation of the ritual.

134. McDowell, *Image of God*, 150, remarks of Adam, "The notion that his ears, mouth, and eyes were opened is not stated but it is implied by the fact that God spoke to him about what he could and could not eat, that he named all the animals paraded before him, and by his exclamation of delight at the creation of Eve."

begin with, the Genesis section is introduced by the first *toledot* formula in Genesis (2:4). The noun *tōlədōt* is a derivative of the verb *yālad*, "to bear," a cognate with Akkadian *walādu*, the term used to denote the creation of the deity in the ritual's texts. The Genesis author could not imagine God as giving birth to Adam. In the heading, however, he alluded to the birthing terminology of the ritual. The verb's application in the ritual's texts and Genesis 2:4's allusion to this may also explain why the formula is not placed before the first creation account.[135]

Schüle notes that God "takes" humankind and "lets him rest."[136] In this picture, he sees the image transported through the wasteland to the garden by human hands and coming finally to rest. There are two points, noticed by Schüle, where the Genesis account departs from its model and these deviations are of crucial significance.[137] First, at the point where God's image in Eden is completed, humankind needs a companion so that he is not alone (2:18) because God's company is insufficient. In my view, that is an ingenious way that the narrator chose to comment or elaborate on 1:27 where both "image" and the qualification "male and female" occur. As we have seen, through the intertextual reference to the ritual, "image" is the "implicit tenor" of chapter 2, while gender separation is the explicit essence of humankind's creation. It is being male and female that makes up humankind being created in God's image.[138]

The second modification concerns the end of the story – at the point where the image is carried from the garden to its final destination in the shrine, humankind leaves the garden to return to the soil he was taken from. This again is a genuine contribution to the divine image concept as well as a motif pointing forward. Even though he was created in God's image, humankind cannot enter the sanctuary. Indeed, humankind is exiled. God will, however, make amends by initiating covenant, first with Noah, then with Abraham, and then with Israel. A major aspect of this covenant will be the sanctuary

---

135. The *toledot* formula often elaborates on an aspect of some motif already mentioned; Baumgart, *Die Umkehr des Schöpfergottes*, 41–46.

136. Schüle, *Prolog*, 163.

137. Schüle, 165.

138. See Trible, *God and the Rhetoric of Sexuality*, 15–21.

designed by God. Israel will worship God and her representative will enter this shrine.[139]

Obviously, the goal of the ritual is the consecration of the divine image so that it can represent the deity. After the night spent with the gods in the garden, the image "belongs entirely to the divine sphere. It has become the bodily appearance of a God [sic], the very medium through which he enters the world of created life and, correspondingly, through which he can be addressed by prayer, worship and sacrifice."[140] Something similar and something totally different can be claimed of the divine image presented in humankind in chapter 2. Humankind is created in order to represent God in a bodily appearance and therefore belongs entirely to the sphere of creation, this world. There is no consecration. However, that does not make humankind less precious. Indeed, in the subsequent narrative, human life will be seen as the highest asset (4:10–11; 9:6). And it is humankind bearing God's image who can address the Creator in prayer, worship, and sacrifice.

The two-day pattern of the ritual has virtually no parallel in Genesis 2, as, in chapter 1, the creation of humankind is executed on day six. Still, with the "anesthesia" motif and by not making it two days (2:21), the narrator provided a parallel and, at the same time, made the two creation accounts concur with each other as to how long the creation of humankind took (see 1:27; 5:1–2).[141] And finally, unlike idols, human beings cannot be adorned with precious stones and gold leaves. That is why these commodities are transferred to Havilah, the land of the river Pishon with its fountain in Eden.

After these parallels, let us now turn to the theological import of the second creation account in relation to the ritual and the first creation account.

> The texts reflect the major ideological problem of these procedures as their being carried out by human hands, although only the God or the Goddess [sic] whose image it was about to

---

139. There may be yet another modification in Genesis of the ritual. As clear from extant texts, the *mīs pî* was to be done "on a favorable day;" see Walker and Dick, "Induction of the Cult," 72–73, 84–85. As opposed to this, the "partition" of the human being ends successfully after a trial-and-error procedure. The man's acclamation, however, makes it a favorable day.

140. Schüle, "Made in the 'Image of God,'" 12.

141. The author of ch. 2 could have easily made his account resemble the ritual to a higher extent by dividing the one day in ch. 2 into two with God performing the "operation" on Adam at night. By sticking to the one-day pattern, he made the two accounts on the creation of humankind correspond to a higher degree.

become was seen to be the real craftsman. No human being, but only the deity was able to lay his/her features into the statue so that it was really his/her image.[142]

By this observation, Schüle has put his finger on one of the crucial issues. For the *mīs pî* ritual, it is a dilemma how a deity can be fashioned by human hands. To solve the problem, at one point during the ritual, the hands of the craftsmen were cut off in a symbolic way and they were to take an oath of having never even touched the statue.[143] Genesis 2's solution of the problem is more radical and, concerning the ritual, this appears to be the most important aspect that has escaped the attention of interpreters. By a profound recasting, the narrator turns the ritual and the roles in it upside down – now, it is not humans shaping the divine image but the divine craftsman forming, *yāṣar*, the human being in his image.[144] God is involved in a rather dirty process of creating in chapter 2: he plants a garden, shapes various animals as well as humankind, then, performs surgery on him. This is a very material God in a very material world.[145]

In Genesis 1:26–27, the reference point of God's image was the king in Mesopotamia, as the representative of the deity. In Genesis 2, it is the image of the deity that is to be consecrated and used to represent the god. Priestly connotations are present here.[146] The underlying question that moves the narrative forward is To what extent is humankind the image of God?

In David Carr's view, the P creation account was placed before the non-P account in order to replace it.[147] Mark Smith sees it slightly differently: "To my mind, the effect was not so much to replace but rather more to redirect and refocus the audience's attention by giving the initial account pride of

---

142. Schüle, "Made in the 'Image of God,'" 12.

143. Schüle, 12.

144. Only P calls humankind the image of God, as Schüle, *Prolog*, 86, correctly claims; but cf. McDowell, *Image of God*. This does not entail as Schüle thinks, however, an antagonistic stance toward the concept of humankind's creation in ch. 2. As he himself makes it clear the second creation account is based on the creation of the *god's image*.

145. Contra Dauphinais and Levering, *Holy People, Holy Land*, 32.

146. Cf. Chapman, "Breath of Life," 246–47.

147. Carr, *Reading the Fractures*, 74–75, 317.

place."¹⁴⁸ This approach seems to better account for both the similarities and dissimilarities of the two chapters.

> In conclusion, one could say that the first account seeks to found a sort of theocracy of the God of Israel over the entire world, while the second account wants to show how much the creator God was attentive, from the beginning, to the conditions of life for the humanity which populates the promised land.¹⁴⁹

Bernard Batto has made a good case for the J account's dependence on Atrahasis.¹⁵⁰ As the story stands now, however, it clearly demonstrates signs of reworking. By combining references to Atrahasis and the *mīs pî* ritual, the narrator has achieved something remarkable. By alluding to the detailed procedure of the ritual and Atrahasis' motifs, as well as borrowing and putting motifs of the ritual and the epic into the context of the second creation narrative, he provided a framework of reference. By so doing and placing his account after that of P, the editor has qualified and clarified P's image of God concept, at the same time, however, insisting that it "is the one God Yahweh, also called Elohim, who authors this world-order that is marked out from the type of world-order imagined in the religious environment."¹⁵¹

Marduk's victory over the anti-creation forces in BCS is made complete when the gods are relieved of the burden of labor and when a capital city for Marduk's dwelling is built with a temple and ziggurat (Tablet VI). Marduk had been declared king and endowed with the power of fixing destinies. Tellingly, none of these is so much as hinted at in Genesis 1–2. There is no kingship, no city, no temple-ziggurat – the triad of Babylonian mythology

---

148. Smith, *Priestly Vision in Genesis*, 215. I think Smith hits the nail on the head here. His argument, however, of the priestly tradition defeating the other creation traditions, including that of ch. 2 (226–27), seems to run counter to his view quoted above. Ska, "Genesis 2–3," 1–27, also sees in the two accounts more incompatible views and political-theological interests behind them. Note also that in his *opus magnum*, Carr, *Formation*, 295, by using milder language and referring to P as reworking "earlier alternate traditions to offer a different account of events," seems to have modified his former stance.

149. Ska, "Genesis 2–3," 21.

150. Batto, *Slaying the Dragon*, 41–72. See also his comparative study of 2:18–24 where he convincingly argues for its dependence on Atrahasis. I can well imagine that the original J account was based on Atrahasis and as such was more reminiscent of it, as "reconstructed" by Batto, 41–72. P certainly could have used J's "Yahweh" by modifying it into "Yahweh Elohim," and added some details like the river account and the tree motif.

151. McConville, *God and Earthly Power*, 24.

is absent.¹⁵² Creation in Genesis is fine and complete without them. What remains is a garden. Humankind created in the image of God is the ruler of earth. The garden is the city where the first couple are at home, the temple and the ziggurat where God dwells (see 3:8). It is the garden that bridges heaven and earth, it replaces the achievements that Mesopotamian people were so proud of. There is no talk of fixing fate as this will depend on humankind's decisions.¹⁵³ The end result of the creation narrative of Genesis, both by what it narrates and what it keeps quiet about, is the dethronement of Marduk: without capital city, without shrine, without kingship he is unable to rule.

The image of God concept introduced, in chapter 1, by God's decision to create humankind in his image and set against the background of the Mesopotamian king image is both liberating and democratizing as well as a polemic against the status quo – there is no need for kings as humankind is the image of God, and they as a community will perform their mission to rule over creation. Even if the term is not mentioned the concept is very much present in the creation of humankind in chapter 2. By being set in the ritual context of mouth washing with no temple and city, we can hear a definite anti-cult polemic – there is no need of cult statues, as the image of God is humankind themselves consecrated to represent the Creator in this world.¹⁵⁴ Humankind is simultaneously image *and* worshipper of the image maker. Stemming from two different traditions, the creation accounts are still a literary unity.¹⁵⁵ Indeed, they are a theological unity. In the Babylonian exile, creation was formulated in its unexcelled version, trying to give hope by announcing the end of the old and outlining a new world.

---

152. Comparing the two-stage creation of humankind or possibly the creation of two classes of humankind in the late Assyrian epic Creation of the King (see Foster, *Before the Muses*, 496–97) with creation in Genesis, Schüle, *Prolog*, 121–24, observes that the stem מלך is not used in Genesis 1 possibly to avoid a two-class society consisting of kings and commoners.

153. Cf. Otto, "Die Paradieserzählung," 190–91.

154. Cf. Brueggemann, "From Dust to Kingship," 1–18, where he, after studying several OT texts, argues that the point of 2:7 is the enthronement of humankind. A royal interpretation of 2:7 may be boosted by the fact that the mouth washing ritual was performed on kings too; see Berlejung, *Theologie der Bilder*, 182.

155. Cf. Stordalen, "Genesis 2,4," 173; Sawyer, "Image of God," 64–66; Otto, "Die Paradieserzählung," 73; Wenham, "Priority of P," 253–56. Otto, "Die Paradieserzählung," 183–88, considers the first account the elaboration of the second while Smith, *Priestly Vision of Genesis*, 216–28, views the first as a commentary on the second. Wenham, "Sanctuary Symbolism," 404, claims of Gen 1–3, "Whatever the stylistic differences between the sources, our interpretation suggests that ideologically the J and P sources are much closer to each other than is usually held."

In the Garden (3:1–24)

For ANE people, including Israel, one of the vexing existential questions was, "why is man so like the gods in that he has knowledge and yet so unlike the gods in that he is mortal?"[156] What is the explanation Genesis provides for this? How does Genesis communicate its worldview so that it makes sense to exilic Jews? And how does Babylon fare in Genesis' view? After the BCS and Atrahasis, the Genesis narrator here has stories like Adapa and Gilgamesh as well as various mythical characters and motifs in mind. The following interpretation will be an attempt at highlighting the multiple threads of this colorful fabric.

Whereas, in Mesopotamian thought, the created world was not very good (i.e. evil was inherent in creation), in Genesis, God creates a very good world (i.e. evil is subsequent to creation).[157] Eternal life was something desired in Mesopotamia. In the Adapa story, Anu is angry with Adapa who broke the wings of the South Wind. When Adapa is ordered to report to Anu, Ea deceives him by advising him not to accept food or drink from Anu.[158] Meanwhile, however, Anu changes his mind due to the good impression Adapa made on him, and what he offers is the bread and water of eternal life. In obedience to Ea's advice, however, Adapa refuses them, so unwittingly robbing himself of eternal life. In this myth, eternal life is represented by food as in Genesis.

The motifs of eternal life, plant, and, importantly, serpent occur in the Gilgamesh epic (Tablet XI). Gilgamesh, intent on acquiring eternal life, travels to Utnapishtim. After failing the first test, he is given a second chance. Gilgamesh gets the plant from the bottom of the sea but, alas, when taking a bath in a pool, a serpent smells the fragrance of the plant and steals it. When Gilgamesh realizes what happened, he breaks down in tears.

The most significant similarities between Mesopotamian myths and Genesis 3 are summed up by Skinner,

> In both we have the idea that wisdom and immortality combined constitute equality with the deity; in both we have a man receiving the first and missing the second; and in both the man

---

156. Clark, "Legal Background," 266.
157. See Blenkinsopp, "P and J in Genesis," 7; LaCocque, *Trial of Innocence*, 49–50.
158. See, e.g. Joines, "Serpent in Gen 3," 7; Batto, "Malevolent Deity," 207–8.

is counseled in opposite directions by supernatural voices, and acts on that advice which is contrary to his interest.[159]

There are differences too, however, between the Mesopotamian myths and the biblical account. The first is that both Adapa and Gilgamesh sought to acquire something they had not possessed. As opposed to them, Adam and Eve forfeited the eternal life they had possessed. Adapa and Gilgamesh are postdiluvian heroes as, in Mesopotamia, humankind seems to have enjoyed eternal life which, however, changed after the flood when humankind was decreed mortal. Again, what the Genesis story does not explicate but implies is that humankind was not created immortal; with an open access to the tree of life (2:9), however, they practically had eternal life.[160] This is buttressed by God's preventive action of expelling the first couple from Eden after their disobedience so that humankind is unable "to reach out his hand and take also from the tree of life and eat, and live forever" (3:22).

Now, does the serpent, the antagonist of the story, represent a benevolent or an evil force?[161] Serpents in ANE world had an ambiguous role. They were linked to wisdom, fertility, and health, now, to chaos, threat, and destruction.[162] Since what the serpent says comes true but the effects of his words are partly negative for humankind in particular and creation in general, the answer to the question is as ambiguous as the serpent itself. I suggest that to evaluate the serpent's role correctly, we need to look for clues in Babylonian mythology. I shall draw particular attention to some specific parallels ignored so far.

In Mesopotamia, snakes not only accompany major "gods, but are also their allies against evil, acting as fearsome champions of law and order. From the late third millennium B.C.E. onwards, inscriptions attest to the

---

159. Skinner, *Critical and Exegetical Commentary*, 92.

160. Similarly, Beattie, "*Peshat* and *Derash*," 68; Herion, "Why God Rejected," 56; LaCocque, *Trial of Innocence*, 99–102; cf. Schmid, "Loss of Immortality," 64; McKeown, *Genesis*, 33; Stordalen, "God of the Eden Narrative," 12. Batto, *Slaying the Dragon*, 57, claims "that humankind's status was not as yet entirely defined, that the human experiment was still in the developmental stage."

161. Westermann, "Der Mensch im Urgeschehen," 238, does not deem the identity of the serpent, a creature of God, important, only its words. Then he adds, "The words of the serpent are certainly directed against God, but this does not become the theme of the narrative. We are not justified by the text in seeing behind these words a complete orientation of the serpent against God or a being at enmity with God."

162. Cf. Charlesworth, *Good and Evil Serpent*; Walton, *Genesis*, 34; Day, *From Creation to Abraham*, 44–46.

presence of snake-dragons guarding the entrance to temples."[163] Three dragons (*ušumgallu*, *mušḫuššu*, *bašmu*) are known as guardians of temples.[164] Because of its appearance, history, and perceived significance, one of them is of particular importance for the interpretation of Genesis 3.

Babylonia's patron god, Marduk is often depicted or associated with his symbol, a snake-dragon, the "most important dragon in ancient Mesopotamia . . . known from the Old Akkadian period down to the Seleucid period,"[165] called *mušḫuššu*, "fearsome serpent."[166] Nabu, the god of science, who gained prestige in the Neo-Babylonian empire as Marduk's son, was also associated with the *mušḫuššu*. It became associated with the supreme god(s) of Babylon after a long and battered history of changing masters from Ninazu to Ningishzida to Tishpak, tutelary god of Eshnunna, who is said to have vanquished it.[167] With Hammurabi's conquest of Eshnunna, the monster became related to Babylon's patron deity and his son Nabu. These two, as opposed to the previous deities, were never associated with other dragons, only with the *mušḫuššu*.[168]

At earlier times, the *mušḫuššu* had a beneficial, apotropaic function in Babylonian religion and was regarded as a champion of law and order. A fearless warrior, it was supposed to watch over the just rule of its masters and attack evildoers. Also, it was among those that repelled evil influence.[169] From Middle-Babylonian times on, however, it became associated with Tiamat and her monsters (BCS I.121; II.27; III.31, 89), and so had a somewhat qualified positive function. This was mainly due to the fact that in BCS IV.116, after his defeat of Tiamat, Marduk sets up the images of the vanquished monsters in the gate of Apsu with the *mušḫuššu* among them.[170]

> Thus the new theology preserves the apotropaic quality of images of the m. [*mušḫuššu*] (and of the other monsters): whereas earlier they reminded evil of the m.'s active intervention on behalf

---

163. Takayoshi, "Snake-Dragon," 26.
164. Takayoshi, 26.
165. Takayoshi, 25.
166. Lambert, "History of the muš-ḫuš," 87n1.
167. See Lewis, "CT 13.33–34," 29.
168. Wiggermann, "mušḫuššu," 457–59.
169. Wiggermann, *Mesopotamian Protective Spirits*, 159.
170. Wiggermann, "mušḫuššu," 455, 458–61.

of law and order, they now discourage it by exemplifying the fate of rebels at the hands of Marduk.[171]

The *mušḫuššu* is generally portrayed with the long neck and head of a snake, with a forked tongue protruding from its mouth and with the front paws of a lion and, as hind paws, the talons of an eagle. The body, neck, and tail are scaled.[172] Lambert aptly highlights that "Here, then, is a combination of three of the most awesome creatures from the animal kingdom: the lion, king of beasts; the snake, feared and admired everywhere for its uncanny gait and power to inflict sudden death; and the eagle, king of the birds."[173] Of the many depictions of the *mušḫuššu*, specimens can be seen in rows 2 and 4 on Babylon's Ishtar gate reconstructed by Nebuchadnezzar II.[174] They were supposed to guard the gates of the city against enemy attack as other representations of the serpent from the Neo-Assyrian and Neo-Babylonian periods make it clear.[175] Nebuchadnezzar boasted of having placed snake-dragons at the gates of Babylon obviously to guard the city from intruders.[176]

I suggest that the Genesis account draws on various Mesopotamian myths and motifs related to the immortality *topos*, as recognized by many, and the character of the Genesis serpent is modeled on ANE serpents, particularly the *mušḫuššu*. I propose that (1) its association with Marduk and Nabu in sixth-century Babylonia; (2) its being endowed with some protective function;[177] (3) its portrayal as a legged serpent; and (4) its perceived significance in contemporary society makes the *mušḫuššu* a particularly good candidate for being cast in Genesis' subversive counter-narrative through, instead of protecting

---

171. Wiggermann, *Mesopotamian Protective Spirits*, 169, and "mušḫuššu," 461. This positive evaluation of the *mušḫuššu* had only gradually come about, however. Originally "a death dealing monster," Wiggermann, "Tišpak," 117–33, suggests, it was created by Enlil and Tiamat to restore order in the society bent to anarchy without a king by, paradoxically, killing off the population. Wiggermann, "Tišpak," 125–26, therefore calls it a "death demon." Its negative and positive sides will concern the discussion of Gen 3.

172. Wiggermann, "mušḫuššu," 456.

173. Lambert, "History of the muš-ḫuš," 456; cf. Gen 3:1.

174. See Lambert, 87–88.

175. Lambert, 87–89. The portrayals of the *mušḫuššu* are more or less consistent from the late-third millennium to Neo-Babylonian times, "a striking testimony to continuity in ancient Mesopotamia of the use of these creatures" (93).

176. Langdon, *Building Inscriptions*, 85.

177. In Middle-Assyrian times, figurines of the *mušḫuššu* were used to prophylactic ends under house floors; Albenda, "Of Gods, Men and Monsters," 18.

God's garden,[178] leading humankind astray and being the main instigator of humankind's disobedience. The *mušḫuššu* is a metonymic representation of Marduk and his son Nabu.

One minor, and less serious, aspect may buttress this metonymic interpretation. As noted above, the *mušḫuššu* had changed hands quite a few times in its long history. Its frequent handing-over must have had a harmful effect on its psyche. On its appearance in Genesis 3, it may be fed up with its present master and has its own scheme by intending to change hands once again, this time from Yahweh/Marduk to humankind. Moreover, as observed, the serpent might be envious of the woman for taking its place in chapter 2.[179] These are possible reasons for it to instigate humankind to eat from the tree so that they become gods too. By finally wanting one of its kind, another animal-like creature, to rule over the animal world, it tries to sneak out of Yahweh's control.[180]

Genesis 3 starts by calling the serpent "more crafty" than any other animal God created (3:1).[181] Moberly sees the epithet ambiguously, claiming it should alert the reader's suspicion. Also, the serpent misquotes God's order. The enmity between humans and snakes and the persistent opposition of the serpent to God again raise the alarm in the reader.[182] In any case, the "serpent recognized the prohibition for what it was, a ploy on the part of the Creator to preserve his own turf."[183]

On the other hand, by its introduction, the serpent is associated with Nabu the god of wisdom. It is noteworthy, though, that it is one of the creatures of God, not an autonomous being. It appears as God's antagonist by its attempt to induce the first couple to disobey their Creator. The serpent's

---

178. Dragga, "Genesis 2–3," 6–7, also claims that the serpent's role was to guard the tree.

179. E.g. LaCocque, *Trial of Innocence*, 174.

180. Despite being animal-like, humankind enjoys a special relationship with God (see 3:8), so much so that, Bailey, "Initiation," 143, speculates, the serpent was envious of this.

181. I fail to see that this note is supposed to warn the "audience to beware of the serpent" as Boomershine, "Structure of Narrative," 117, suggests, without giving rationale.

182. Moberly, *Theology of the Book of Genesis*, 79–80.

183. Batto, *Slaying the Dragon*, 59. In a comment, Batto clarifies his stance, "Certainly mythology contains ample evidence of gods lying. But in the case of Genesis 3, I am inclined to think that the Yahwist intended to portray Yahweh as innocently mistaken" (Batto, 61).

suggestion for the woman to eat from the tree of knowledge of good and evil[184] seems noble but leads to unwanted consequences, even if, as it turns out, it is based on truth.[185] With their eyes opened (3:7), the final act of the *mīs pî* ritual is completed: by becoming animated, the divine image gets fully functional.[186] By persuading them, the serpent rules humankind and so subverts creation order (cf. 1:26). Having eaten the fruit, "the nature of their newly acquired knowledge was the kind that made them aware of their nakedness."[187] Children "are not ashamed of their nakedness, but mature people, wise people, those who have a knowledge of good and bad, are."[188]

This is the conventional interpretation of the nakedness motif. Bernard Batto, however, looks at the Mesopotamian evidence afresh. In both Sumerian and Akkadian texts, primitive, unclothed humans are as good as animals, in need of the gifts of civilization, clothes among them, to be bestowed by the gods. Clothes made humans different from animals and closer to the gods, who were also clothed. As we have seen, the first human being, even with God's breath in his nose, was closer to animals than to the divine world. Batto thus takes 2:25, "Adam and his wife were both naked, and they felt no shame," as a statement of their animal-like status. Similarly, he sees 3:7 as the recognition "that they were closer to animalhood than to the divinity to which they aspired."[189] Their making clothes (3:7) is then "an act of defiance of their creator and a grasping at divinity."[190] Batto thus argues, "Ashamed of their nakedness but unable to make proper clothes for themselves, they hide from the deity whose status they aspired to. For his part the deity, in recognition that these humans had indeed proven to be more godlike than animallike, eventually clothes them."[191]

---

184. Clark, "Legal Background," 267, claims that the phrase "good and evil" (3:5) is not original but does not provide reasons. I see it as an epexegetical remark.

185. See Barr, *Garden of Eden*, 8, 60–61; Dragga, "Genesis 2–3," 7; Stordalen, "Man, Soil, Garden," 24.

186. Schüle, "Reluctant Image," 43–44.

187. York, "Maturation Theme," 405.

188. York, 409.

189. Batto, *Slaying the Dragon*, 56.

190. Batto, 56.

191. Batto, 56. Cf. Jacob, *Genesis*, 31: "nakedness is animal-like." Galambush, *Reading Genesis*, 32, asks from where the human couple "got the idea of clothing and belts in the first place." In effect, similarly to Batto, she suggests that they saw God, obviously clothed, walk in the garden. Thus, they decided that, to demonstrate their new and more exalted identity, they

Reading Genesis 3 against the background of the Adapa myth may yield a parallel interpretation. For an audience well-versed in Babylonian mythology, one character of the myth might be dimly recognizable in the Genesis story. The two guardians of heaven granting Adapa entrance were Tammuz, god of vegetation, and Ningishzida, likewise god of vegetation and gate-keeper of the underworld as well as a tree god, his name meaning "Lord of the right/reliable tree" or "The lord who makes the tree be right."[192] He is often associated with snakes, as on the libation vase of Gudea where he is flanked by two *mušḫuššu*; elsewhere, he is often depicted as a serpent with a human head. Ningishzida is a reliable god, as is evident from his name. He is involved with law both on earth and in the underworld. His most common title refers to his function, "chamberlain of the netherworld," and, in standard Babylonian texts, he is called "lord of the netherworld." In this capacity, he upholds world order. To this end, reliability is essential to him, "encoded in his name (-zi-da)."[193] Ningishzida was evidently a serpent with a human head – that is why he could speak. Indeed, the guardian of heaven opened the door not to eternal life but to his realm, the underworld. Death, previously unknown to humankind, is now part of their fate.[194]

How are the serpent and God respectively to be evaluated? In his *The Theology of the Book of Genesis*, after a discussion of James Barr's treatment of the Eden story,[195] Walter Moberly sums up the problem:

> The words that YHWH speaks (2:16–17) are the first words of direct, personal address, such that one might reasonably suppose them to have keynote significance: Here are the creator's instructions for his creation, in some way determinative of the relationship between them. What context other than that of creation could be more weighty? If this is a foundational portrayal

---

needed clothing; cf. Smith, *Genesis of Good and Evil*, 60. Westermann, *Genesis 1–11*, 269, notes that providing clothes to the human couple is the only reference to God's making something which, in the OT, as opposed to Mesopotamia, is regarded as human, cultural achievement.

192. Wiggermann, "Nin-ĝišzida," 368.

193. Wiggermann, 371.

194. The Ningishzida connection is only valid if his relevance in the Neo-Babylonian era was perceptible. For Adapa as representative of humankind, despite being an *apkallu*, see Lowery, *Toward a Poetics*, 223–24.

195. Barr, *Garden of Eden*, considered "Gnostic" by Moberly, *Theology of the Book of Genesis*, 71–78.

> of the God whose people Israel know themselves to be, then high expectations naturally attach to the portrayal of God here. Specifically, if God's warning of death as the penalty for disobedience here (2:17) is an empty warning, then why should other warnings from God elsewhere be taken seriously? The heuristic assumption for the reader must surely be that God's words here are reliable.[196]

The lack of justification or explanation on God's part of his prohibition and warning, Moberly goes on, is natural – he is the maker and his words are reliable. That is the working assumption of the audience. Again,

> when the snake continues by flatly denying God's warning of death, insists that the result will be beneficial, and fills the silence about God's initial motive in a suspicious way – grudging repression, not benefit, was God's concern (3:4–5) – then the reader's working assumption is that the snake will be proved wrong.[197]

Since trust in God is a weighty issue in the opening chapters of the Bible, with enormous theological ramifications, "the classic Christian instinct to resist a reading of Genesis 2–3 in which God is untrustworthy and his words unreliable fully deserves to be tried out heuristically."[198] Moberly does so by taking alienation, hostility, burdensome work as the outworking of death in God's threat. Thus, because our initial expectation, the "prima facie sense of the warning," is not fulfilled, a new look at the words may find that they hold true "in a sense other than that initially imagined."[199] So, Moberly suggests that we

> look again at those principles already held and dig deeper, as it were, so as to ask whether they may indeed be true even if such truth is no longer at a surface level in the kind of way that was initially supposed. This, I propose, is the strategy employed within Genesis 2–3 – to lead the reader into deeper

---

196. Moberly, *Theology of the Book of Genesis*, 78–79.
197. Moberly, 80.
198. Moberly, 83.
199. Moberly, 83–85.

understanding of what is, and is not, meant by "death" as the consequence of disobedience to God.[200]

I feel somewhat ambivalent about Moberly's interpretation. He seems both to ignore the ANE background and to downplay the fact that the snake's words come true as opposed to those of God. He also appears to disregard the positive effect of the act of the first couple, namely that they acquire wisdom – the result is double-sided. On the other hand, he has rightly emphasized (the partly) harmful outcome of the snake's offer, often overlooked. And most importantly, he has put his finger on a nerve of the passage: What deity do we have portrayed here? How can we trust such a god? I will discuss this question in due time, after the flood narrative when we are given more pieces of the puzzle to fill in the picture.[201]

John Day raises the similar question of why God wants the couple to remain ignorant of wisdom. His answer is that God disapproves of the first human beings' aspiration to acquire the knowledge of good and evil by their assertion of autonomy so disobeying God's command not to eat of the tree. This knowledge should be gained by obedience to God as "The fear of the LORD is the beginning of knowledge/wisdom" (Prov 1:7; 9:10).[202]

I have mentioned the "crafty" serpent's possible association with Nabu, god of wisdom in Babylonia. The close propinquity to the wisdom tradition of Genesis 3 is well-known. David Carr lists the similarities: (1) The tree often stands for wisdom. (2) The serpent, likewise a symbol for wisdom in ANE, is characterized as "prudent, *'ārūm*," a term used in Proverbs to stress the contrast between the wise and the fool. (3) The woman's perception of the desirability of the fruit (*taăvâ, neḥmād, haśkîl*; 3:6) resembles wisdom terminology. The story is a polemic against wisdom tradition, Carr goes on to say that it "is characterized by a reasoning based more on collected human experience than divine *fiat*."[203]

Mark Smith, comparing Genesis 2–3 to Ezekiel 28, sees the narrative as criticizing not wisdom in general but more specifically the royal worldview

---

200. Moberly, 86.

201. Cf. Stordalen, "Man, Soil, Garden," 22, who applies a Greimasian scheme.

202. Day, *From Creation to Abraham*, 66–67.

203. Carr, "Politics of Textual Subversion," 589–90. For a more comprehensive list of vocabulary and themes, see Stordalen, *Echoes of Eden*, 206–13.

of wisdom.²⁰⁴ Wisdom can be used for good and ill. By using it with ambiguous effects, I suggest that the serpent served as well as betrayed humankind's interests. It furnished them with wisdom but, at the same time, did not guard the garden from enemy attack – rather, it spat its lethal venom at humankind.²⁰⁵ In fact, the narrative implies, it led an enemy attack by sneaking in. Consequently, the garden is to be guarded by cherubim²⁰⁶ rather than by Ningishzida or the *mušḫuššu* (see 3:24).²⁰⁷ The story accounts for both the gains and limits of wisdom.

Divide et impera, that is God's tactic in dealing with disobedient subjects. He acts by doing justice to the divine order, and poetic justice at that. The fate of the serpent, the ringleader of the rebellion against the divine status quo, is humiliation²⁰⁸ and enmity with the woman and her offspring, humankind (3:15).²⁰⁹ The "punishment suggests a crime of arrogance. The one who presumed to be higher than all the other creatures, high enough to dare to enter a conversation with the woman, will be forced to live lower than most animals, on its belly in the dirt."²¹⁰ It took the scene as *'ārûm*, now cursed, *'ārûr*, it departs.²¹¹

Since the woman misled the man, even though she will attempt to control him, she is cursed to a subject status and labor pangs,²¹² *'iṣṣābôn* (3:16), but

---

204. Smith, *Priestly Vision of Genesis*, 43–45.
205. See Van de Mieroop, "Reading Babylon," 267.
206. Cf. Dragga, "Genesis 2–3," 12.
207. Note that the *mušḫuššu* was supposed to guard the city Babylon. In PH's alternative world, however, there is virtually no city – it is a garden that is to be guarded.
208. Sjöberg, "Eve and the Chameleon," 222 (but see George, *Babylonian Gilgamesh Epic*, vol. 2, 896–97), questions that it is a serpent that stole the magical plant from Gilgamesh. The phrase *nēšu ša qaqqari*, "earth-lion," in XI.296 denotes a chameleon instead, he suggests. As a matter of fact, the serpent in Genesis 3 is not said to lose its legs (cf. 3:14) but from now on is to go in a subservient position; Walton, "Genesis," 35. If Sjöberg's suggestion holds the reference to the *mušḫuššu*/Ningishzida is even more likely.
209. See Wenham, *Genesis 1–15*, 79; Phillips, "Serpent Intertexts," 237.
210. Chapman, "Breath of Life," 258.
211. Phillips, "Serpent Intertexts," 237, 241. As opposed to the man and the woman, the serpent is not interrogated by God; Arneth, *Durch Adams Fall*, 118. This might be another hint at the narrator's stance toward it – Yahweh as good as ignores it in the court.
212. Foh, "What is the Woman's Desire?" 376–83. Schüle, *Prolog*, 175–76, claims that the connotation of the verb *māšal* in the OT is always positive and here it contains a function of caring for and representing the woman by her husband in ANE societies that, in the curse, gets distorted. What is negative is not the competence but the fact that the woman/wife is not allowed to perform this. In other words, it is a patriarchal society into which she is cursed. I find Foh's

not disabled or dead children as in Atrahasis.²¹³ The relationship between man and woman, that the man so much needed, is now ruined.²¹⁴ Man's work is also cursed into *'iṣṣābôn*, along with the ground, the sphere and subject of his work. As a result of man's eating from the forbidden plant, his work will be futile, producing "thorns and thistles," plants, he cannot eat, whereas the subject of his work will become his grave (3:17–19).²¹⁵

Yahweh's judgment thus affects his initial blessing of and mandate to humankind (1:28) negatively. Humans will multiply but only through painful childbirth. They will subdue the earth but this will come by sweat, thistle, and thorns. Their rule over animals will be an ongoing struggle. (Note the chapter's underlying theme of humankind's original place in the animal world.) Since animals were subjected to human rule (1:28), the curse on the serpent is rather double-edged. On the one hand, in their struggle with humankind, animals prove their equal, which rather than a demotion is a promotion. On the other hand, human dominion over the animal world will result in the latter's inferiority and defeat. As Turner notes, "3.14–15 announces a decisive shift in human-animal relations. Conflict has replaced simple dominion, with the guarantee of victory going to the human side."²¹⁶ Indeed, the serpent's initial intention might be to reverse God's creation mandate of humankind to rule over the animal world.²¹⁷

---

argument more compelling though; cf. Longman, *Genesis*, 67. She argues on the basis of 4:7, where *təšûqâ* recurs, that the noun has no sexual overtones (see Lohr, "Sexual Desire," 227–46) but, in both passages, a desire to control, the man and sin respectively. Turner, *Announcements of Plot*, 24n3, seems to have got her wrong as well as the evidence in Genesis where not only Rebekah (27:5ff) but Sara (21:9–14), Leah (29:23; 30:16), and Rachel too (31:34–35; cf. 35:2–4) got their ways.

213. As the harlot initiated Enkidu into civilization, so does the woman, an agent of civilization and not a temptress, with the man. The result of the initiation is knowledge of good and evil. But, whereas in Gilgamesh, Enkidu alone is initiated, in Genesis, both woman, the initiator, and man are. When discovered, the man blames the woman for her role as the initiator. This is analogous to the curse of the dying Enkidu of the harlot. "Come, Shamhat, I shall fix a fate for you! [Curses (?)] shall not cease for ever and ever" (VII.iii.6–7). At Shamash's challenge, Enkidu retracts this, wishing the harlot a successful life of a courtesan: "Because of you, the mother of seven, the honoured wife, shall be deserted" (VII.iv.11); Bailey, "Initiation," 147–48.

214. Walsh, "Genesis 2.4b–3.23," 168.

215. Westermann, *Genesis 1–11*, 265 (quote from King, *Babylonian Boundary-Stones*, 41) refers to an Akkadian curse "May Adad, the ruler of heaven and earth overwhelm his fields, so that there may spring up abundantly weeds in place of green herbs and thorns in place of grain!"

216. Turner, *Announcements of Plot*, 23, 45.

217. Turner, 30–31.

The enmity between the serpent and the woman (3:15) can be illuminated by reference to the wisdom motif outlined by Carr.[218] Even though wisdom, for which the woman stands, has proved an ambiguous blessing, Yahwistic wisdom or faith is both something to be followed and ever at loggerheads with any other, that of the empire, represented by the *mušḫuššu*, in particular. But in the long run, the former will triumph over the latter. This interpretation also makes the puzzling reference to the woman's offspring – the adherents of Yahwistic wisdom, as opposed to those of the serpent – less problematic.

Yahweh's curse strikes Adam and Eve in their very existence – Eve in her function as wife and mother, Adam in his providing for the family. Both curses are etiological, not unlike Enkidu's curse and blessing of the harlot. Finally, Eve's naming by Adam and becoming the mother of all humankind underlines the difference between the two women. The harlot is never elevated above the role of an agent and a seductress. Eve is an equal companion, a spouse, a mother.[219]

This is obviously not what was meant in 1:26–28's commissioning of humankind to rule and subdue creation. We have seen that the peaceful cohabitation of humans and animals is over. Man and woman are not helpers at each other's side – the egalitarian world of creation gives way to a world of kings and subjects.[220] The vegetarian diet of humankind is cursed too, by implication, along with work which becomes hard and futile toil.

I have referred to the Adapa myth and Gilgamesh. They demonstrate that, in Mesopotamia, it is only kings or sages who come close to acquiring eternal life. In Genesis, however, it is humankind en bloc that possesses eternal life only to forfeit it. One of the basic differences from the biblical story is that Adapa is the prototype of priesthood, Gilgamesh that of kingship, whereas Adam stands for humankind.[221] Genesis' world is egalitarian in its outlook.[222]

---

218. See Carr, "Politics of Textual Subversion," 589–90, discussed earlier.

219. Bailey, "Initiation," 149–50. One more similarity to Gilgamesh is when the couple realize that they are naked and clothe themselves. This echoes the harlot's clothing Enkidu; Bailey, "Initiation," 149.

220. The husband's royal superiority to his wife, expressed by the verb *māšal*, is even more poignant, given PH/Genesis' egalitarian attitude.

221. Liverani, "Adapa," 22.

222. But cf. Batto's observation that Adapa is more than the prototype of priesthood as he is elsewhere parsed as amīlu and is thus the equivalent of Hebrew 'ādām, "humankind" (Batto, *Slaying the Dragon*, 194–95, footnote 23). I still think that Adapa (and Atrahasis) is

God's first commission is not abolished but upheld – in a cursed form though. God's image is not shattered but corrupted; humankind cannot, in a benevolent way, completely and exclusively rule for creation's sake, but does it in a self-centered, violent, and destructive way. Humankind has achieved knowledge with its ambivalent consequences.[223] Thus, with God's recognition that humankind has become godlike, knowing good and evil (3:22), it is underscored "that in the area of intelligence and understanding, and perhaps even in moral decision, humans are more godlike than animal-like. What it means to be human has become clearer."[224]

"Humankind has now become like one of us, knowing good and evil" (3:22 AT), God states before driving them out of Eden. But what exactly is it for human beings, above animals and below gods, to "know good and evil?"[225] In the reference to human subjugation by humans (3:16), humankind's failure to execute their original mandate and instead rule over each other has been hinted at. Chapters 1–3 thus narrate why rule by humankind over creation has gone awry. By chapter 11, it will only get worse. Reading on, we see the story unfold.

"Adam named his wife Eve, because she would become the mother of all the living" (3:20). By naming, the man assigns the function to the woman, and through names relationships are established.[226] More importantly, the remark is out of place here and would rather fit right before 4:1. By placing it here, however, the author created a chiasm thus providing for a transition between humankind's primitive status and multiplication.

---

portrayed as a social and religious authority, i.e. king (and priest) rather than a commoner (see Tablet 1 in particular).

223. Cf. Schüle's statement (*Prolog*, 158): "The theme of Gen 2–3 is the wisdom and its ambiguous consequences." Schmid, "Die Unteilbarkeit," 21–39, seems to understand "good and evil" not just as a reference to wisdom but in the sense I do.

224. Batto, *Slaying the Dragon*, 61.

225. Westermann, *Genesis 1–11*, 274, discusses the divine envy motif. Goldingay, "Postmodernizing Eve," 50n1, gives a short list of the uses of "good and evil" in the OT.

226. Cf. Walton, *Genesis*, 31. O'Connor, *Genesis 1–25A*, 53.

A Adam speaks and names his wife: she is mother of all living (3:20)
     B God's care (3:21)
       C God speaks: his statement and decision (3:22)
       C' God acts: his preventive/punitive action (3:23)
     B' God's judgment (3:24)
   A' Adam knows his wife: she becomes mother and names her son (4:1)

In A and A', we see Adam and Eve, with the emphasis on Eve, even though she acts only in 4:1, as well as the two naming actions. B is about God's recognition of humankind's deed, anticipating the statement in C. By clothing them, God does not just acknowledge humankind's rising above animals and becoming godlike but demonstrates care toward them.[227] God's judgment in B' is the reverse. In C, we read first God's judgment about humankind's newly acquired status as well as his determination to stop them from eating from the tree of life and live forever. In C' God's decision is put into action. Note the verbs *šlḥ* and *lqḥ* in C–C': "humankind" has become godlike; so that they cannot "send" their hand and "take" from the tree of life (C), God "sends them away" to work the "humus" from which they were "taken" (C'). In this way, the opposing intentions of humankind and God are once again underlined: while the former strive for divine status the latter is intent on maintaining the present order.[228]

Finally, it is not immaterial that the way the Pentateuch commences Israel's history is prefaced by the creation of humankind "which place[s] humanity

---

227. Importantly, it is God who dresses humankind and not themselves (cf. Enkidu being dressed by Shamhat). The human and divine roles of Mesopotamia are subverted in Genesis.

228. As well-known, in the first creation account, God is referred to by his generic name, Elohim, while, in the second by his proper name, Yahweh. The combination of the two names as well as "Elohim" (3:1, 3, 5; J source), however, has given a headache to scholars; see, e.g. Nielsen, E., "Creation and the Fall," 12. I wonder whether we are not witnessing to the reworking and literary strategy of the narrator. That is to say, the narrator attributes the creation in the first account to "Elohim," the universal godhead. When, however, he starts the second account of the creation of humankind (2:4), the narrator uses "Yahweh Elohim" through the end of ch. 3. Yahweh, the national god of Israel, takes the scene in ch. 4 only. In this way, the narrator has not only equated the two gods but created a smooth transition from general cosmogony to a more particular anthropogony, as well as from the universal creator god to that of Israel's national deity who are one and the same; similarly see Westermann, *Genesis 1–11*, 198–99; Sarna, *Genesis*, 17; McConville, *God and Earthly Power*, 24. Otto's suggestion ("Die narrative Logik," 597–99) concerns narrated and narrative times but in effect points in the direction I have delineated. See also LaCocque's different explanation (*The Trial of Innocence*, 57–58). Van Seters, *Prologue to History*, 108, regards the technique as "a deliberate use by one author (or redactor)" but fails to elaborate. Outside Gen 2–3, the compound "Yahweh Elohim" occurs in Exod 9:30 only.

as such in universal or unspecified settings."²²⁹ Aspects of this universalism will be elaborated on in what follows.

Challenging Imperial Hegemony: The Multiplication of Humankind and the Beginning of Civilization (4:1–5:32)

Uniformity and centralized empire go hand in hand just as equality and diversity do. Genesis values a diverse culture and an egalitarian society. This is emphatic in chapters 4 and 5.

A Diverse Culture of Commoners: God's Image and Knowing Good and Evil (4:1–26)

The story of the creation of humankind is fraught with theology. Its apex is the theme of God's image. In this chapter, I will study Genesis 4 and its antecedents with an eye on this concept. Then, I will discuss the concept's recurrence in the subsequent chapters.

On day six of creation, God sets out to do his ultimate job.

> "Let us make mankind in our image, in our likeness [*bəṣalmēnû kidmûtēnû*], so that they may rule over the fish in the sea and the birds in the sky, over the livestock and all the wild animals, and over all the creatures that move along the ground." So God created mankind in his own image, in the image of God he created them; male and female he created them. (1:26–27)

To clearly see the term's meaning, a comparative religion approach is indispensable as I have shown. However, cannot we expect the concept to unfold as the narrative unfolds? This expectation of ours seems to be justified by Robert Alter's narratological observation that, in OT narrative, there is no "free motif," each phrase or motif serves the intention of the narrative.²³⁰ Now, what is this intention? Does this concept have any import beyond chapters 1–2? In what follows, I will read the first chapters of Genesis in the light of this motif, humankind created in the image of God, assuming that its relevance

---

229. McConville, *God and Earthly Power*, 35.
230. Alter, *Art of Biblical Narrative*, 79.

reaches beyond chapters 1–3. I will note the ways in which the narrative makes use thereof in implicit or explicit ways and consider the implications.

In PH, humankind's creative activity is a major theme. This, however, is prepared by two motifs. In the act of creation, God first blesses sea creatures and birds, "Be fruitful and increase in number and fill the water in the seas, and let the birds increase on the earth" (1:22; cf. 8:17). Second, God's first command or blessing to humankind is, "Be fruitful and increase in number; fill the earth" (1:28). This blessing is repeated after the deluge in 9:1 and, with some modification, in 8:17 and 9:7.

> Then God blessed Noah and his sons, saying to them, "Be fruitful and increase in number and fill the earth." (9:1)

> Bring out every kind of living creature that is with you – the birds, the animals, and all the creatures that move along the ground – so they can multiply on the earth and be fruitful and increase in number upon it. (8:17)

> As for you, be fruitful and increase in number; multiply on the earth and increase upon it. (9:7)

Procreation belongs to humankind's humanness.[231] The blessing in 1:28 is preceded by God's deliberation to create humankind in God's own likeness. Smith notes that to be fruitful and increase, "is suggestive of a further, priestly sense of the image and likeness, namely that the human person is also a creator in a manner somewhat analogous to the divine creator."[232] The blessing of humankind differs from that of other creatures in that it is supplemented. Humankind is to subdue the earth and "Rule over the fish of the sea and the birds of the air and over every living creature that moves on the ground" (1:28). Turner notes that "Just as God previously created light (day 1) and, then, transferred this responsibility to the heavenly luminaries (day 4), so, here, he transfers dominion over creation to human beings."[233]

Humankind's creative capacities and activities begin to unfold only when they are out of Eden. God's creating activity is carried on by humankind so that by acquiring the knowledge of good and evil and so becoming

---

231. Cf. Miles, *God*, 25–84.
232. Smith, *Priestly Vision of Genesis*, 224.
233. Turner, *Genesis*, 24.

godlike humankind does not need the mediation of gods and *apkallu* of Mesopotamian culture.[234] We can see this happen right at the beginning of chapter 4: "Adam lay with his wife Eve, and she became pregnant and gave birth to Cain. She said, 'With the help of the LORD I have brought forth a man'" (4:1).

Cain's birth is a confirmation of the strength of the command in 1:28 – the first couple has started their mandate to fill the earth, corroborated by the subsequent genealogies.[235] The naming is typical of Genesis, a popular etymology with some theological flavor. "Cain" can be derived from Hebrew *qānâ*, "to get, acquire."[236] Borger refers to two Assyrian personal names, Itti-ili-a-šam-šu, "I have bought him from God," and Iš-tu-aš-šur-a-šam-šu, "I have bought him from Ashur." In these, the Akkadian *itti/ištu* stands for "from" which, Borger argues, is similar to the rather odd *'et* in Gen 4:1.[237] Van Seters refers to the myth Marduk's Creation where line 21 states, "The goddess Aruru created the seed of mankind together with him [i.e. Marduk]." He considers Genesis 4:1 corresponding, phrase by phrase, with the above sentence.[238]

In six instances and in relation to God, the verb *qānâ* means "to create" (Gen 4:1; 14:19, 22; Deut 32:6; Ps 139:13; Prov 8:22). Taking the preposition *'et* in its simplest sense, the meaning of Eve's words is, "I have created/acquired a son with the help of Yahweh." Confirming this explanation, Kikawada calls attention to the creation scene in Atrahasis (1.201) where the corresponding Akkadian phrase is applied.[239] Here, the creatress Mami modestly declines Enlil's order by claiming the task is "with Enki." In Atrahasis, Mami does not do anything on her own but only in cooperation with the other creator god, Enki. Genesis 4:1 may be dependent on this motif in which case Eve's success is seen as coming from Yahweh. Thus, Eve's words can properly be rendered, "I have gained/created a man with the help of/together with Yahweh."[240] The "first woman, in her joy at giving birth to her first son, boasts of generative power. The Lord formed the first *man* (ii 7), and I have formed the second

---

234. Melvin, "Divine Mediation," 2–15.
235. Turner, *Announcements of Plot*, 25.
236. E.g. Gen 47:22; Jer 32:9; Neh 5:16; see Cassuto, *Genesis*, 198–202.
237. Borger, "Gen. iv 1," 85–86.
238. Van Seters, *Prologue to History*, 123–24.
239. Kikawada, "Two Notes on Eve," 35.
240. Kikawada, 36–37; but see Westermann, *Genesis 1–11*, 289–92.

man."²⁴¹ Eve is deprived of the associations with Mami's divinity but preserves some remarkable vestiges of the parallel: Mami is the creatress, Eve is the first created woman. "Eve receives some of the attributes of the creatress in addition to the character of the created, and thereby a transparent added image is superimposed upon her."²⁴² This interpretation is backed up by the LXX: *ektēsamēn anthrōpon dia tou theou*, "I have acquired a human being by God."²⁴³

Still, Eve does not claim that the birth is identical to God's creating planets, plants, animals, and humankind. For this very reason, the verb used here is not one used in the creation account. Thus, her wording is pretty exact: she produced Cain with the help of Yahweh. Due to the events in chapter 3, humankind's work and existence are doomed to decay. This is emphasized by the naming of Abel (4:2), meaning "breath."²⁴⁴ The names and deeds of Cain and Abel (farmer and stock-breeder; God's rejection and approval; the anger of the "One Acquired" at and envy of "Breath"; and finally the slaughter of "Breath" by "The One Acquired") characterize created existence in a kind of merism by mentioning both good and bad possibilities open for human beings (see my interpretation of 3:22). Through begetting and birthing, however, humankind creates new life. It is this paradox that characterizes human existence: it seems futile but not to the extent it was considered in Mesopotamia.

The beginning of the next genealogy confirms humankind's creative capacity by reapplying the phrase known from 1:26: "When Adam had lived 130 years, he had a son in his own likeness, in his own image [*kəṣalmô bidmûtô*]; and he named him Seth" (5:3). By begetting a son, Adam reiterates God's

---

241. Cassuto, *Genesis*, 201, emphasis his; cf. van Wolde, "Story of Cain," 27–28; Alter, *Genesis*, 16. I do not share Cassuto's rather negative conclusion that Eve saw her birthing equal to God's creating, hence standing equally with Yahweh "*in the rank of creators*" (Cassuto, *Genesis*, 201; his emphasis).

242. Kikawada, "Two Notes on Eve," 35; cf. Batto, *Slaying the Dragon*, 63; Day, *From Creation to Abraham*, 78–80.

243. In a novel way, Stordalen, *Echoes of Eden*, 296–97, suggests that "man" refers to Adam, not Cain, thus ironically recording the coming-of-age of the man, in Eve's view, and finally attaining sexuality.

244. Day, *From Creation to Abraham*, 81, does not find it credible that Eve would name her son "breath", thus ignoring the mythic character of the primeval story. Day, *From Creation to Abraham*, 100, demonstrates the same ignorance in his objection to why Irad (see 4:17–18) cannot denote the city Eridu as being inappropriate in a Kenite genealogy.

creating deed.²⁴⁵ Offspring take after parents as humankind bears the image of their Creator. This is reminiscent of BCS that states, "Anshar made his son Anu like himself, and Anu begot Nudimmud in his likeness" (I.15–16). In this picture, heredity is implied as the image of God.²⁴⁶

Regarding Genesis 4:2 ("Now Abel kept flocks, and Cain worked the soil"), Turner highlights that "Not only do the Man and Woman reproduce (multiplication), but their progeny keep sheep (dominion over the animals) and till the ground (subjugation of the earth)."²⁴⁷ In this way, the narrator not only signals a fulfillment of God's initial blessing in 1:28 but indicates the division of agriculture into cultivation of plants and animal husbandry as well as the antagonism concomitant with this, well-known from Mesopotamian literary works.²⁴⁸ The Sumerian poem The Disputation between Ewe and Wheat is built on this motif. In this epic, however, the two branches of production providing for the life of humankind are as good as deified in that they are metonymically represented by the deities Ezina-Kushu, wheat, and U, sheep, respectively. However, in Genesis, the two branches of production are the products of humankind's invention, not divine creation.²⁴⁹ Indeed, religion in PH is a human invention.²⁵⁰

Cain's gift, rejected by God, is a crux for interpreters.²⁵¹ Spina has argued that the ground for the rejection was the ground: Cain's close association as a farmer, *'ōbēd hā'ădāmâ* (4:2), with the cursed ground (3:17) and that the plants Cain offered were the products of this "ground."²⁵² In any case, Cain is envious of his brother, which catches God's attention, "Why art thou wroth? and why is thy countenance fallen? If thou doest well, shall it not be lifted up?" (4:6–7 ASV). For Moberly, "YHWH's words do not have Cain's supposed wrong in view, but rather make the point that the disappointment written

---

245. See Alter, *Genesis*, 23.

246. See Walton, "Genesis," 43. Importantly, and as opposed to ANE religions, however, in Genesis, and the OT, this did not have, as a consequence, fertility cults nor the imaging of Yahweh.

247. Turner, *Genesis*, 35.

248. Turner, *Announcements of Plot*, 25.

249. Cf. Miller, "Eridu, Dunnu, and Babel," 239.

250. Kawashima, "*Homo Faber*," 496–98.

251. Note that at this point, there being no institutionalized religion, PH knows only of "gift, *minḥâ*," presented to God and of no altar and "sacrifice, *'ōlâ*" (cf. 8:20).

252. Spina, "'Ground' for Cain's Rejection," 319–32.

large in his face can be remedied if he handles the situation well."²⁵³ Moreover, Schlimm suggests that לַפֶּתַח of 4:7 be repointed into לְפֶתַח and interpreted: "But if you do not do good, then at sin's entryway is a רֹבֵץ," read as an active participle, or as *rabiṣ* and referring to a Mesopotamian demon (*rabiṣu*), a lion or a similar beast of prey. He states, "Ancient readers of Genesis 4,7b would likely have caught one or both of these associations and understood the verse as warning Cain about the potential consequences of his anger by alluding to these threatening creatures."²⁵⁴ Figures of monsters were used at entrances to apotropaic ends.

> They presented a threat to those outside the gate or door, warning that entry may entail great harm to themselves. By evoking this leonine imagery, Gen 4,7 briefly but vividly makes clear the warning given to Cain. Should he enter sin's doorway, his life will become endangered. In what follows 4,7, Cain enters the doorway to iniquity by killing his brother (4,8), and he consequently fears for his life (4,14), much as God's words here forecasted.²⁵⁵

Adopting Crouch's suggestion,²⁵⁶ Schlimm argues that the crouching beast craves for Cain who must rule over it.²⁵⁷ But Cain is defeated – he kills Abel. The Creator's curse is visible in that humankind will return to the soil whence he was taken: it received Abel's blood, who fell victim to Cain's rancor. In a similar way, it will open its mouth to receive the perpetrator's corpse. Here, Abel is seen as one returned to the ground prematurely and violently.²⁵⁸

In chapter 3, alienation between husband and wife, humankind and ground, humankind and vegetation, humankind and the animal world, was the result of humankind's independent action. Now, it is alienation of kinship.

---

253. Moberly, *Theology of the Book of Genesis*, 96–97.
254. Schlimm, "At Sin's Entryway," 411–12; Walton, *Genesis*, 38; Day, *From Creation to Abraham*, 86.
255. Schlimm, "At Sin's Entryway," 413. As opposed to ancient translations the MT does not cite Cain's words in 4:8. Simon, *A ki nem mondott*, 56–57, interprets this very feature of the story by claiming the narrative's gist is the dialogue that dissolved into thin air.
256. Crouch, "חטאת as Interpolative Gloss," 256.
257. Schlimm, "At Sin's Entryway," 413; cf. Crüsemann, "Autonomie und Sünde," 65–67.
258. See Hauser, "Genesis 2–3," 302.

Humankind, created in the image of God, has really gotten to know good and evil.[259] Murder, however, threatens humankind's mandate to fill the earth.[260]

The ground is doomed to be infertile because of man's disobedience (3:18), the fruit of which man eats (3:17, 19, and 4:12a). God sees Cain's deed as a crime more severe than that committed by his father. Because of Adam, the ground was cursed (3:17–19). Now, Cain is more cursed than the ground (4:10). Adam's lot was a cursed ground that made work and life difficult. Cain's fate is worse: the ground will not yield its fruit, compelling him to a permanent unsettled life.[261] Due to his sin, Cain is to become "a restless wanderer on the earth" (4:14). He will have no hope of settled life but will have to move on and on. No wonder that, hearing God's curse, Cain is desperate: "Today you are driving me from the land, and I will be hidden from your presence; I will be a restless wanderer on the earth, and whoever finds me will kill me" (4:14).

Kawashima suggests, then, that "The city makes possible human existence at some remove from the soil, and it may even function here as a type of asylum, allowing Cain to settle in the land without polluting it."[262] Cain finds a place to settle down – in Nod, the land of "wandering" (4:16). Walton notes, "As in Mesopotamia, Cain's status as a wanderer marks him as undesirable. This wandering is in contrast to being a city-dweller. In fact, it is in his line that the arts of civilization are developed (4:17–22)."[263] Given this and his achievements in city building, for a cursed wanderer, Cain does pretty well.[264]

"Cain lay with his wife, and she became pregnant and gave birth to Enoch. Cain was then building a city, and he named it after his son Enoch" (4:17). Whereas building cities is seen as all-important in Mesopotamia, in Genesis 4, it is only marginal. Due to God's punishment and with the non-farming skills of Cain's descendants indirectly affirming God's curse on the ground,

---

259. Smith, *Genesis of Good and Evil*, 69, sees Cain and Abel "emblemize two different moral capacities and potentialities issuing from the human knowledge of good and evil gained in Genesis 3."

260. Turner, *Announcements of Plot*, 26.

261. Spina, "'Ground' for Cain's Rejection," 327. Even though Spina has noticed these important links, he does not abandon the conventional translation, "from the ground," in 4:11 (327).

262. Kawashima, "*Homo Faber*," 490.

263. Walton, "Genesis," 39; see also Steinmetz, "Vineyard, Farm, and Garden," 203.

264. Cf. Westermann, *Genesis 1–11*, 324.

Cain's line, with the exception of Jabal (4:20), become city dwellers.²⁶⁵ They are also the first musicians and smiths (4:21–22). In this way, God's curse of the ground is made ineffective for his offspring.²⁶⁶ Theirs are achievements of human endeavor and neither of these lifestyles is superior. In 4:15, Yahweh is seen as having pity on Cain and showing compassion.

From a Mesopotamian perspective, it is definitely a paradox that the first man-slaughterer becomes the first city builder, a role, if not divine, much honored in Mesopotamia. Hallo presents that "In the context of the Kenite genealogy, which stresses the novelty of arts and sciences attributed to this line of 'culture-heroes,' this can only imply that he became the first builder of a city, i.e. that the building of cities began with him."²⁶⁷ Further, he elsewhere states, "In the biblical version of antediluvian traditions, we hear of no kings, and of only one city, named for the son of its builder Enoch, Irad, reminiscent of the city Eridu mentioned as the first city in the SKL."²⁶⁸ If the proposal put forward by Hallo holds, city in general and the first city Eridu (or the famous "divine" cities founded in primordial times), in particular, once again, are rendered relative. In the book of Genesis, Eridu is not even referred to as a city but, in the person of Irad, only as the son/grandson of the founder of the first city. It is more pertinent to our topic as in one Babylonian poem at least, Marduk, Creator of the World, Babylon is referred to as Eridu.²⁶⁹ In Genesis, it is humankind that are assigned important cultural, social, and political functions, not cities. And as opposed to the SKL, the word "king" does not even occur in PH.

---

265. Galambush, *Reading Genesis*, 37.

266. Cf. Crüsemann, "Eigenständigkeit der Urgeschichte," 18; Schüle, *Prolog*, 184; Waschke, "Zum Verhältnis," 76.

267. Hallo, "Antediluvian Cities," 64. The subject of the Hebrew can be Cain just as well as his son Enoch, overlooked by Hallo. Kvanvig, *Primeval History*, 247–49, argues for Enoch's being the subject claiming "Enoch, the founder of the first city, Irad/Eridu, [comes] fairly close to the first sage in Mesopotamian traditions, U-an/Oannes, who taught humankind how to build cities." Miller, "Eridu, Dunnu, and Babel," 240, deems the text, or tradition, unstable by seeing a gloss here and reconstructs 4:17–18. I wonder, however, whether the ambiguity is intended, and thus the author succeeded in tainting the identity of the founder of the first city, so significant in Mesopotamia.

268. Hallo, "Royal Hymns," 669; similarly Hallo, "Antediluvian Cities," 64; Hess, *Studies in the Personal Names*, 40–41.

269. See Foster, *Before the Muses*, 488n2. Indeed, Babylon had a district called Eridu.

Wilson has observed the similarities between Mesopotamian genealogies and that in Genesis 4.

> Both the Mesopotamian and biblical traditions speak of seven figures or seven generations of ancestors who lived before the flood and who were the founders of the various arts of civilization. Both agree in placing the origins of artistic skills and the building of cities in this period, and both also place the beginnings of cultic worship at this time (cf. Gen. 4:26).[270]

The seven antediluvian *apkallu*, creatures of Ea, first referred to in the third millennium but "becoming very popular in the art of the Neo-Assyrian and Neo-Babylonian periods,"[271] are said to have brought learning and the arts to Sumer. Just like the seven antediluvian sages, the seven generations starting with Cain are portrayed in terms of cultural inventions like city building, the crafts, and arts. The divinization of cultural inventors is rejected in Genesis, however. In addition, the "seven-day divine creation of the cosmos is paralleled by these seven generations of human creativity."[272] As Lowery highlights, "Genesis removes technological progress from the realm of the gods and places it solely within the sphere of human activities."[273] The other side of the coin is that, through their behavior, the *apkallu* occasionally angered the gods.[274] Cain's offspring are no demigods but human to the core. They bring arts and craft to humankind, but at least one of them shows the human capability of evil (4:23–24) – like father, like son.

In his commentary, Westermann discusses at length the aspect of creating. He notes that in Mesopotamia the act of creation is not restricted to heaven, earth, and humankind. Rather, creation is "the established, ordered and cultivated world, including artificial irrigation, the cultivation of plants, cattle breeding and finally the most important farming implements."[275] In short, nature and civilization are no distinct entities; the gods are responsible for

---

270. Wilson, *Genealogy*, 154; cf. Hess, "Genealogies of Genesis," 246.
271. Takayoshi, "Near Eastern Fish Men," 22; cf. Greenfield, "Apkallu," 73.
272. Sarna, *Genesis*, 36.
273. Lowery, *Toward a Poetics*, 93.
274. See Reiner, "Etiological Myth," 4–5.
275. Westermann, *Genesis 1–11*, 58.

any achievement, humankind is only the beneficiary of divine inventions. Creation thus includes civilization and technology.[276]

The similarity of the genealogies in Genesis 4 and 5 has been noted.[277] Albeit not concerned with Genesis, Finkelstein has observed that several members of the Assyrian King List correspond to members in the genealogy of the Hammurabi dynasty.[278] This harmonizing tendency may be behind the correspondence between the genealogies of Genesis 4 and 5. That is to say, the resemblance of Genesis 4–5 to the Mesopotamian king lists (MKL) may suggest that the narrator adopted from the king lists the correspondence device in order to democratize his genealogies.

To another descendant of Cain, Lamech, significant cultural feats are attributed:

> Adah gave birth to Jabal; he was the father of those who live in tents and raise livestock. His brother's name was Jubal; he was the father of all who play the harp and flute. Zillah also had a son, Tubal-Cain, who forged all kinds of tools out of bronze and iron. (4:20–22)

Cain was not only the father of city dwellers but nomadic people also originated with him. Genesis in this way signals two defining ways of life, that of city life and that of country life. In Mesopotamia, city life was considered superior to country life,[279] with cities occasionally deified.[280] Genesis 4 does not refer "to an achievement (e.g., domestication) but to a lifestyle. Just as Mesopotamians believed cities and kingship originated with the gods, so did pastoralism, agriculture, and other lifestyles. Again, in contrast, Genesis

---

276. Westermann, 58. Later on, Westermann adds "The theological significance of what is said about human achievements in the primeval story is restricted to freeing them from the realm of mythology. What humans achieved was neither divine nor was it extolled as such. Human endeavor and cultural progress were desacralized in Israel from the very beginning" (Westermann, 67).

277. Finkelstein, "Antediluvian Kings," 50n41, has noticed that each of the seven *apkallu* bore names similar to the particular king in whose reign they appeared. This, again, makes the dependence of Gen 4–5 on Mesopotamian material as well as its soft polemical intention possible (cf. Hess, "Genealogies of Genesis," 246–47).

278. Finkelstein, "Genealogy of the Hammurapi Dynasty," 98.

279. Oppenheim, *Ancient Mesopotamia*, 110–11; Hallo, "Antediluvian Cities," 57.

280. Hallo, "Antediluvian Cities," 59.

sees them as human developments."[281] Culture "is a human invention."[282] Significantly, within the same genealogy, city life and country life are presented as originating with the same ancestor. Cain is the forefather of musicians as well as of metal workers.[283] He knows both evil and good,[284] he "constitutes a type of every-man."[285] But how does the account of Lamech fit in here?

"Zillah also had a son, Tubal-Cain, who forged all kinds of tools out of bronze and iron. Tubal-Cain's sister was Naamah" (4:22). First, apart from Eve who names Cain and Seth (4:1, 25), only this entry of all the antediluvian genealogies mentions women by name, a characteristic of WSL.[286] The names of Lamech's wives and daughter could have easily been dropped or the entry reformulated as they are not essential. Surprisingly, however, they are included in the list. Also, Lamech is the seventh from Adam. He boasts, "Adah and Zillah, listen to me; wives of Lamech, hear my words. I have killed a man for wounding me, a young man for injuring me" (4:23). Cassuto senses here

> a kind of antithetic parallelism to the statement at the beginning of the section [4:1] . . . Eve gloried in the fact that she had formed and given birth to a *man*; Lamech prides himself on having cut off the life of a *man*. The earlier boast was *with the Lord*; the later, *against the Lord*."[287]

While Eve's "creation" was a manifestation of being created in God's image, Lamech's violence is the undoing of this creation, which is ethically

---

281. Walton, "Genesis," 41.

282. Kawashima, "*Homo Faber*," 485.

283. Wenham, *Genesis 1–15*, 111, also recognizes that one of the themes in ch. 4 is that technology is not God(s) given but a human achievement. However, while he thinks "that all aspects of human culture are in some way tainted by Cain's sin" (111), in my view, culture in the chapter, and in Genesis in general, is more positively portrayed. Wenham sees Genesis as a black zebra striped with white, I see it as white with black stripes.

284. Cf. Van Wijk-Bos, *Making Wise the Simple*, 96–97; Longman, *Genesis*, 102–3.

285. Kawashima, "Violence and the City," 264. Machinist claims, "the knowledge of good and evil is a knowledge of what rules or conventions govern earthly society, as part of the larger cosmos, and further that this knowledge is not simply pure information; it is knowledge that is implemented in action" (Machinist, "How Gods Die," 212).

286. See Malamat, "King Lists," 163.

287. Cassuto, *Genesis*, 242–43; his emphasis. Note that, in 4:1, Eve gives birth, *yālad*, to a "man," *'îš*, not, what might be expected, a *yeled*, while Lamech boasts of having killed a man, *îš*, and a boy, *yeled* (4:23). It is also noteworthy that the two nouns, *peṣaʿ* and *ḥabbûrâ*, occur in the *ius talionis*, Exod 21:25.

reprehensible for Yahweh.[288] Moreover, Lamech boasts of committing a bigger crime than Cain.[289] Humankind's knowing good and evil is on full display in chapter 4. In this context, Wilson's observation of linear genealogies (as that, partly, of Genesis 4) stressing the relational aspect is of interest as it is relations that suffer the most in this chapter.[290] "There is an increase of violence throughout (vv. 8, 15, 24), and the verb 'to kill' appears five times (vv. 8, 14, 15, 23, 25)."[291]

Westermann also notes that the first narrative of the chapter on fratricide warns of the possibility of people bearing God's image and living with each other as brothers murdering each other. Lamech's song cautions that human progress may entail the possibility of enmity and mutual destruction. The increase of human capacities leads to a growth of self-esteem and self-assertion which demands disproportionate revenge.[292]

The beginning and closing of the chapter may contain another hint at Genesis' view of culture. Thematically the protagonist is Cain, whose main acts are his fratricide as well as cultural inventions. Structurally the chapter is enclosed by an *inclusio*. Its first half reports the births of Adam and Eve's first and second son, while the second half that of their third son.

> Adam lay with his wife Eve, and she became pregnant and gave birth to Cain. She said, "With the help of the Lord I have brought forth a man." Later she gave birth to his brother Abel. (4:1–2)

> Adam lay with his wife again, and she gave birth to a son and named him Seth, saying, "God has granted me another child in place of Abel, since Cain killed him." Seth also had a son, and he named him Enosh. (4:25–26)

Between these birth accounts, Cain's two stories are wedged in. In the fratricide (4:3–16), he, the first perpetrator and embodiment of manslaughter, is pictured in a bad light. Yet, Genesis 4:17–24 is the other side of the coin. Cain is being depicted as, by Mesopotamian standards, someone starting

---

288. See Cassuto, *Genesis*, 244.
289. See Gevirtz, "Lamech's Song," 410–11; Kawashima, "Violence and the City," 268.
290. Wilson, "Between 'Azel' and 'Azel,'" 19.
291. Cotter, *Genesis*, 41.
292. Westermann, *Genesis 1–11*, 337.

successful and noble projects. He founds cities and his seven descendants prove rather innovative in the realm of culture paralleling God's creative acts in chapter 1. In this way, the narrative unveils the paradox of creating culture and civilization.

Chapter 4 concludes with the sentence: "Seth also had a son, and he named him Enosh. At that time men began to call on the name of the Lord" (4:26). At this point of human history, there is no chosen people as yet, only human beings exist (Enosh means "human being") who feel in need of turning not only to the transcendent but to Yahweh.[293] In Mesopotamia, cult is derived from creation and humankind is created to relieve the gods from labor and to provide food for them – culture and cult are closely linked. In Genesis, cult and religion originate in primeval times.[294] In some myths (Rulers of Lagash; Ewe and Wheat), humankind is created in two steps: bare existence is followed by the divine grant of culture.[295] Developing human culture contributes to the welfare of the gods.[296] In Genesis, humankind is created to care for creation and to create culture – no reference is found to cult in chapters 1–11. Genesis 4:26 mentions the worship of Israel's deity thereby exemplifying a universalistic conviction that, before and outside Israel, there was Yahweh worship.[297] For this, neither shrine nor ziggurat is needed. It is the more remarkable,

> As with the other beginnings in the chapter, in the ancient Near East the beginning of religion is not associated with humans but with the gods (oddly enough). That is, the gods establish cultic sites for themselves (since the temples were their dwelling places). When humans are created, they are to serve the gods— the implication being that sacred space existed before humans.[298]

---

293. See Westermann, 339.
294. Waschke, *Untersuchungen*, 113.
295. Clifford, *Creation Accounts*, 44.
296. Westermann, "Der Mensch im Urgeschehen," 240.
297. Alter, *Genesis*, 21, speaks of "the universalism of the monotheistic idea." Note also Moberly's judicious analysis of the verse (Moberly, *Theology of the Book of Genesis*, 67–70) as well as McConville's support for Moberly's interpretation (McConville, *God and Earthly Power*, 41–42), adding that "The unexpected allusion to Yahweh-worship in antediluvian times is a careful splicing of the universal and particular."
298. Walton, "Genesis," 42.

It is not religion only that is the invention of gods. In Mesopotamia, "the prerogative of invention reverts to the gods, who assign arts and crafts to humanity and thereafter stay in control, maintaining the responsibility for good running order."[299] The seven *apkallu* taught humans the crafts before the flood. The Sumerian epic Enki and Ninmaḫ attributes to Enki the invention of crafts, while SKL to kings. SKL refers to kings Etana and Lugal-banda, both shepherds (Col. 2, line 16 and Col. 3, line 12), that is kings; Mes-he, a smith (Col. 3, line 31); Magalgalla, a skipper (Col. 4, line 24); Nannia, a stonecutter (Col. 6, line 19). These references might be to culture and civilization, similar to those in Genesis 4.[300] SKL mentions these occupations with reference to kings who are often demigods. It is thus no coincidence that the craft *par excellence*, kingship "was lowered from heaven," as stressed in various Mesopotamian literary works, most notably SKL, which emphasizes it twice. As opposed to this, PH does not take notice of kingship. What is more, both arts and crafts are human achievements with no divine assistance, and social order is human responsibility.[301]

Related to this is how work is seen. In Mesopotamia, it is something troublesome, possibly avoidable, and detested by gods, meant for human beings or smaller deities only. This is succinctly hinted at in Atrahasis' incipit,

> When gods were man,
> They did forced labor, they bore drudgery.
> Great indeed was the drudgery of the gods,
> The forced labor was heavy, the misery too much . . . (1.1–4)

This existence is unbearable; gods are not supposed to work. So, they decide to create humankind to be relieved of the burden of labor. Albertz notes that all the Akkadian phrases related to work in the epic, due to the concept of hard labor, have negative connotations.[302]

In the Genesis account, God himself does work (see 2:2–3, 7, 19, 22) and, after the well-done job, rests unchallenged and contented so setting an example. By being an extension of God's creating activity, in Genesis, work belongs to the goodness of creation. Humankind, created in God's image,

---

299. Castellino, "Origins of Civilization," 93.
300. See Cassuto, *Genesis*, 188.
301. Cf. Melvin, "Divine Mediation," 11.
302. Albertz, "Kulturarbeit im Atramḫasīs," 56.

is to emulate the Creator. Adam is placed in the garden of Eden "to work it and take care of it" (2:15). It is humankind that names the animals (2:19–20) as a sign of being made in the image of God and of humankind's creative faculty. In Sumerian mythology-cosmogony, naming is an important literary motif denoting divine power and skills as it is only gods who are involved in naming tools and cities, among other things (see The Song of the Hoe; Enki and Inanna). Only after work is cursed (3:17–19) is it troublesome in Genesis, so matching human experience. Only after the curse does the keeper become the one from whom the garden is to be kept (see the verb *šāmar* in 2:15 and 3:24). Sweat, thorns, and thistles notwithstanding, work remains humankind's creative and hence satisfying activity, as implied in Genesis 4. "Human sin has not changed God's good creation into an evil creation."[303]

As opposed to Mesopotamian epics, the first book of the Bible implies culture's potential of creating works of art, human innovation, and ingenuity while at the same time hinting at the capacity of human inventions and ingenuity to destroy. Beneficial and harmful effects are both inherent to humankind's ingenuity. Forged tools, of hunting or agriculture, can also be used to kill (see 4:22); wine can cause drunkenness and nudity (see 9:20–21).[304] Being mindful, however, of these risks and "side effects," by virtue of their creative and procreative activity, humankind carries on God's creating work thus witnessing to being created in God's image.[305] Ironically, this might be suggested by the serpent's enticing words to the humans, "For God knows that when you eat of it your eyes will be opened, and you will be like God [or: gods], knowing good and evil (3:5)."[306] And God's statement after their disobedience, "The man has now become like one of us, knowing good and

---

303. Fretheim, *God and World*, 78.

304. Cf. Westermann, "Der Mensch im Urgeschehen," 240.

305. Cf. Niskanen, "Poetics of Adam," 421–34; see 1:27; 5:1. Schüle, "Made in the 'Image of God,'" 17, considers knowing good and evil "wisdom as a source of human creativity," being fruitful, and taking dominion. Sarna view is that "each act of procreation is an imitation of God's original creation of man," (Sarna, *Genesis*, 41; cf. Fretheim, *God and World*, 60–61).

306. The Hebrew is ambiguous and can mean "like God" or "like gods." Only a minority of interpreters has entertained taking the phrase plural; see Speiser, *Genesis*, 23; von Rad, *Genesis*, 88–89; Alter, *Genesis*, 11–12.

evil. He must not be allowed to reach out his hand and take also from the tree of life and eat, and live forever" (3:22).[307]

Indeed, humankind has become like God, knowing good and bad.[308] The first thing the couple realize with their eyes open is that they are "naked." They may have become like God, but what they first learn entails the awareness of incompetence. Paradoxically, their "knowing good and evil" is the result of the serpent's being more crafty than not just other animals but themselves. In fact, humankind's previous naive, thus immature, status has matured into one that is capable of making decisions for good and bad.[309]

As God created nature so does humankind culture. Nature and culture, created by God and humankind respectively, are manifestations of God's blessing.[310] The beauty and goodness of both are to be maintained and enjoyed. Their enmity, however, brings about curse. The peaceful living together of human beings and animals has given place to enmity of the two realms commenced at humankind's disobedience. As a consequence, the animal world is cursed as well. God's creatures are set against and live in fear of each other: "And I will put enmity between you and the woman, and between your offspring and hers; he will crush your head, and you will strike his heel" (3:15).

We have seen a snapshot of PH's diverse view and egalitarian attitude toward the world. In Genesis 5, there is more to come.

---

307. In conventional Christian theology, God is denied attributes associated with evil. But what if, as this verse may be taken to imply, God is really capable of both good and bad but has restricted himself? That is to say, in Genesis, God is portrayed as a deity who creates a good, indeed, very good world and who is perhaps not as wanton as deities in Babylon are. Still, there are two stories (chs. 3 and 6–7), at least, in PH where God's motives are not clear, to say the least. God's furnishing cloth for the first couple right after their curses (3:21) as well as his words in 8:21–22 make him appear to be sorry for the judgment. God, Schüle, *Prolog*, 417, thus claims, God, "like each deity in ANE, is familiar with feelings, is moved by inclinations as well as questionable motives such as suspicion and jealousy". For Babylonian Jews, acquainted with destructive and benevolent deities alike, this god certainly made sense.

308. Contra Reicke, "Knowledge Hidden," 201, who claims that "the paradise narrative regards knowledge as a dangerous matter." Rather, it regards knowledge as neutral with the potential of being used for good and ill.

309. Ezekiel 28, often referred to when interpreting this verse (e.g. Wenham, *Genesis 1–15*, 64), seems to support this: Having misused his privileges and power, the king of Tyre is cast down from God's presence.

310. Cf. Goldingay, *Old Testament Theology*, 187.

An Egalitarian World of Commoners: The Ten Generations (5:1–32)

Genesis 5 connects the flood to the preceding story of creation and humankind's growth.[311] Its function, however, is not just this but, by virtue of the genealogy, to provide an alternative to the Mesopotamian view of civilization. SKL, one of the obvious parallels to Genesis 5, contains a number of names of mythic heroes.[312] It purports to go back to times before the flood. Between the extant SKL manuscripts dating from the early centuries of the second millennium and Berossus's Babyloniaca from the early third century, there is a considerable time gap with one small fragment from Ashurbanipal's libraries that lists nine antediluvian kings and has the beginning of a bilingual version of the deluge.[313] Thus, it seems that, in at least one literary composition of mid-first-millennium Mesopotamia, the flood story was prefaced by a genealogy, just as it is in Genesis.

The SKL is divided into two parts, the kings before and the kings after the flood. The reigns of the former are incredibly long. The shortest is 18,600, the longest 43,200 years. After the flood, reigns are rarely longer than 1,000 years.

In PH, the deluge also marks a disruption with genealogies preceding and following it. Genesis 5 lists ten antediluvian generations. Before the flood, SKL mentions eight kings. The antediluvian section of SKL does not list the first man nor the flood hero though. Hence, Walton suggests that, in Genesis 5, they should not be counted.[314] This is, however, not the only list related to our topic. In Mesopotamian sources, including the chronicle by Berossus, prior to the flood, eight, nine, or ten kings ruled,[315] or in one list perhaps seven.[316] The similarity of, approximately, ten generations in the lists is striking just as the difference is: most of the Sumerian, Assyrian, and Babylonian lists have kings[317] as opposed to the list of Genesis where commoners are named. Ten generations

---

311. See Levin, "Understanding Biblical Genealogies," 33.
312. Cf. Sarna, *Genesis*, 40; Carr, *Reading the Fractures*, 71–72.
313. Lambert, "New Fragment," 270.
314. Walton, "Antediluvian Section," 207.
315. See Lambert, "New Look," 292–93.
316. Lambert, 272.
317. See Walton, "Genesis," 44.

seem to have been the optimal pattern of genealogies in Mesopotamia.[318] Borrowing from Mesopotamia on the part of the Hebrews appears certain.[319]

In Mesopotamia, numbers had both numerical (the real value) and numerological (representing the sacred or pointing beyond the mundane) significance. In mythical texts, such as SKL, the latter was seen as more important. In Babylonia, the numbers 3, 5, 6, 7 and 101 were granted special significance. Bearing that in mind, the total of the six generations before Methuselah, from Seth to Enoch, for example, is 4,949 years – 7 x 7 x 101 years, of which the total of the first three generations (Seth, Enosh, Kenan) is 2,727, or 3 x 3 x 3 x 101 years. Abraham's age is 175 – 7 x 5 x 5 years; Isaac is 180 – 5 x 6 x 6 years; Jacob is 147 – 3 x 7 x 7 (note that the multipliers in these three cases add up to 17); Joseph is 110 – 5 x 5 + 6 x 6 + 7 x 7 years. In Mesopotamia, "holy numbers" were used in connection with gods, kings, famous individuals as well as, in mythic-religious contexts, lending religious dignity to the individual or holy text.[320]

Enoch, special in chapter 5 by virtue of being taken by God, is similar to Enmeduranki/Enmeduranna in two versions of SKL as the seventh in the list, but only in Berossus is he seventh in the ten-member list. "Enmeduranki was specifically associated with Sippar, the city of the sun god Shamash, and is also said to have entered the presence of Shamash as well as of Adad."[321] Enmeduranki's relation to Shamash is matched by Enoch's age 365 in chapter 5, corresponding to the days of a solar year.[322]

It may also appear important that in 5:1–18 (without "Enoch") there are two-hundred words; after "Enoch", 5:18–24 contains sixty-five words; and 5:25–32 has one-hundred words. This makes up a total of 365, the days in a solar year as well as the age when Enoch begot his first son.[323] In addition to

---

318. Malamat, "King Lists," 165, 169; cf. Malamat, "Arameans," 135.

319. Lambert, "New Look," 293.

320. Hill, "Making Sense," 241–42; Johnson, "Patriarchal Ages," 152–53; Lowery, *Toward a Poetics*, 185–89; cf. Ruppert, "Der alte Mensch," 272n5; Heinzerling, "'Einweihung' durch Henoch," 581–89; Ziemer, "Erklärung der Zahlen," 1–18. After considering Sumerian and Babylonian evidence, Young concludes that the authors of both SKL and PH were educated in the same mathematical curriculum (Young, "Influence of Babylonian Algebra," 321–35). Young sees Babylonian mathematical evidence for the background of figures in the Noah story as compelling (Young, "Application of Numbers," 331–61).

321. Day, "Flood and the Ten Antediluvian Figures," 69.

322. Hutzli, "Procreation of Seth," 151; see also Day, *From Creation to Abraham*, 106–7.

323. Heinzerling, "'Einweihung' durch Henoch," 582–83.

Enoch's solar-year age, "Lamech's 777 years (5:31) equal the synodic periods of Jupiter + Saturn, and Yared's 962 years (5:20) equal the synodic periods of Venus + Saturn."[324] (Note that Jupiter was associated with Marduk, Venus with Ishtar, Saturn with Ninurta.) Kraeling also notes that the Babylonian flood hero was a solar figure while, in the Priestly source, the flood lasts a solar year and 6:9 has Noah, like Enoch in 5:24, walk with God.[325]

SKL states, "After the Flood had swept thereover, when the kingship was lowered from heaven" (Col. 1, lines 40–41). In Genesis (and the Pentateuch), kingship is never seen as heavenly. It is a late, limited, and human institution (see Deut 17:14–20). The preoccupation with kings in Mesopotamia is partly owing to the fact that it was kings that bore the image of god. As we have seen, the worldview of PH is different: each human being bears the image of God, regardless of their color of skin, social status, or gender. Enoch was taken as an "everyday mortal," not as someone distinguished in his royal or heroic capacity but due to his ethical stance: he walked with God (5:22, 24).[326] Like Enoch, Enmeduranki is said to have had an intimate relationship to the gods Shamash and Adad.[327]

It can be objected that even though no antediluvian person is named a king in PH, the named figures can be regarded as archetypal and not as mere humans. In Genesis 5, each of the named characters not only had a named son (i.e. the successor archetype) but also had additional, unnamed sons and daughters (i.e. the true commoners archetype).[328] I find it significant though that the ten patriarchs are not referred to as kings, which is in keeping with PH and Genesis' general socio-political stance.

---

324. Waltke, *Genesis*, 111.

325. Kraeling, "Earliest Hebrew Flood," 292.

326. Cf. Wenham, *Genesis 1–15*, 146. Hoopen, "Where Are You, Enoch," 8, 17, argues that Utnapishtim in Gilgamesh XI.205–206 is similarly "taken" (Akkadian cognate *leqû*). The two stories thus attest to a similar "taking" concept. Hoopen adds, "Although the author remains vague about this location, the connections between Adam and Enoch laid out above make it likely that Enoch was perceived to be taken to the place where one walks with God: a place like the garden in Eden" (Hoopen, 11). Hoopen claims that, as opposed to Utnapishtim in Gilgamesh, in Genesis, it was Enoch "taken" and, because of his drunkenness, not Noah (Hoopen, 17). In my view, however, PH tried to discredit the Mesopotamian tradition in this way transferring to Enoch the "being taken" motif from Noah so as to emphasize both heroes' humanness.

327. Day, *From Creation to Abraham*, 107.

328. Batto, developed from personal communication with the author.

Regarding the similarities in the genealogies in chapters 4–5, it is worth comparing the individuals bearing identical names. Interestingly, they are among those who deviate from the monotonous scheme of the list by revealing some further information. Enoch in 4:17, in one reading, is the first city builder, whereas his namesake is the one to have walked with God (5:24). Lamech in chapter 4 is the embodiment of brute force; indeed, he boasts of his violence as if claiming that it is power that solves problems. His counterpart in 5:29 is the embodiment of resigned hopefulness as, possibly, a consequence of the experience of what violence entails. "Furthermore, Lamech's age of 777 years in the MT of Gen 5 functions as a nod to the seventy-sevenfold revenge in Gen 4:24."[329] These two individuals in chapter 5 counter the highly ambitious and doubtful project of city building as well as violence, two aspects of kingship itself. The two Lamechs are transitional figures each bringing an era to its conclusion.[330] "Though the Cainites contribute some material and cultural gains to the human enterprise (Gen 4,17.20 – 22), the Sethites provide the needed religious and spiritual dimension."[331] Cain brought about a number of achievements of culture but, by slaying his brother, he failed in morality. Enoch did not achieve anything worth mentioning. Indeed, he lived the shortest life in his genealogy but "walked with God." For PH, ethics matters as much as achievement.

Genesis 5 nearly always follows the next pattern: "And N was x years old when he begot O. And, after the birth of O, N lived another Y years begetting sons and daughters. And N's total age was thus Z years and he died." All this in three verses each. The monotony is interrupted at three points: at the first one on the list, Adam (5:1–5), at the last one of the list, Noah's father Lamech by whom Noah was named (5:28–31), and at Noah's great-grandfather, Enoch. He is the seventh member in Seth's line and as such contrasted with the seventh member of Cain's line, Lamech, the "vengeful murderer who boldly sings of his violent deeds."[332]

Both Enoch and Noah, men who walked with God so deserving special attention, have their Mesopotamian forerunners in the *apkallu* and the flood

---

329. Hoopen, "Genesis 5," 181.
330. Hess, "Lamech in the Genealogies," 25.
331. Spina, "'Ground' for Cain's Rejection," 329.
332. Waltke, *Genesis*, 112.

hero-priest figures who were instrumental in culture and cult. The Genesis narrator, however, robs Enoch and Noah "of their primary prerogatives. Neither sacrificial cult, nor revelations of divine wisdom could be placed in primeval time."[333] There is no institutional cult in PH's world.

Clines has pointed out that the second part of this pattern (total age and "he died") is rather unnecessary.[334] They add nothing to the information, instead emphasize their mortality. This is in stark opposition to SKL which, by never mentioning their deaths, is virtually a list of semi-divine kings.

In their different forms, MKL served to legitimize dynastic claims to power. As such, they were mutually exclusive.[335] The two genealogies of Genesis 4–5, with many similarities or overlaps,[336] were apparently included to demonstrate that although they appear different and exclusive of one another both are part of humankind's universal history.[337]

All the three extant SKL tablets have a total of a six-digit year period. In comparison to SKL, the patriarchs before the flood in Adam's genealogy (ch. 5) died as infants. Longest lived Methuselah, dying aged 969 (5:27) not reaching year 1,000, seen as the threshold of virtual immortality.[338] He too died a mortal.[339] In addition, while the SKL in particular, and king lists in general, were written to justify power claims of cities and dynasties, Adam's genealogy lacks any such purpose – it has the whole of humankind in view.

Having listed the most relevant characteristics of Mesopotamian genealogies, SKL in particular, we can consider their basic differences from the

---

333. Kvanvig, *Primeval History*, 255–58. He adds, "these prerogatives came much later in history, linked to Aaron and Moses" (Kvanvig, 258). His conclusion is somewhat different from mine.

334. Clines, "Theme in Genesis 1–11," 492; but see Ziemer, "Erklärung der Zahlen," 10.

335. Alternative "versions are not viewed as contradictory by the people who use them, however, for the people know that each version is correct in the particular context in which it is cited" (Wilson, *Genealogy*, 166).

336. Wilson, *Genealogy*, 161, links each member, except for Jabal, Jubal, and Noah, in the list in ch. 5 with a member in ch. 4.

337. For a different interpretation, see Hoopen, "Genesis 5." It may be noted that, in Assyrian and Babylonian king lists, there is a King Adamu and a King Atamu, second and fourth in the lists respectively; see Malamat, "King Lists," 165. Adam's role in his genealogy seems to be that it is "Adam," the forefather of humankind who matters, not kings.

338. Barr, *Garden of Eden*, 79–81.

339. Alter, *Genesis*, 23. Lambert and Millard, *Atra-Ḥasis*, 17, refer to three copies of SKL with a total of 241,200, 456,000, and 186,000 years respectively. The total of the nine patriarchs' years in Genesis 5 is a modest 7,625.

genealogies of Genesis 5. The long ages in SKL are countered with relatively short lifespans in Genesis. As opposed to "semi-divine" kings in SKL, in PH, we see mortal humans – commoners versus kings. To PH, the existence of god-kings or divine men is as good as unheard of. There are commoners only, no kings, no priests.

Semi-divine men will appear at the start of the next chapter. But first is the transition,

> When Lamech had lived 182 years, he had a son. He named him Noah and said, "He will comfort us in the labor and painful toil of our hands caused by the ground the Lord has cursed." After Noah was born, Lamech lived 595 years and had other sons and daughters. Altogether, Lamech lived a total of 777 years, and then he died. After Noah was 500 years old, he became the father of Shem, Ham and Japheth. (5:28–32)

Since the soil is cursed, Lamech expresses his hope "that, through Noah, the curse on the soil will be mitigated if not revoked."[340] In 8:21, this "prophecy" is, in a sense, fulfilled.[341] Lamech's hopeful resignation aptly concludes the section characterized by the despair of the curse and exile, fratricide and violence (cf. 6:11) in humankind's most recent history. But how will Noah bring comfort?

---

340. In the Atrahasis introduction to the flood, it is Enlil who has no rest because of the noise of humankind, created in the first place to relieve the gods from labor. The Genesis narrator may have this in mind. It is not just rest that is needed, and it is not the gods who need it, but comfort to humans laboring with the ground cursed by Yahweh. Noah is the only hope of a new creation after the divine judgment and the futility of human toil. This aspect is underlined by the series of namings in PH. Noah's is the fourth naming so far followed by some rationale. On the first occasion, Eve was named as "the mother of all the living" by Adam (3:20). Then, Eve named her firstborn in a rather triumphant way, full of hope and vigor (4:1). Her third son Seth was named in full awareness of the need of divine assistance and in a hopeful tone, though marked by the previous loss (4:25). Lamech's naming of Noah (5:29) is even more desperate, defined by resignation to the inevitable, with only a glimmer of hope. This series shows a deterioration of the human condition from creation to the flood. This is only implied in these namings, never explicitly stated nor elaborated on.

341. Herion, "Why God Rejected," 63.

A Diverse Creation and Society: "According to Their Kinds" – Excursus

Genesis' emphasis on diversity as opposed to uniformity is already seen in the first creation story. The way God created the world has implications for society. In Genesis 1, one of the key expressions is "according to their kinds," *ləmîn*. The narrator applies this to the creation of the flora (day 3) and fauna (days 5–6).

> Then God said, "Let the land produce vegetation: seed-bearing plants and trees on the land that bear fruit with seed in it, according to their various kinds [*ləmînô*]." And it was so. The land produced vegetation: plants bearing seed according to their kinds [*ləmînēhû*] and trees bearing fruit with seed in it according to their kinds [*ləmînēhû*]. And God saw that it was good. (1:11–12)

> So God created the great creatures of the sea and every living thing with which the water teems and that moves about in it, according to their kinds [*ləmînēhem*], and every winged bird according to its kind [*ləmînēhû*]. And God saw that it was good. (1:21)

> And God said, "Let the land produce living creatures according to their kinds [*ləmînâh*]: the livestock, the creatures that move along the ground, and the wild animals, each according to its kind [*ləmînâh*]." And it was so. God made the wild animals according to their kinds [*ləmînâh*], the livestock according to their kinds [*ləmînâh*], and all the creatures that move along the ground according to their kinds [*ləmînēhû*]. And God saw that it was good. (1:24–25)

In these five verses, the phrase "according to their kinds" occurs ten times, so stressing the diversity of the created world. Seeing the beauty and usefulness of this colorfulness, it is stated each of these days "And God saw that it was good" (1:12, 21, 25). What delights God is "the sheer, abundant variety of creatures."[342]

---

342. Bauckham, *Living with Other Creatures*, 219.

The term's (*mîn*) "focus is on the comprehensive nature of God's work of creation. It is its ability to express *variety* (not division, differentiation, or delimitation)."³⁴³ The "expression conveys variety in order to establish the comprehensiveness of God's creative work. God created everything of every kind."³⁴⁴ Bauckham argues that,

> To say that this passage recognizes biodiversity is an understatement. It *celebrates* biodiversity. It paints a picture of a world teeming with many, many different forms of life. Another formula that occurs in the accounts of the fifth and sixth days is the statement that "God blessed them" (1:22, 28). God's blessing is his gift of fecundity. He enables the creatures to "be fruitful and multiply". Not only diversity but also abundance belongs to the Creator's will for his creation.³⁴⁵

Later on, in chapter 6, when God decides to annihilate creation, he does so, however, by making sure diversity is upheld. God instructs Noah:

> You are to bring into the ark two of all living creatures, male and female, to keep them alive with you. Two of every kind of bird [*lamînēhû*], of every kind of animal [*lamînâh*] and of every kind of creature [*lamînēhû*] that moves along the ground will come to you to be kept alive. (6:19–20)

And that is what Noah does; the phrase occurs another four times in 7:13–15. After the deluge recedes, the narrator emphasizes that the animals leaving the ark to repopulate the earth did so "according to their kinds [*lamišpəḥōtêhem*]" (8:19). Here, adherence to a colorful, multifaceted world is articulated, and this theme is elaborated in the book in greater detail.³⁴⁶ The diversity of creation is emphasized here as well as in the following narrative.

In chapters 10 and 36, diversity is reemphasized. This time it is not nature's species, as in chapter 1, but the organizing units of socio-political life. In the

---

343. Neville, "Differentiation in Genesis," 218, his italics.
344. Neville, 226.
345. Bauckham, *Living with Other Creatures*, 218, his italics.
346. Whereas, in 1:28, God commanded humankind to subdue creation, here, God refrains from saying so. "With this phrase omitted, we know that God has learned something about man" (Gros Louis, "Genesis 3–11," 47).

genealogy of Noah's three sons in chapter 10, the three genealogies conclude with a similar wording:

> From these the maritime peoples spread out into their territories by their clans [ləmišpəḥōtām] within their nations [bəgōyēhem], each with its own language [lilšōnō]. (10:5)

> These are the sons of Ham by their clans and languages [ləmišpĕḥōtām lilšōnōtām], in their territories and nations [bəʼarṣōtām bəgōyēhem]. (10:20)

> These are the sons of Shem by their clans and languages [ləmišpĕḥōtām lilšōnōtām], in their territories and nations [bəʼarṣōtām ləgōyēhem]. (10:31)[347]

The next sentence in its turn concludes the genealogy of chapter 10: "These are the clans [mišpəḥōtām] of Noah's sons, according to their lines of descent, within their nations [lətōlədōtām bəgōyēhem]. From these the nations [haggôyîm] spread out over the earth after the flood" (10:32). At the same time, this sentence hearkens back to the first sentence of the genealogy: "This is the account [tōlədōt] of Shem, Ham and Japheth, Noah's sons, who themselves had sons after the flood" (10:1). Thus 10:32 and 10:1 form an *inclusio*, embracing the genealogy.

The theme of chapter 10 is clearly the division of languages, lands, and nations. If some taxonomy is granted, "language" denotes culture, "nation" denotes society and politics, "clan" within nation denotes a smaller socio-ethnic unit, while "land" denotes the geographical territory necessary for society. It is worth noting in this context that the word "spread out," *pārad*, in 10:5 and 10:32, first occurs in 2:10: "A river watering the garden flowed from Eden; from there it was separated into four headwaters." The separation, or spreading out, of the river is meant to provide for the abundance of the created world. Its dividing (*pārad*) into four creates life as well as diverse cultures.

The "spreading out" of Noah's descendants in 10:5 and 10:32 can be taken as the basis for ethnic diversity. Genesis 25:23 uses the same verb (*pārad*, niphal) in the sense of ethnic differentiation. Desperate Rebekah is encouraged about the twin brothers in her womb, "Two nations are in your womb,

---

347. Schüle, *Prolog*, 273, has also noticed the relationship between the creation account and the genealogy in ch. 10.

and two peoples from within you will be separated [*pārad*]; one people will be stronger than the other, and the older will serve the younger" (25:23). The genealogies of Abraham's descendants, those of Ishmael (25:12–18), Isaac (35:28–9), Esau (ch. 36), and Jacob (37:2), are introduced by the *toledot* formula.[348] The pattern of ethnic identity recurs in the genealogies of Ishmael and Esau. That of Ishmael begins as follows:

> This is the account [*tōlədōt*] of Abraham's son Ishmael, whom Sarah's maidservant, Hagar the Egyptian, bore to Abraham. These are the names of the sons of Ishmael, listed in the order of their birth [*bišmōtām lətōlədōtām*] . . . (25:12–13)
>
> These were the sons of Ishmael, and these are the names of the twelve tribal rulers [*nəśî'im lə'ummōtām*] according to their settlements and camps [*ḥamōtām bəḥaṣrêhem ûbəṭîrōtām*]. (25:16)

Origin denoting identity ("tribe") is emphatic here as well as the origin of individual tribes ("in the order of their birth", or alternatively, "according to their names and origin") just as the phrase "according to their settlements and camps" (in Hebrew, two phrases denoting camps) is underlining the nomadic way of life. The tribal rulers, *nəśî'im*, and subunits ("settlements and camps") are noted as well; in contrast to Babylonian values, nomads are not ignored. The word "tribe," *'ummâ*, used in the OT, in addition to 25:16 only three times (Num 25:15; Pss 2:1; 117:1), emphasizes socio-political organization, similarly to "nation," *gōy*, and unlike the other frequently used phrase for "nation," *'am*, which rather connotes religion and individuals.

Esau's genealogy consists of different subunits from that of Ishmael's. This is just what one expects as Ishmael's descendants were nomads, while Edom settled down. The genealogy uses patterns known to us from the previous parts of the book: "These were the Horite chiefs [*'allûpê haḥōrî*], according to their divisions [*lə'allûpêhem*], in the land of Seir. These were the kings who reigned in Edom before any Israelite king reigned" (36:30–31). And the list of Esau's "aristocratic" descendants starts, "These were the chiefs descended from Esau, by name [*bišmōtām*], according to their clans [*ləmišpəḥōtām*] and regions [*limqōmōtām*]" (36:40).

---

348. See Wilson, *Genealogy*, 182.

Again, "kind," which is the category of socio-political stratification (chief, clan, region, individual), is emphatic. It makes the organizing of Esau's tribal descendants into a nation possible. "Chief" (or "tribe"; *allúf*) is used in the OT with reference to Edom only (Gen 36:15–19, 21, 29–30, 40–43; Exod 15:15; 1 Chron 1:51–54).[349] The king list in Genesis 36:31–39 is reminiscent of those in Kings, even if simpler. Its pattern is plain: (1) N, the son of O reigned after P; (2) the name of N's capital city (or his birth place); (3) N died. A comparison with Israel's and Judah's kings might not be far from the narrator's intention as the commencing sentence makes it probable: "These were the kings who reigned in Edom before any Israelite king reigned" (36:31). This note can be considered a homage to Edom, the kingdom, and so the statehood, which long preceded that of Judah or Israel (cf. Num 20:14). Edom's offspring, however, does not only consist of kings. Indeed, the chapter begins with Esau's genealogy (36:1–30).

The genealogies of Ishmael and Esau are interesting examples of creating civilization.[350] Conspicuously, the genealogies in chapters 25 and 36 deal with Abraham's descendants. The related tribes of the Ishmaelites and Edomites, however, were seen as foreigners. Edom (after Genesis, the Ishmaelites are not referred to), even though not to be annihilated in Deuteronomist theology (see Deut 2:1–8), was a permanent nuisance for Israel (see e.g. 2 Sam 8:13–14; Isa 34). Edom's role in Jerusalem's looting in 586 begs the question: If the Pentateuch took its final shape after the exile, what made the editor view Edom in such a positive way? Why is Esau, exceptionally, allotted two *toledot* formulas (36:1, 9)? And why are Esau's descendants listed at this length (forty-three verses)?[351] In any case, it is to be explained why the narrative of Genesis got to contain these two *foreign* genealogies. The narrator drew the contours of an alternative world to that of the Babylonian empire. This alternative world provided place not just for relatives, but for those not belonging to the family as well.[352] This also explains the placement of Esau's genealogy.[353]

---

349. The phrase is used also in Zech 9:7 and 12:5–6 where, however, several scholars read it with a different punctuation, *'elef*.

350. Cf. McConville, *God and Earthly Power*, 37.

351. Cf. Wenham, "Priority of P," 244.

352. Cf. Goldingay, "Place of Ishmael," 146–49; and, *Old Testament Theology*, 159.

353. Contra Wilson, *Genealogy*, 199. In this way, the promise to Abraham (12:2; 15:5; 17:6, 16) is fulfilled; McConville, *God and Earthly Power*, 37.

It is worth comparing MKL with Edom's and Ishmael's lists of rulers. Malamat has pointed out the difference between Mesopotamian and West Semitic genealogies. Whereas the former are vertical or linear – tracing the family from father to son to grandson – the latter tend to take account of horizontal relationships as well, often mentioning female members, so forming a family tree and "revealing a genealogical panorama of a single tribe or of an entire group of peoples."[354]

The list of Edom's kings resembles MKL with an emphasis on continuity in the royal line. This is, however, counterbalanced by the impression given by its kings being apparently elected rather than hereditary, as well as by the first list that is more in the fashion of WSL stressing tribal relations. The same holds for Ishmael's offspring.

Like the stratification of flora and fauna, the coming about of countries, nations, and languages, as well as that of the socio-political stratification of Ishmael's and Esau's descendants, are regarded in Genesis as something valuable. The former (ch. 1) entails natural, the latter (chs. 10, 25, and 36) socio-cultural diversity. Both are indispensable in the world.[355] They not only make life bearable but diversity grants the world and life their God ordained role.

The only exception in the diversity of creation is humankind. The author, most strikingly, does not stratify humankind as opposed to flora and fauna; "the multiplicity of animals is contrasted with the 'unity' of human beings, an opposition also indicated by the consistent absence of *mîn* whenever references are made to human beings."[356] Having seen how much God enjoys diversity in creation, the explanation must be: there is only one human race and any subordination within humanity is a denial of the Creator's intention. In other words, diversity in the socio-cultural world is not a "creation order" but, like culture itself, a human achievement.

Equality within the human race is established in the account of Genesis 1. God sets out the creation of humankind:

"Let us make man in our image, in our likeness, and let them rule over the fish of the sea and the birds of the air, over the

---

354. Malamat, "King Lists," 163.

355. The deconstructionist reading offered by Slivniak, "Garden of Double Messages," 439–60, stresses the opposition and interdependence of nature and culture.

356. Beauchamp, "מין *mîn*," 290; cf. Cotter, *Genesis*, 18.

livestock, over all the earth, and over all the creatures that move along the ground." So God created man in his own image, in the image of God he created him; male and female he created them. (1:26–27)

Clearly, animal species consist of male and female individuals as well. Still, the narrator notes only of humankind that it was created male and female. The human race bears God's image only through its being "stratified" into male and female.[357]

The Flood: A New Beginning by Destruction (6:1–9:19)

Genesis 6–9 relates the flood, preceded by an enigmatic story of supernatural beings. As is well-known, Mesopotamia also had its own versions of the flood predating that of Genesis, as well as myths and epics about supernatural beings. These provide the background to the Genesis story that draws on its Mesopotamian source and polemicizes with its theology.

Before the Flood: Of Demigods, Giants, and Heroes (6:1–8)

"This is unquestionably one of the obscurest sections of the Torah, and all the varied views advanced concerning it by later generations not only did not contribute to its elucidation, but, on the contrary, served to cloud its significance and make it more and more incomprehensible."[358] Even though we have gained much insight on the section since this statement by Cassuto was first made in the 1940s, it has not become entirely dated. Certainly it is still, now as before, one of the obscurest sections of the Pentateuch. Part of the problem lies in the fact that it is arguably the most mythic section of the OT, without preceding or succeeding discussion.[359] It is about divine beings and demigods, heroes and giants, and, related in some way to these, the limitation of the human life span and Yahweh's decision to destroy creation.

This enigmatic passage presupposes acquaintance with the mythological background of *năpilîm* and *gibbōrîm*, gods' sons and their marriage with

---

357. See Trible, *God and the Rhetoric of Sexuality*, 17; Goldingay, *Models for Interpretation*, 94.
358. Cassuto, "Sons of God," 25.
359. Petersen, "Genesis 6:1–4," 49.

The Primeval History: An Alternative to Babylon's Metanarrative 119

women,[360] or "underlying versions of the flood story" differing from and alluded to by 6:1–4.[361] I will study this putative background and try to determine the function of the passage as the introduction to the flood story.

Genesis 6:1–4 is placed in its narrower and wider contexts of 6:1–8 and the flood. Having a new context, it receives a new content as well. That is to say, whatever the original was, it is now to be understood as the preface to the flood.[362] As such, it is difficult to read it as not providing a rationale for the flood. Of 6:1–4, Cassuto claims again, "The passage is in no way connected with the account of the Flood."[363] Though noticing the discordance, Wenham disagrees. While it "appears to have little connection with the preceding genealogy, it is in fact closely integrated with it. . . . By focusing on God's 'making' and 'creating man' in 6:6, 7 and 5:1, 2, it also forms a loose *inclusio* with the opening paragraph 5:1–5."[364] So, 6:1–7 serves as the introduction to the flood.[365] Seen in this light, the concordant elements of the section are emphasized, with discordance acknowledged. To be sure, there are quite a few of the latter,[366] with the first word signaling a new time setting in contrast to the foregoing.[367]

The genealogies in chapters 5 and 10 are reminiscent of SKL, consisting of ante- and postdiluvian sections and interrupted by a reference to the flood. Chapter 5 leads up to the flood hero (5:29, 32). Readers familiar with SKL should at this point expect some remark on the flood. And, indeed, the flood starts in 6:9. It is, however, prefaced by the strange section on demigods, giants, and heroes.

---

360. Schüle, *Prolog*, 225.

361. Kvanvig, "Gen 6,1–4," 90.

362. This canonical context is often ignored by interpreters. A good case in point is Kvanvig's otherwise excellent study. He puts 6:1–4 in context with a short sentence (Kvanvig, "Gen 6,1–4," 111): "First when we read 6,1–4 in the context of 6,5 ff the perspective changes: The multiplication of humans in v 1 increases the multiplication of sin in v 5." Petersen, "Genesis 6:1–4," 50, suggests that the function of 6:1–4 is the ordering of human cosmos but fails to demonstrate this in context.

363. Cassuto, "Sons of God," 25.

364. Wenham, *Genesis 1–15*, 136, makes these statements of 6:1–8 and 6:5–8 but, apart from "Yahweh," the keywords he mentions ("man," "God," "sons," "daughters," "make," "create") do not occur in v.8. In addition to this, disregarding the chiasm of 6:5–8, v.8 is not material to the introduction of the flood but rather starts the story itself.

365. Cf. Longacre, "Discourse Structure," 93.

366. See Kvanvig, "Gen 6,1–4," 79–90.

367. Kvanvig, "Gen 6,1–4," 81; cf. Baker, "Diversity and Unity," 191–92.

The following structure may help us recognize the main motifs and thrust of 6:1–7. In demarcating the unit's limits, it is necessary to bear in mind that the episode does not end at verse 4 as if it were an intrusive remnant of some myth.[368] Indeed, it has integrating features.

A Humankind increases, "and daughters were born to them [*ûbānôt yullǝdû lāhem*]" (6:1)

    B "The sons of God saw [*wayyir'û*] that the daughters of men were good, and they married any of them they chose" (6:2 AT)

        C Yahweh utters his decision (*wayyōmer yhwh*): humans will have 120 years to the flood (6:3)

A' "The giants were on the earth in those days – and also afterward – when the sons of God went to the daughters of men and had children by them [*wǝyālǝdû lāhem*]" (6:4)

    B' Yahweh sees (*wayyar' yhwh*) that humankind's makings are evil, so, he regrets having created them (6:5–6)

        C' Yahweh utters his decision (*wayyōmer yhwh*) to destroy the earth (6:7)

A and A' portray the first step leading to the crisis. A' (along with B) refers to mythical beings who marry the daughters of humankind. Led by theological considerations interpreters sometimes deny or play down the story's mythical character, thought to be foreign to the Bible.[369] They do not take the "sons of god" in its obvious ANE sense as divine beings (see Pss 29:1; 89:7; Job 1:6; 2:1; 38:7; cf. Deut 32:8, LXX).[370] The LXX renders the term *'uioi tou theou*. The oldest Jewish interpretations also took it in this sense,[371] and

---

368. Contra Cassuto, "Sons of God"; Westermann, *Genesis 1–11*, 363–69; Gowan, *Genesis 1–11*, 82–86. This seems to be the upshot of Schüle's analysis too (*Prolog*, 219–46) who in a novel way suggests that 6:1–4 is a creation text. Genesis 6:1 clearly "dates" the episode at the period of the multiplication of humankind though.

369. E.g. Calvin, *Genesis*, 104; Keil, *Pentateuch*, 131–34.

370. Cassuto, "Sons of God," 20n18, does not make a distinction between "divine beings" and "angels," a consequence of his preference for an "angelic interpretation." He regards both the plural and singular genitive as of the same semantic content, his argument, however, is not compelling. He distinguishes between angels of lower and higher ranks and thinks 6:2 refers to the former (Cassuto, 23). Angels of higher and lower ranks might be known in some passages of the OT, acknowledged by Cassuto elsewhere (Cassuto, *Genesis*, 294). The Pentateuch does not know of a developed angelology though.

371. Cassuto, "Sons of God," 21.

the mythic content of the phrase is not only supported but elaborated on by several ancient translations. The Hebrew term's possessive can be singular, "God's sons," or plural, "gods' sons."[372] This latter rendering can be found in Aramaic rabbinic sources (*bənê 'ĕlāhayyā'*) as well as in Aquila's translation (*'uioi tōn theōn*).[373] Alternatively, "sons of god" sometimes refers to kings in Babylonian texts.[374] For the first audience, this equivocalness perhaps granted the opportunity to see the "sons of God/gods" as, first of all, heavenly beings but also as rulers.

The difference and similarity between B and B' are that B refers to the perception of God's sons while B' to that of God, expressed in both cases by the verb "see." Whereas the latter, as far as its result is concerned, is negative, the first is positive – they are contrasted. The perception of the sons of God underlines that God's creation is good, stressed in the creation account seven times (1:4, 10, 12, 18, 21, 25, 31) and implied in the account of the woman's creation (2:18–24).[375] Opposed to this is God's perception. But what exactly does God see as evil?

C and C' report Yahweh's two decisions: (1) human lifespan is cut or, alternatively, humans will have 120 years to the flood; and (2) the annihilation of created life. Regarding neither of God's decisions is there a consensus among scholars. The structure above points in the direction that the giants (6:4) and Yahweh's decision (6:7) are in some way related, as were Yahweh's decision in 6:3 and the cohabitation of divine and human beings in 6:1–2. At the same time, it should be emphasized that no sin or transgression is explicitly pinpointed in the preface.

The next section starts at 6:9, signaled by the *toledot* formula.[376] The two units, 6:1–7 and 6:9–22, make 6:8, however, appear as a redundant, disjunctive

---

372. In some instances (e.g. Deut 14:1; 32:5; Ps 73:15; Hos 2:1), the phrase obviously refers to Israel, but is to be taken in a polemic sense: it is not divine beings but Israel who is Yahweh's sons. Calvin, *Genesis*, 238 (see also Keil, *Pentateuch*, 131–34), expresses his stupefaction over the mythic interpretation: "That ancient figment, concerning the intercourse of angels with women, is abundantly refuted by its own absurdity, and it is surprising that learned men should formerly have been fascinated by ravings so gross and prodigious." Barr, *Garden of Eden*, 84, deems interpretations of Calvin's kind as demythologizing the passage. On the three main interpretive options and one similar to mine, see Wenham, *Genesis 1–15*, 139–41.

373. Cassuto, "Sons of God," 20.

374. Kline, "Divine Kingship," 187–204; cf. Millard, "New Babylonian 'Genesis,'" 12.

375. Contra Kaminski, "Beautiful Women," 457–73.

376. Cf. Longacre, "Discourse Structure," 93; Wenham, *Genesis 1–15*, 155.

note. The reference to Noah's finding mercy with Yahweh, a preparatory sentence, can be seen just as isolated in its context as Noah himself was in his generation.

Genesis 6:1–2 speaks of the multiplication of humankind to whom daughters are born, *yulladû*. Immediately before it, however, we read of Noah fathering, *yôled*, three sons (5:32). This is repeated in 6:10 so enveloping the section on the events on earth and God's reaction to them. Also, the second note on Noah's sons is right after the note on Noah's righteousness (6:9) and before mentioning Yahweh's perception of humanity's corruption (6:11–12). By juxtaposing the births of humankind's daughters and Noah's sons, human violence and Noah's righteousness, two human groups and two ways of life are contrasted and God's decision and choice become clearer.

Importantly, in A the protagonist is humankind, while in A' it is the sons of God and giants; in B, it is the sons of God,[377] while, in B', C, and C' it is God himself. Seeing the developments on earth, God gets more and more involved, finally taking over the initiative. God does not do this because of rebellion – vertical sin – but because of ethical concerns – horizontal sin – as I will argue. God's growing frustration and taking the initiative are signaled by the multiple references to God's perception in 6:5–13.

In Greek mythology, gods and goddesses frequently established intimate relationships with mortals. In Hellas, this was such a well-known *topos* that, risking an overstatement, human beings without some divine pedigree or demigod relation were the exceptions to the rule. While, in ANE, divine-human marriage, disregarding the sacred marriage *topos*, does not seem to occupy such an important place, it is not unknown.[378] Indeed, there is evidence that the motif of divine-human marriage was well-known in Israel's neighborhood. From Egypt to Canaan to Mesopotamia, fertility cults were practiced, in which the marriage of the fertility goddess (Innin in Sumer,

---

377. Sure, it is the sons of God who act in 6:2. Their action may be an "acting upon," still, their "taking" the daughters of humankind is not against the will of their future wives as if they were just puppets in the hands of male power; so Baumgart, *Umkehr des Schöpfergottes*, 113–14.

378. Contra Fockner, "Reopening the Discussion," 436, who claims marriage between gods and humans in ANE was unknown; cf. Schüle, "Divine-Human Marriages," 116–28.

Ishtar in Babylonia) was dramatized. This resulted in cultic prostitution, an abhorrent thing for Israel.[379]

In the Gilgamesh epic, popular in seventh-century Assyria and in sixth-century Babylonia, the goddess Ishtar happens to see Gilgamesh bathe and falls in love with him. Gilgamesh himself is a demigod, the son of King Lugalbanda and the goddess Ninsun.[380] In Tablet VI, Ishtar resorts to sweet-talk. But Gilgamesh plainly rejects the proposal by reminding Ishtar of her fickleness.

By supplying "unsolicited" information,[381] this passage seems self-explanatory: although rarely attested, human-divine marriage or cohabitation is assumed as something obvious or possible in Mesopotamia.[382] The epic begins by introducing its hero Gilgamesh. He is two-thirds god, and is of enormous stature: eleven cubits, roughly five meters.[383] The height of his companion Enkidu is noteworthy too.[384] They were attributed feats like the killing of the lion, the heavenly bull, and the monster Huwawa.[385] At the same time, Gilgamesh was dreaded in Uruk for his tyrannical rule and, importantly, the *ius primae noctis*. Wenham thus notes, "it is clear that even if specific sources for Gen 6:1–8 cannot be identified, Genesis is making use of well-known

---

379. Lambert, "Myth and Ritual," 106–7, claims that we have conclusive evidence of the sacred marriage as far back as the III dynasty of Ur. Note, however, that, by Neo-Babylonian times, the sacred marriage ritual was celebrated but not re-enacted; Sefati, *Love Songs*, 46–47. Also note that many scholars now are skeptical about the existence of cultic prostitution.

380. Even though "demigod" might be a controversial term, I use it in its general sense, "a minor god, or a being that is partly a god and partly human" (Turnbull, *Oxford Advanced Learner's Dictionary*, 403). On Gilgamesh's being a demigod, see George, *Babylonian Gilgamesh Epic*, vol. 1, 119–35. Bührer, "Göttersöhne und Menschentöchter," 512, has also noticed the link with the Gilgamesh tradition.

381. See Kreuzer, "Saul," 42.

382. See similarly Walton, "Sons of God," 202–3.

383. Cf. Walton, "Genesis," 45. Buttressed by line 34 of a Gilgamesh fragment from Ugarit found in 1993; see George, "Gilgameš epic," 240, 242.

384. Batto, *Slaying the Dragon*, 66–67, also sees the Enkidu parallel as significant. The "giants," he considers a reference to the *lullû*, the divine-human primeval man in Gilgamesh and Atrahasis.

385. Not only mythic prehistory, however, but historic memory too reports of such heroes. Naram-sin attributed to himself divine prerogatives. Tiglat-Pileser I gained fame as a builder and hunter. Reportedly, he embarked on a sea trip to hunt big sea animals. Still, he was remembered not only for his hunting or building achievements but as a conqueror who pushed the borders of his empire as far to the West as the Mediterranean. Wenham, "Genesis 1–11 as Protohistory," 90, mentions the ancient belief that Gilgamesh, Alexander the Great, and Augustus, among others, were great men of the past, fathered by gods.

oriental ideas."³⁸⁶ Gilgamesh belongs to the "heroes of old."³⁸⁷ The *apkallu*, the semidivine sages and heroes before the flood, also marry human daughters, whose descendants were considered infamous.³⁸⁸

Yahweh's decision to shorten human life may thus be seen as a soft polemic against the high view of the Mesopotamian antediluvian kings on the respective lists. "Even this race of supermen, or a humankind with superman at its head, is still *bāśār*, is Yahweh's appropriate dictum."³⁸⁹ Divinely sired men do not live immensely long lives either.³⁹⁰ The problem with this interpretation is that there is only one major character in Genesis who did not live 120 years, Joseph who dies at 110.³⁹¹ Based on a comparison with Atrahasis, Kvanvig argues for the alternative that the 120 years in 6:3 are the time gap between God's decision and its execution by the flood. He also proposes that *yādôn* in 6:3 might be a derivative of Akkadian *danānu*, "be strong, powerful." If so, it is a nice play on the word "heroes" in 6:4.³⁹²

Positing a Mesopotamian background, Clines suggests that the phrase *bəšaggam* consists of the preposition *b* plus a noun cognate with the Assyrian verb *šagāmu*, "to bellow, howl," echoing the Atrahasis epic where people begin to multiply (see 6:1) and their bellowing disturbs Enlil.³⁹³

The obscure word *nəpilîm*, recurring in Numbers 13:33 only, is translated by the LXX as *gigantēs*. The narrator of Genesis 6:4 may have giants of ANE

---

386. Wenham, *Genesis 1–15*, 138.

387. See Wenham, 146. Another Mesopotamian tradition, along with a late tale of Ailianos, intimates that the circumstances of Lugalbanda and Ninsun's marriage resulting in Gilgamesh's birth were highly unusual; Wilcke, "Genealogical and Geographical," 563. It is not less unusual for the readers of Genesis to learn of these divine-human marriages. In addition, Kilmer, "Mesopotamian Counterparts," 39–41, notes that four semi-divine postdiluvian *apkallu* could probably mate with the daughters of humankind and were endowed with special powers and wisdom. By using those powers for good or ill, they could both offend and impress the gods. In addition to Gilgamesh, heroes like Enmerkar or Lugalbanda were also born of such marriages; cf. Schüle, *Prolog*, 222. On the poem Lugalbanda and Ninsuna, narrating King Lugalbanda and the goddess Ninsun's wedding, see Jacobsen, "Lugalbanda and Ninsuna," 69–86.

388. Kilmer, "Mesopotamian Counterparts"; cf. Walton, *Genesis*, 45–46.

389. Kraeling, "Significance and Origin," 198.

390. Kraeling, 200.

391. Hartley, *Genesis*, 96.

392. Kvanvig, "Gen 6,1–4," 98–99; cf. Fockner, "Reopening the Discussion," 451–52.

393. Clines, "Significance of the 'Sons of God,'" 39–40; similarly Kvanvig, "Gen 6,1–4," 107–10 and *Primeval History*, 285.

myths like Gilgamesh in mind.³⁹⁴ These figures lived both before and after the flood, were heroes, and were venerated.

Three further remarks on 6:4 seem in order. First, whatever its origin, the verse's present "mutilated" form suggests that the narrator, by not dwelling on these heroes, wanted to limit their perceived significance to a minimum. Second, and related to this, the identity as well as ancestry of the giants and the heroes remain enigmatic. Both seem to be introduced on the assumption that the audience is familiar with them. To the present-day reader, at least, the clause "They were the heroes of old, men of renown" is ambiguous as to its reference. Is it the giants now identified with the heroes or, rather, is it the offspring of the human-divine marriages to whom the narrator refers? If this syntactical ambiguity is intended and the referent was not clear to the first audience either, the narrator may intend to make an ambiguous distinction between giants and heroes and shroud them, and their descent in particular, in mystery. In this way, he leaves more room for interpretation by the first audience.³⁹⁵ Third, the narrator has managed to populate his narrative world with sons of gods, giants, and heroes by, at the same time, making God the main protagonist of pre-flood events.

PH views the heroes in an ambiguous way. In the religion of Babylonia where giant heroes and demigods had an enormous religious significance, their import cannot be overlooked. Although low-key, it still appears to be a polemic against Mesopotamian myths and religion. On the other hand, these heroes did achieve something to become men of renown. Therefore, they are not to be regarded as "horrible people."³⁹⁶ The narrator would have had plenty of possibilities to characterize them more negatively but he did not. Rather, bearing the reservations above in mind, these heroes are presented in a positive light, while at the same time, in a tongue-in-cheek fashion, relativized.

---

394. Of the *nəpilîm* Westermann, *Genesis 1–11*, 378, similarly remarks that "it must have been originally a term to describe mythical beings, semi-gods, like Gilgamesh who was said to be two-thirds god and one-third human."

395. I am inclined to see "they" (6:4) as referring to the "giants/nephilim," thus equating the giants and heroes; see also Hamilton, *Book of Genesis*, 270; contra Kraeling, "Significance and Origin," 196. Kraeling attributes the identification of giants and heroes to an editor's correction of the author's work (Kraeling, 203). Gese, "Der bewachte Lebensbaum," 77–85, sees in the note a critique of Mesopotamian death cult. Ingeniously, Sarna, *Genesis*, 46, suggests that "nephilim" is used "for oratorical effect, much as 'Huns' was used to designate Germans during two world wars."

396. See Waltke, *Genesis*, 118.

Rüdiger Bartelmus has studied the concept of heroes in Sumer, Ugarit, and Greece, of which Sumer concerns us. He has found that the hero concept is linked to a heroic age and probably aims at the legitimation of the reigning dynasty or king.[397] Clearly, the effect of 6:1–4 is just the opposite: by relativizing these heroes, royal claims are downplayed. And there is no follow-up on kings or dynasties.

This interpretation seems to be underscored by a look at early Mesopotamian kingship. Sjöberg's extensive list of Sumerian and Old Babylonian kings shows that divine descent was the norm. Sjöberg mentions by name some three dozen kings descended from Mesopotamian deities from the three senior gods Anu, Enlil, and Enki to Marduk, Shamash, Sin as fathers, to Ninlil, Ninhursag, Ninsun, Nanna, and Nanshe as mothers. No doubt, this development in Mesopotamian royal ideology was used for political ends.[398] This may be a parallel to 6:2. As for the lack of any reference to kings in Genesis 6:1–4, we should not miss them – PH's narrator is not aware of royals.

If human-divine marriage was well-known in ANE and something abominable to Israel, Yahweh's decision (6:3) can be explained as a punishment for crossing the boundary between the divine and human worlds[399] or as a preventive action.[400] "The sexual mingling of the Sons of God and the daughters of men creates an imbalance and a confusion in the cosmic order. The birth of the demigods threatens the fabric of the cosmos," Hendel claims.[401] But is it really the cosmic order God is concerned about? Is it not rather the social order, becoming disorder, that is giving God a headache? I will interpret the

---

397. Bartelmus, *Heroentum in Israel*, 46. Unfortunately, he does not study Akkadian literature.

398. Sjöberg, "Die Göttliche Abstammung," 87–112.

399. Wenham, *Genesis 1–15*, 146.

400. Hendel, "Demigods and the Deluge," 18–19, calls attention to Hesiod's Catalogue of Women where Zeus is intent on preventing the birth of demigods stemming from the wedding of gods and human beings. Gese, "Der bewachte Lebensbaum," emphasizes the similarity to ch. 3 where the boundary between humankind's mortality and God's immortality is established. Oden, "Divine Aspirations," 214–15, sees divine order breached by humankind's violence as the main reason contributing to the flood. He points out that both Atrahasis and the Genesis flood story conclude with divine regulations, similar or dissimilar in content, portraying "humans aspiring to divine status – which status is ultimately denied them" (Oden, 215).

401. Hendel, "Demigods and the Deluge," 23; cf. Brueggemann, *Genesis*, 72.

section with an eye on PH's view of egalitarian society and its broader context. As for this context, I have referred to Sasson's chart, which I slightly modify.[402]

A Creation (1:1–2:15)	A' Flood: Anti-creation (6:9–9:3)
B Prohibition and warning (2:16–17)	B' Prohibition and warning (9:3–17)
C In and out of the garden (2:18–4:16)	C' In the garden (9:18–29)
Curses (3:14–19; 4:11–12)	Curse (9:25)
D Genealogies (4:17–5:32)	D' Genealogies (10:1–32; 11:10–26)
E Heroes (6:1–8)	E' Tower of Babylon (11:1–9)

Concluding their respective sections, E and E' correspond to each other in vocabulary and theme. Genesis 6:1 speaks of the beginning of multiplication of humankind, whereas 11:6 of the beginning of what humankind will do; 6:1–4 relates actions of the "daughters of humankind" and "sons of God," whereas the tower is built by the "sons of humankind" (11:5); 6:4 refers to "heroes of old, men of name" (AT), whereas Nimrod, another "hero" (10:8), is implicitly among Babylon's builders making themselves a name (11:4). I see in both cases the sin committed against creation and not the Creator directly.

Regarding theme, I argue that 11:1–9 is about an attempt at a centralized, homogeneous empire defying the Creator's original plan. Reading 6:1–4 in this light means that humankind's sin here is not a violation of human-divine boundaries either. Rather, their elevation above their fellow humans creates a boundary between themselves and the rest of humankind – the heroes violated interhuman relations. God's original creation was meant for one human species. This is changing with the appearance of heroes and superhumans – human society becomes stratified and hierarchic.

Finally,

> The LORD was grieved [*wayyinnāḥem*] that he had made [*ʿāśâ*] humankind on the earth, and his heart was filled with pain [*wayyitʿaṣṣēb*]. So the LORD said, "I will wipe humankind, whom I have created, from the face of the earth [*hāʾădāmâ*] – humankind and animals, and creatures that move along the ground,

---

402. Sasson, "'Tower of Babel,'" 218; cf. Tomasino, "History Repeats"; Carr, "Βίβλος γενέσεως Revisited (Part Two)," 329.

and birds of the air – for I am grieved [*niḥamtî*] that I have made them [*'aśîtim*]." (6:6–7 AT)

God's grief plays on Noah's naming by Lamech: "He named him Noah [*nōaḥ*] and said, "He will comfort us [*yənaḥămēnû*] in the labor [*mimma'ăśēnû*] and painful toil [*mē'iṣṣābōn*] of our hands caused by the ground [*hā'ădāmâ*] the LORD has cursed" (5:29). For Richard Hess "Lamech's hope for comfort turns into God's repentance for the creation of humanity. This leads to the Flood in which Noah continues to play a key role."[403]

Hess observes of the conclusions of the respective genealogies (chs. 4 and 5) that

> both Lamechs play pivotal roles in their lines and both have statements recorded in the text. But Cain's Lamech utters a cry of vengeance and with that terminates his line; while Seth's Lamech expresses the hope for a better life for his descendants, and with that introduces the offspring who will continue his line and play a role in trying to fulfill his wish.[404]

The fulfillment of Lamech's wish takes place in the flood to which I now turn.

The Flood (6:9–8:19)

Ever since George Smith delivered his groundbreaking lecture on "The Chaldean Account of the Deluge" that came to be known as the Gilgamesh epic, comparing Gilgamesh and the Genesis flood account has been a preferred way of approach.[405]

In ancient Mesopotamia, the flood was a landmark event of orientation. In historiography, there were antediluvian and postdiluvian times.[406] The flood not only divided "real" human and primeval histories but also marked a qualitative shift. Before, humankind was immortal and essential cultural inventions were mediated by the mythic sages, the *apkallu*, who were therefore instrumental in Mesopotamian culture. Afterward, it was "normal" human history.

---

403. Hess, *Studies in the Personal Names*, 116–17.
404. Hess, 142.
405. Smith, "Chaldean Account," 213–34, on 3 December 1872.
406. See Lambert and Millard, *Atra-Ḫasis*, 18.

The Atrahasis epic begins by reference to the hard labor the junior gods have to suffer as a consequence of the senior gods' ordering the world. After forty years, the Igigi mutiny and the rebellion results in a compromise between them and the Anunnaki. The decision of creating humankind is made and duly executed. Now, it is humankind who bears the load of the Igigi – the gods are relieved and can enjoy the fruit of humankind's work, which is the offerings. Apparently, however, an unforeseen problem mars the life of the gods: through multiplication, humankind gets noisy and rebellious so depriving Enlil of much needed sleep. He decides to decimate the human populace first by plague, then by famine, by drought, and finally by other calamities. All these do not, however, achieve the aim intended as there is a saboteur within divine ranks, Enki, who frustrates Enlil's plans by communicating them to the pious and wise Atrahasis. Finally, Enlil grows suspicious and orders the annihilation of all humankind by a worldwide flood. But again, Enki outsmarts his colleague by telling Atrahasis to build an ark. During and after the flood, the gods are portrayed as terrified as well as angry with Enlil because the destruction of humankind in the seven-day flood robs them of sacrifice food. With the waters receding, Atrahasis disembarks from the ark and offers sacrifice to the gods who gather "like flies over the offering." Enlil is of course angry on learning that there are survivors. An argument between Enlil and the other gods ensues, concluded by a compromise of making humankind mortal and stopping unlimited multiplication by birth control measures.

This account of the deluge was not acceptable without modifications for the Jewish sages.[407] Thus, Genesis offers its own version with remarkable similarities as well as telltale differences. The reason for the annihilation is made clear. It is evident that overpopulation, a rather questionable *casus belli*, is not Yahweh's concern in Genesis.[408] Indeed, after the flood, God commands humankind to be fruitful and multiply (9:1, 7).[409] Instead of overpopulation or opposition to divine authority, it is wickedness on earth that impacts Yahweh, coupled with the establishing of boundaries in human society. In God's perception, conditions are pretty bad: "The LORD saw how great the wickedness

---

407. See Müller, "Motiv für die Sintflut," 299.
408. See Kilmer, "Mesopotamian Concept of Overpopulation," 172–74.
409. Kilmer, 174–75.

of the human race had become on the earth, and that every inclination of the thoughts of the human heart was only evil all the time" (6:5).

This statement is surprising for two reasons. As we have seen, chapter 4 presents a balanced picture of humankind's capability of good and evil: even the first murderer achieves things that, in Mesopotamian mythology, were attributed to gods or divine beings. Second, 6:1–4 addressed some issues like the cohabitation of divine and human beings, the existence of giants and heroes that can be interpreted negatively. Still, the narrator did not draw the conclusion Yahweh did; in his view, humankind knows good and evil and not "every inclination of the thoughts of the human heart was only evil all the time" (6:5). The narrator's and Yahweh's perceptions do not seem to match.

Genesis 6:11–12 further underlines Yahweh's view of a world beyond redemption. "Now the earth was corrupt in God's sight, and the earth was filled with violence. And God saw the earth, and behold, it was corrupt; for all flesh had corrupted their way upon the earth" (RSV). If Yahweh's perception does not match reality and it is his overreaction that partly causes the flood, this may be morally disturbing. It is, however, in line with the cause of the deluge in Atrahasis. There, the gods, with their ringleader Enlil, similarly overreact.

The state of affairs on earth is emphasized by the term in verse 1 "the face of the earth" recurring in verse 7 thus forming an *inclusio*:

> When men began to increase in number *on the face of the earth* (6:1 AT)
>
> So the Lord said, "I will wipe mankind, whom I have created, *from the face of the earth*" (6:7)

Importantly, it is "in God's sight" that the earth is corrupt (6:5, 11). Yahweh has taken a big step from his rather reserved, matter-of-factly-observing self in 3:22 noting the change in the conditions of humankind, to a more agitated and involved deity. And it is not only Yahweh's overreaction that he has in common with Mesopotamian gods. There are other features shared by Genesis and Atrahasis.

In Atrahasis, Enlil grows angry because of the noise of the growing human masses, or because of their rebellion.[410] Here, it is human violence and evil that lead to Yahweh's judgment. Even though violence is not elaborated on, in 4:1–16 and 17–26, it is dominant.[411] Indeed, Batto claims that the narrative in chapter 4 intends to provide rationale for the flood.[412] This is emphasized by the parallel arrangement of Cain and Lamech who concludes Cain's genealogy which is, in this way, enveloped by two murderers.[413] In 6:11–13, both the narrator and Yahweh state once again that due to the spread of violence earth cannot be spared.

> Now the earth was corrupt in God's sight and was full of violence. God saw how corrupt the earth had become, for all the people on earth had corrupted their ways. So God said to Noah, "I am going to put an end to all people, for the earth is filled with violence because of them. I am surely going to destroy both them and the earth." (6:11–13)

"Violence," *ḥāmās*, occurs here for the first time, and, the lack of previous usage notwithstanding, must be connected with the shedding of blood.[414] The same earth God created and saw as very good (1:31) has become corrupt (6:12)[415] and humanity has corrupted itself, *hišḥît* (6:12), so God decides (6:13) to destroy it, *mašḥîtām*.[416] This only reaffirms what 6:5 has already claimed of Yahweh's concern about human wickedness. God intends to destroy corrupt creation and start all over with humankind. God is troubled by what he "sees," humankind's wickedness and corruption (6:5, 12). For God, horizontal aspects are decisive in his decision of annihilation of the world. Thus, the punishment is justified even if it seems to be out of proportion. God in

---

410. See Pettinato, "Die Bestrafung," 165–200; Batto, "Sleeping God," 160; Batto, "Covenant of Peace," 192–93; Kvanvig, "Gen 6,1–4," 107–10; differently Albertz, "Das Motiv für die Sintflut," 3–16.

411. Cf. Carr, *Formation*, 293.

412. Batto, *Slaying the Dragon*, 86.

413. See Hess, "Lamech in the Genealogies," 21–22.

414. Stoebe, "*ḥāmās*, Gewalttat," 586; Frymer-Kensky, "Atrahasis Epic," 153. The word *ḥāmās* "is virtually a technical term for the oppression of the weak by the strong" and denotes sins like that of Lamech and Cain (Clines, "Noah's Flood," 133).

415. See Hendel, "Tangled Plots," 46.

416. Clines, "Noah's Flood," 135.

Genesis is concerned with social and inter-human realities. Vertical aspects are not mentioned. Seeing this, Pettinato's claim that Atrahasis provides a firmer ethical basis than Genesis where humankind's sin and sinful behavior are described in rather vague terms seems off the mark.[417]

In chapter 7, two apparently insignificant statements are made: "Noah was six hundred years old when the floodwaters came on the earth" (7:6); "And after the seven days the floodwaters came on the earth" (7:10; but cf. 7:17 too). These may be allusions to SKL which also mentions twice that the flood came. Needless to say, Noah's story, introduced by the *toledot* formula (6:9), is not one of a king nor is his a royal genealogy, as Babylonians would expect, but of a commoner – unlike Atrahasis/Ziusudra/Utnapishtim, Noah is no king and no priest.[418] He is a commoner and a just one at that (6:9). His righteousness is as much emphasized as that of Atrahasis or Utnapishtim (Gilgamesh XI.27).[419] The Genesis story seems to imply that Noah was righteous in that he was innocent of the violence of his society. This might be hinted at by the unusual *toledot* formula. "This is the account of Noah. Noah was a righteous man, blameless among the people of his time, and he walked with God. Noah had three sons: Shem, Ham and Japheth" (6:9–10).

The brief genealogy is interrupted by the reference to Noah's righteousness. Since PH is the story of the whole of humanity and Noah is the post-flood ancestor of all humanity, this reference adumbrates God's goal for creation. Noah's righteousness "is the quality that must characterize humanity if the world is to survive."[420] The reference to Noah's walking with God makes him resemble his ancestor Enoch (see 5:24) which raises the question What will

---

417. Pettinato, "Die Bestrafung," 200.

418. In the Eridu Genesis, Ziusudra is king and priest. Davila, "Flood Hero," 199, sees Ziusudra only as a king. He is right in that neither Atrahasis nor Utnapishtim is called king. However, Jacobsen, "Primitive Democracy," 166n44, draws attention to an incident in Gilgamesh. Before setting out against Huwawa, Gilgamesh consults the city council. Similarly, in XI.35, Utnapishtim is supposed to confer with the elders of Shuruppak about building the ark. Atrahasis likewise speaks to the elders of the city about leaving it. Thus, even if neither of the Akkadian flood heroes are *called* kings they are definitely *depicted* in royal capacities; cf. Kvanvig, *Primeval History*, 246.

419. Noah is six hundred years old at the flood. In Atrahasis, periods of six hundred years divide the plagues before the flood.

420. McConville, *God and Earthly Power*, 36, 42.

happen to Noah, since Enoch was taken by God? Will he be likewise rescued from his generation?[421]

Anderson structures the flood story as follows (letters denoting the chiasm are provided by me):[422]

Transitional introduction (6:9–10)
   A Violence in God's creation (6:11–12)
      B First divine address: resolution to destroy (6:13–22)
         C Second divine address: command to enter the ark (7:1–10)
            D Beginning of the flood (7:11–16)
               E The rising flood waters (7:17–24)
                  F God remembers Noah (8:1a)
               E' The receding flood waters (8:1b–5)
            D' The drying of the earth (8:6–14)
         C' Third divine address: command to leave the ark (8:15–19)
      B' God's resolution to preserve order (8:20–22)
   A' Fourth divine address: covenant, blessing, and peace (9:1–17)
Transitional conclusion (9:18–19)

This scheme may help us see the ascending water of destruction and its descent, the undoing of creation and the advent of new creation, as well as Yahweh's change of determination from destruction to blessing and covenant. The turning point is provided in F when God remembers those in the ark. It makes God's change of mind clear. The chain of events starts when

> The LORD regretted that he had made human beings on the earth, and his heart was deeply troubled. So the LORD said, "I will wipe from the face of the earth the human race I have created – and with them the animals, the birds and creatures that move along the ground – for I regret that I have made them." (6:6–7)

God's conversion is denoted by the verb "regret," *nīḥam* (6:6–7). Seeing the violence compels him to undo creation. Even though the verb does not

---

421. Baumgart, *Die Umkehr des Schöpfergottes*, 106–7.
422. Anderson, "From Analysis to Synthesis," 38. For a similar albeit more detailed structure, with 8:1 marking the turning point though, see Wenham, "Coherence of the Flood," 336–48.

recur after the flood, God undergoes a change. "Never again will I curse the ground because of humans, even though every inclination of the human heart is evil from childhood. And never again will I destroy all living creatures, as I have done" (8:21).

The Genesis flood account is a story about God's conversion or, more precisely, God's conversions. Baumgart has studied from this perspective the roles of the different divine protagonists in Atrahasis and Gilgamesh.[423] The gods together make the decision of destroying life on earth. Wise and benevolent Enki, however, resolves to save the world. The mother goddess is also deeply touched by the death of her people and makes an emotional and successful attempt in the midst of the gods to save humankind and restrain them from all such actions in the future. In Genesis' monotheism, Yahweh embodies all these characters and the characteristics of Enlil, Enki, and Mami. The teamwork of the gods and the conversion in their world present Yahweh in terms of a drama of conversion. The mother goddess characteristics could not have been developed for the male deity as pointedly as they characterize Mami in the Akkadian myths, still, the conversion dimension is the most decisive for Yahweh. In the monotheistic theology of Genesis, these observations imply that Yahweh is not an apathetic, unchanging deity.[424]

In comparison with Gilgamesh, Baumgart states, the analysis of 6:5–8 and 8:20–22 demonstrates that Yahweh is converted at the flood. Before, he finds humankind and what it produces are ripe for destruction. Nearly the same humankind and what it produces, Yahweh states, are not to be destroyed after the flood. In Atrahasis the mother goddess, a party to deciding the destruction, being struck by the wide-scale destruction came to take a liking for humankind. In Genesis, the reason for God's change is that humankind and life have captivated Yahweh's innermost self.[425]

Baumgart further notes that, in Genesis and in Atrahasis, the phrase "all living creatures," occurs in comparable places, such as before the first births of children of humankind.[426] "Adam named his wife Eve, because she would become the mother of *all the living*" (3:20). Genesis 3:20 concerns not just

---

423. Baumgart, *Die Umkehr des Schöpfergottes*, 419–95.
424. Cf. Kessler, "Rhetorical Criticism," 16.
425. Baumgart, *Die Umkehr des Schöpfergottes*, 444.
426. Baumgart, 444–45.

Eve's particular birthing but the origin of all lives. "Mother of all living" in turn alludes to Mami's title, *belet kala ili*, "mistress of all gods" in Atrahasis I.246–48.[427] Baumgart sees it as probable that the Genesis text alludes to the Mesopotamian mother goddess. More importantly, he links 3:20 to 8:21 where we find the phrase *kol-ḥay* after Noah's sacrifice, when Yahweh declares his resolution never again to destroy humankind. Besides, both 3:20 and 8:21 are in contexts with future life in view – "And never again will I destroy *all living creatures*, as I have done" (8:21).

This happens exactly at the point when, in the Akkadian tradition, at Atrahasis/Utnapishtim's sacrifice, the mother goddess makes a similar declaration (Atrahasis III.5.30–6.4; Gilgamesh X.156–59). Baumgart concludes that having witnessed the large-scale destruction of life, the phrase *kōl-ḥay* is used by Yahweh to make clear that he has changed his mind. In this, he may have been touched by his mother goddess part. The mother goddess does not only reproach the gods but also manipulates Anu lest such a disaster should happen again.[428]

After comparing the Genesis and the Mesopotamian accounts, Baumgart notes the conversion process Yahweh is going through between 6:5–8 and 8:20–22. In this process, Yahweh is confronted by the death of his own creatures, which entails a defining experience for him.[429]

On balance, the result is that the Jewish sages who used the Mesopotamian theology saw the only one God, Yahweh, as taking over roles and functions as well as the cooperation of the Mesopotamian gods and goddesses. Genesis thus portrays Yahweh as an amalgamation of Mami, Enlil, and Enki, with Mami and Enki's compassion and commitment to humankind prevailing.[430]

It was first Mallowan, followed by Holloway's two studies, who suggested that, in the Mesopotamian flood story, the ark is modeled on a ziggurat.[431]

---

427. Kikawada, "Two Notes on Eve," 33–35. For more Mesopotamian parallels with 3:20 and 4:1, see Kramer, *History Begins at Sumer*, 144; Uehlinger, *Weltreich*, 32.

428. Baumgart, *Die Umkehr des Schöpfergottes*, 447–48, 476.

429. Baumgart, 135–41, 163–73.

430. Baumgart, 493–94. Note that one of the cult cities of Enki was Babylon: Ebeling, "Enki (Ea)," 378.

431. Mallowan, "Noah's Flood Reconsidered," 65; Holloway, "What Ship Goes There," 328–55; Holloway, "Shape of Utnapishtim's Ark," 617–26. See also Blenkinsopp, "Structure of P," 275–92; Zenger, "Beobachtungen zur Komposition," 35–54; Pola, *Die ursprüngliche Priesterschrift*, 367.

Following them and drawing on Benno Jacob's commentary as well as establishing links between Genesis 2:2–3 and Exodus 24–40, Baumgart states the tabernacle is related to creation. He goes on to claim that the tabernacle in Exodus is modeled on the ark as well as the Jerusalem Temple. Like the tabernacle, the ark is the vehicle of salvation.[432]

Divine conversion is the basis for life of the re-created world. Frymer-Kemsky sees the flood stories in Gilgamesh and Genesis as "so far removed from each other in focus and intent that one cannot compare the ideas in the two versions of the flood without setting up spurious dichotomies."[433] I hope to have proved the opposite. Obviously, the Genesis flood story is not a slavish adaptation of its Mesopotamian counterparts, it is a story with significantly new emphases – it is a new story. Its thrust and main theme is the judgment and end of the old and the re-creation of a new world.

Genesis 8:1 marks the end of the old and the start of the new, "But God remembered Noah and all the wild animals and the livestock that were with him in the ark, and he sent a wind over the earth, and the waters receded." The structure as well as motifs make the starting-all-over theme emphatic. The wind sent by God to dry up the water in 8:1 is evocative of God's *ruaḥ* in 1:2 moving magnificently above the water. "The *ruaḥ* in both i 2 and viii 1 represents the presence and creative power of God transforming a watery waste into a habitable world."[434]

PH did not just incorporate the flood story but, by adopting and somewhat modifying the motif of God's conversion, presented a coherent storyline as well as a deity who, much reminiscent of his Mesopotamian colleagues and having gone through a change in his character and attitude toward humankind, tallies with Israel's historical experience.

At the end of the day, the difference is that of the theodicies of polytheism and monotheism. Polytheism attributes opposing forces and motives to different gods. Atrahasis solves the question of theodicy by a disagreement within the divine council. Enlil, the god in charge of destinies and, in particular, of destruction,[435] is against humankind, whereas Enki, the benevolent creator

---

432. Baumgart, *Die Umkehr des Schöpfergottes*, 504–53.
433. Frymer-Kensky, "Atrahasis Epic," 148.
434. Moberly, "Why Did Noah Send out a Raven?" 352.
435. See Nötscher, "Enlil," 383–85.

of humans, is for. Monotheism cannot resort to a conflict within the divine council. Thus, in Genesis, it is a tension within God himself, resolved in God's conversion.[436] It is God who first decides to wipe out humankind (6:6–7) just as, in chapter 8, it is God being sorry for their destruction.[437]

But does not all this make the world an unsafe place, at the mercy of a volatile deity? This question will be dealt with in the next section.

God's Covenant (8:20–9:19)

The full implications of Yahweh's judgment and "conversion" can be properly seen in the context of the whole flood story. On disembarking, Noah builds an altar to the Lord, and takes of every clean animal and every clean bird to offer burnt offerings.[438] Earlier, both the narrator (6:6) and Yahweh (6:7) claimed that Yahweh "regretted" to having created humankind. Whereas, before the flood, Yahweh was convinced "that *every* inclination of the thoughts of his heart was *only* evil *all the time*" (6:5; cf. 6:11–12), after the flood, this is qualified. Genesis 8:21 is not a universal statement like that in 6:5 but a tempered view on the evil capacity of human heart.[439] "Yahweh smelled the pleasing aroma and said in his heart: 'Never again will I curse the ground because of humankind, even though the creation of humankind's heart is

---

436. See Batto, "Malevolent Deity," 226–28.

437. Similarly, Loewenstamm, "Flood," 108.

438. Gen 8:20 is the first and last time one builds an altar to offer a sacrifice in PH (cf. the different terminology in 4:3–5).

439. Importantly, neither 8:21 nor 6:5 contains statements about human "inclination/imagination," as the NIV and the RSV would have it, but about human "creation." That is what God judges evil. Out of nine occurrences, in eight instances at least (Gen 6:5; 8:21; Deut 31:21; Isa 29:16; Ps 103:14; Hab 2:18; 1 Chron 28:9; 29:18), the word's plain meaning is "creation" (*yēṣer*, a derivative of the verb *yāṣar*; see Gen 2:8; cf. Carr, *Reading the Fractures*, 64). In its context, Isa 26:3 seems to speak of a (solid) creation, i.e. a strong city: "A solid creation—you will keep it in peace, for it felt safe in you." An important parallel to Gen 6:5 and 8:21 is 1 Chron 29:18 (cf. 1 Chron 28:9), where the phrase concerned is used, "keep this forever so that your people's heart's creation [i.e. the Temple] might be realized, *ləyēṣer maḥšəbōt ləbab 'amməkā*" (AT). Smith, *Genesis of Good and Evil*, 76–77, similarly takes *yēṣer* to mean "formation" the root of which "denotes what the human person 'forms' or 'designs'" (Smith, 76). He emphasizes the linguistic connection between 8:21 and 2:7 and seeing here a pun. Goldingay, *Old Testament Theology*, 164, has also noticed the discrepancy between God's perception and Genesis'/OT's description of things.

evil from childhood. And never again will I destroy all living creatures, as I have done'" (8:21 AT).[440]

The sacrifice causes God to realize that human evil cannot be wiped out by force.[441] A clean slate is no viable option. Humankind has not changed; they are still capable of doing evil and good (see 3:22). Both God's words in Genesis 8:21 and the background of 6:1-6, as well as humankind's creating culture in chapter 4, seem to suggest that, with the flood, God went too far.[442] This may be the main reason why God, uniquely, establishes a covenant with creation that is binding only on him.[443] This is also the reason for God's decision to never again to curse the ground. The flood effectively cancels or at least moderates God's curse on the ground (3:17), "thereby fulfilling the prediction in 5:29 that Noah would bring us 'relief . . . from the suffering of our hands from the grounds that Yhwh cursed.'"[444]

We see both similarity and dissimilarity between PH and the Mesopotamian accounts. PH is similar to what we find in Atrahasis where Nintu and some of the gods not only disagree with the general destruction but weep over creation destroyed (III.4). At the same time, the protagonist's fate certainly reveals a huge difference between divine commitments. Whether because of a compromise in the divine council or by merit of the hero, Utnapishtim/Ziusudra is transferred to the land of immortality. Noah is not transferred nor does Yahweh's commitment in Genesis concern one person only but the whole of humankind, indeed, all of creation, fauna included. God sets "Noah's family on the path of fulfilling the creation project in the world."[445]

God makes certain his commitment, "As long as the earth endures, seedtime and harvest, cold and heat, summer and winter, day and night will never

---

440. Cf. Sarna, *Genesis*, 59. Note that the term "only" is missing and "all the time" is replaced by "from childhood." Rendtorff has argued that *qālal* means not so much "to curse" but "to describe something as cursed" (Rendtorff, "Gen 8,21"). Petersen, "Yahwist on the Flood," 438–46, however, has challenged Rendtorff's interpretation claiming the evidence does not support this. Turner, *Announcements of Plot*, 40–41, suggests that God's curse in 3:17–19 has rendered human work, including the subjugation of the earth, impossible, reflected in the omission from 9:1 of the command "subdue the earth" in 1:28. See Goldingay's similar discussion, *Old Testament Theology*, 176–77.

441. Cf. Petersen, "Yahwist on the Flood," 444–45.

442. Cf. Clines, "Failure of the Flood," 74–84.

443. Cf. Van Wijk-Bos, *Making Wise the Simple*, 85.

444. Galambush, *Reading Genesis*, 45–46.

445. Goldingay, *Old Testament Theology*, 179.

cease" (8:22). Through this rhythmic change of opposites, Yahweh demonstrates his commitment to diversity and integration while Enlil was more intent on the decline into chaos without difference and form.[446]

Again, humankind is commanded to multiply and fill the earth (9:1; cf. 1:28). The command, however, "to subdue the earth and have dominion over the animals" (1:28) has, with the curse in 3:17–19 still in force, not just been omitted but taken on a cruel aspect, underlined by the fact that it is seen from the viewpoint of the animals.[447] They will go "in fear and dread" of humankind, no longer under his responsible dominion (cf. also 2:19–20). Violence has become part and parcel of the natural order: every living creature is delivered into the power of humankind (9:2). It is, however, not to be unrestrained violence.[448]

Then, God utters the first prohibition in the post-flood world, "Whoever sheds the blood of man, by man shall his blood be shed; for in the image of God has God made man" (9:6). Jack Miles observes that this sentence would rather fit at the end of the first bloodshed in chapter 4 than at the conclusion of the flood story. It is placed after the biggest homicide – by God. Bloodshed is prohibited to humankind for only God is creator and destroyer of life.[449] God seems to have learned the lesson and wants no more killing. At the same time, we should not forget what caused God to annihilate creation: it was *ḥāmās*, "violence" (6:11, 13). Through this solemn warning (9:6), God is intent on forestalling further violence and bloodshed.[450] The prohibition, seen in the light of Noah's righteousness, has more universal import.

> The flood-narrative is therefore framed by the postulate of *tsedaqah* and the prohibition of murder by appeal to humanity's god-likeness. In this Old Testament version of the well-established ANE topic of flood-survival by an individual, a

---

446. Müller, "Das Motiv für die Sintflut," 307. It may also be a polemic against the fertility cults of Mesopotamia. E.g. summer, in The Disputation between Summer and Winter (lines 69 and 90), is called the "heroic son of Enlil" and winter his "proud son." By this claim of continuity in the created order, 8:22 "denies the basic dynamics of the fertility cult by making it clear that man's actions, for good or ill, can have no effect on the pattern of the seasons" (Fisher, "*Gilgamesh* and Genesis," 401).

447. Turner, *Announcements of Plot*, 40–41.

448. Clines, "Noah's Flood," 138.

449. Miles, *God*, 45.

450. Cf. Fretheim, *God and World*, 84.

foundation is laid for human interrelationships, rooted in the essential nature of humanity.[451]

What, then, has changed? Neither humankind, nor the natural world – only God. The flood and its wide-scale destruction impacted God to the effect that he has committed himself to the world. To drive this home, God makes a covenant with the world. As opposed to the gods in Atrahasis, Yahweh commits himself to the world of his own will, not as a compromise with the divine council.

Yahweh's commitment to the world is underscored by the sign of the war instrument, the "bow" placed in the sky. It is used to express peace, which, as some rabbis note, is even more emphatic as it is turned upward so that the arrows are shot toward the sky and not the earth.[452] BCS may serve as a parallel.[453] After Marduk's victory, Anu raises Marduk's bow and addresses the assembly of gods,

> He kissed the bow. "May she go far!"
> He gave to the bow her names, saying,
> "May Long and Far be the first, and Victorious the second;
> Her third name shall be Bowstar, for she shall shine in the
>   sky."
> He fixed her position among the gods her companions. (Tablet VI)[454]

In Genesis, the general rule is that God designs and man executes. On making the decision to destroy the world, God purposefully prepares Noah for the flood and life afterward. That is the reason of the detailed instructions for the construction of the ark. As, at creation, God ordered and structured the world, God now orders and structures the means of survival at length. Indeed, he does not only advise Noah but commands, and God's command

---

451. McConville, *God and Earthly Power*, 42.

452. Turner, "Rainbow as the Sign," 119; Galambush, *Reading Genesis*, 47. Turner's reference (Turner, "Rainbow as the Sign," 122) to Ezek 1:26–28, where *rāqiyaʿ* and *qešet* are both applied makes it only clear that *qešet* means both the weapon, and rainbow, the basis for the word's usage. He fails to make clear why that particular image is chosen by Yahweh as the symbol of the covenant. Day, *From Creation to Abraham*, 152, does not see the correspondence between rainbow and bow claiming that "the rainbow is simply an arc and lacks anything corresponding to the string of a bow." Using the same word for both, ancient Hebrews thought otherwise.

453. See Batto, "Covenant of Peace," 195–96.

454. Dalley, *Myths from Mesopotamia*, 263.

is duly obeyed. Thus, it is not just divine competence in the Genesis story but divine providence and it is sufficient.[455] This is reflected in the structure of the story.[456] Even a *ṣōhar*, whatever it means, is ordered by God and furnished by Noah (6:16). If it is some sort of light, as, among others, Alter suggests, it may be a hint at SFS where Utu the sun god sends his light into the interior of the ark (line 208).[457] God also gives detailed orders of the clean and unclean animals to be brought into the ark – life is to resume after the flood. Briefly, God is in control of the events, shown also by God's closing the ark's door, which the gods in Atrahasis leave to Atrahasis.

The Genesis flood is more than a plan designed and executed in good order, however. As a number of scholars have pointed out, it is a story from uncreation to re-creation.[458] In Genesis 1 and 2, the creation of humankind was the climax of God's action. Here, the purpose of creation is undone. In chapter 7, "the destruction takes place in much the same order as creation."[459] Clines notes, "The mitigation of the punishment of the Flood means that the 'uncreation' which God has worked with the Flood is not final; creation has not been permanently undone."[460] Noah is the new Adam who starts all over.[461] This re-creation motif as part of God's purpose in the destruction one cannot find in the Mesopotamian myths.[462] Yahweh's curse (3:17–19) is replaced by the Creator's blessing adumbrating God's relationship to the world. Blessing is not canceled but will determine the world's fate.[463]

Finally, we have to attend to the questions, How does the flood story contribute to the theme of PH? and, What about the startlingly ambiguous portrayal of God in the flood narrative and in PH? To answer them, we will

---

455. See Loewenstamm, "Flood," 108.

456. See Anderson, "From Analysis to Synthesis."

457. Alter, *Genesis*, 29.

458. See Anderson, "From Analysis to Synthesis;" Carr, "Βίβλος γενέσεως Revisited (Part Two)."

459. Blenkinsopp, "Uncreation," 46–47.

460. Clines, "Noah's Flood," 137–38.

461. This is supported by Larsson's chronological analysis of the creation and flood stories; Larsson, "Chronological Parallels," 490–92. He concludes, "The seemingly meaningless and contradictory dates in the Flood story link the Creation and the 'new' Creation together. At the Creation man got his unique position. At the 'new' Creation this position was confirmed and strengthened" (Larsson, 492).

462. Contra Simoons-Vermeer, "Mesopotamian Flood Stories," 17–34.

463. Rendtorff, "Hermeneutische Probleme," 21.

need to go back to chapter 3. I am calling to assistance Walter Moberly's treatment of the story. Yahweh's words in 2:16–17 are his first personal address to the first couple, issuing a command and followed by a warning. If the serpent was right, as many take it, and God's warning proves an empty threat (the couple became like God and did not die), how reliable is God, Moberly asks.[464]

As opposed to chapter 1, chapters 2–3 depict a God less majestic, less transcendent, and more prone to morally questionable actions.[465] The refusal of Cain's offering (4:5) and the sweeping assessment of humankind's heart (6:5, 12) leading to the flood add to this picture. During the flood, however, as we have seen, God goes through a crucial change committing himself to creation. This "conversion" results in God blessing humankind and making a covenant with creation never again to destroy it. It is here that God's reliability, based on his covenanted commitment to creation, is firmly established. This is underlined by the bow motif borrowed from BCS and placed not after the creation narrative but after the flood story in 9:12–16.[466] Needless to say, the flood story and God's renewed commitment to creation were meant as an encouragement to the exilic community after the flood-like experience of the losses of Davidic kingship, Jerusalem, and temple.

Whereas, after the flood in SKL, permanence and security are granted to the world by lowering kingship once again, in Genesis, it is God's blessing and covenant that do the job and curtail the curse (9:1–17). The note on Noah's sons (9:18–19) serves as the transition to the next section.

The Multiplication of Humankind: A New Beginning (9:20–10:32)

The section after the flood provides the essential transition from PH to the patriarchal history by telling the story of a new beginning and focusing on the multiplication of humankind, a concern with the entirety of the human race. The flood hero is being portrayed differently from his

---

464. Moberly, *Theology of the Book of Genesis*, 78–79.

465. Diachronically, of course, it is a difference between P and J. Diachronic study can shed light on the chronological development and refinement of theodicy.

466. See Batto, *Slaying the Dragon*, 87–88. Cf. Römer, "Origin and the Status of Evil," 58 who states, "The Flood story emphasizes the fragility of this creation and God's steady commitment to fight evil."

Mesopotamian counterparts, as well as this genealogies are used differently than in Mesopotamia.

Noah's Stupor (9:20–29)

After the flood, Utnapishtim is transferred to Dilmun or the land between the rivers, the land of no labor (see Gilgamesh XI.2–7) where eternal life is allotted to him by the gods.[467] In Genesis, Noah continues to labor. As opposed to the Mesopotamian view, cultivating the ground in Genesis is not considered bad. Despite God's curse, labor yields its fruits to humankind. Here, it is Noah who "plants;" in chapter 2, it was God.[468] In Gilgamesh, culture was salvaged by the craftsmen in the ark (XI.83–85). Noah, created in the image of God, fulfills his father's yearning (5:29) by the invention of viticulture. But it is not just the fruit of the vine that grants "relief out of the ground" but human work capable of creating culture. Thus, I suggest that, in Lowery's words, "the author was trying to communicate the magnitude of destruction brought about by the flood as God's judgment toward humankind. Destruction was so complete that *even culture itself* was destroyed."[469] After the flood, however, as before, humankind invents culture.

Genesis 8:21 seems to imply that the old era of a cursed ground has come to an end with the flood's devastation. This also makes sense of Noah's being the first farmer (9:20), after the flood. God has cleaned the slate. His "efforts to reduce the effects of previous judgment and curse gave Noah the opportunity to provide the relief" Lamech was yearning for (5:29).[470]

The episode of Noah's stupor is notoriously difficult. Interpreters stumble over it for the obvious reason that there is no obvious reason for the curse or the sin committed by Ham.[471] What the story states, risking an overstate-

---

467. Dalley, *Myths from Mesopotamia*, 43, regards Dilmun and "the mouth of the rivers" as one and the same locale.

468. Gros Louis, "Genesis 3–11," 48.

469. Lowery, *Toward a Poetics*, 233, his italics.

470. Spina, "'Ground' for Cain's Rejection," 330–31; cf. Rendtorff, "Gen 8,21"; differently Crüsemann, "Eigenständigkeit der Urgeschichte," 24.

471. The weakness of Steinmetz's argument is her rash equation of Ham's sin with sexual violence on his father: "Just as 'seeing' nakedness is more than seeing, 'uncovering' is more than uncovering" (Steinmetz, "Vineyard, Farm, and Garden," 199); see also the critique by Embry, "'Naked Narrative' from Noah," 417–33. More sophisticated is Nissinen, *Homoeroticism*, 52–53, who argues that sexual abuse of men in ANE was meant to humiliate them. Thus, "Ham aspired to dominance among post-flood humanity and attempted to show his superiority by disgracing

ment, is laconic. When Noah drank some of the wine he made, "he became drunk and lay uncovered inside his tent. Ham, the father of Canaan, saw his father naked and told his two brothers outside" (9:21–22). What is clear is that the sin is related to Noah's nakedness; what it consisted of is not made evident – the scene, to use Auerbach's famous phrase, is fraught with background, made tangible by varying and conflicting interpretations.[472]

The parallel structures and corresponding features of the Adam and the Noah stories have been noticed.[473] Sasson's chart, modified by me above, makes the similarity of the two sections clear. Tomasino has also studied the parallels between the garden story and that of Noah's drunkenness.[474] He points out that the phrase "man of the ground" (9:20), a *hapax*, refers us back to chapter 2 where Adam is portrayed as a man of the ground. The most important parallels are that both God and Noah "plant" gardens (2:8 and 9:20) and the protagonists' nakedness is covered by others, God and Shem-Japhet respectively (3:21 and 9:23).

The overall similarity of the larger sections is also visible in that

> both sections begin with a primeval ancestor (Adam, Noah) and then move through the following sequence of scenes: from scenes regarding the first generation (Adam and Eve in Gen 2:4b–3:24, Noah in 6:5–8:22), to scenes regarding the children (Cain and Abel in 4:1–16, Noah's sons in 9:18–27), to genealogical information (Gen. 4:17–26; 5:29; 10), to a final shorter story concerning the human community as a whole (Gen. 6:1–4; 11:1–9).[475]

The same holds for the story subsequent to the flood (9:20–27), which parallels the two stories following creation (2:5–3:24 and 4:1–16). These stories have in common the focus on a primary progenitor who is characterized by his relation to the "ground" (2:5, 7–8, 15; 9:20), starts out as an

---

his father sexually" (Nissinen, 53). For a novel redaction-critical approach, see Frankel, "Noah's Drunkenness," 49–68.

472. Auerbach, *Mimesis*, 3–23.

473. Smith, "Structure and Purpose," 310–11; Cohn, "Narrative Structure," 4–6; Steinmetz, "Vineyard, Farm, and Garden"; Carr, *Reading the Fractures*, 235–40; Carr, "Βίβλος γενέσεως Revisited (Part Two)," 328–34; Embry, "'Naked Narrative' from Noah," 423–27.

474. Tomasino, "History Repeats."

475. Carr, *Reading the Fractures*, 236.

agriculturist/viticulturist (2:7 and 9:20), and faces trouble coming from the products of his garden (2:17; 3:2–6; 9:20–21). In addition, in both stories seeing of nakedness (3:7 and 9:22) as well as pronouncement of judgment, divine (3:14–19) or human (8:25–27), are of significance. But there are more parallels. Both 4:1–16 and 9:20–26 begin with references to the sons of Adam and Noah respectively (4:1–2 and 9:18); right after this, both mention the "ground" tilled by Cain and Noah respectively (4:3 and 9:20); both stories signal the recognition of God/Noah of what happened (4:9–10 and 9:24); and both conclude with a curse (4:11–12 and 9:25–26). Thus, 9:20–27 have, in a condensed form, several themes of its pre-flood counterpart. However, God seems rather absent in Noah's story. It is this time not God but Noah who plants the garden, utters the curse, and banishes.[476]

Thus, there are verbal and thematic correspondences with Adam's and Noah's progenies subsequently listed – Noah is a second Adam. Cohn notes that "The parallel structures thus underscore the roles of Adam and Noah as uniquely first men commanded to 'be fruitful and multiply and fill the earth' (1:28; 9:1)."[477] Seen in this light, and, in particular, in the light of the Eden story, the episode is opening up.[478]

I have drawn on Bernard Batto's interpretation of the nakedness motif in chapters 2–3.[479] As opposed to the conventional interpretation, he does not link it to shame in general but to the concept found, among others, in Gilgamesh where being unclothed is a characteristic of animals. Being clothed, humankind was thought of as superior to animals in Mesopotamia. The first couple, Batto argues, achieved human status by eating the fruit of the tree of the knowledge of good and evil. In that very moment, they realized they were naked, thus looking like animals although they were not any longer. By making them garments, God too acknowledges this.

I suggest that, in order to see Ham's sin and the reason of the curse by Noah, we are referred back to the garden of Eden. More precisely, it is Ham

---

476. Carr, "Βίβλος γενέσεως Revisited (Part Two)," 331–32.

477. Cohn, "Narrative Structure," 5. The new beginning is stressed by the strange use of "began," *wayyāḥel*.

478. Various interpretations have been put forward as gap-filling as to what Ham's sin consisted of. But the text does not imply any sin apart from seeing Noah's nakedness; cf. Ross, "Curse of Canaan," 229–30.

479. Batto, *Slaying the Dragon*, 53–56.

who, on seeing his father naked, refers him back to ancient times when humankind was still like animals. In chapter 3, humankind achieved their status above animals and below gods by eating of the tree of the knowledge of good and evil, so acquiring the capability of doing either. By seeing Noah drunk and not appreciating his cultural achievement, Ham implicitly denies his father human status.[480] His is thus not just an act of voyeurism or disrespect but one of not acknowledging what humankind in general and Noah as a second Adam in particular has come to be, represent, and achieve, so relegating him to being an animal.[481] As opposed to their brother, Shem and Japhet recognize that Noah is more than an animal. Therefore, they cover him, as God clothed the first couple, so making manifest his and their non-animal status. Tasting the first fruit led to human status (3:6–7, 22), that of the second to its denial (9:21–22).

God punished the transgression of the serpent by cursing it. Now, it is Noah who utters the curse on Ham. "Ham's role in this episode is analogous to that of the serpent in Eden," Tomasino claims.[482] It is analogous but Ham and the serpent are assigned opposite roles. While the serpent was instrumental in humans' becoming human, Ham repudiates this achievement. By planting a vineyard, Noah has just demonstrated he is more than an animal. Ham's action signals an ill-boding new start. The harshness of the curse can be understood from this perspective: Ham is to become servant of servants (9:25–27) because he denied his father human status (1:28; cf. 9:2–3). In addition to bringing poetic justice, Noah's curse is thus a subversion of PH's values in that, similarly to the fate of the woman (3:16), it makes a human being subject to another. By starting humankind's post-flood story in this way, the narrator expresses his view of the irreversible course of events: humankind has indeed become distinct from the animal world, knowing good and bad.

---

480. Westermann, *Genesis 1–11*, 487, claims that in antiquity drunkenness was not seen as reprehensible: "If a person became drunk at a celebration, it was always good for a story, but no judgment was passed." Westermann interprets Ham's sin as a failure to do his duty by covering him (Westermann, 488).

481. That is how Embry interprets the story. He notes that, "in Noah's account, viewing nakedness is a matter of revisiting the features of the Fall" (Embry, "'Naked Narrative' from Noah," 426) but does not make the connection I do. Blenkinsopp, "P and J in Genesis," 11, has also noticed similarities between chs. 2 and 9.

482. Tomasino, "History Repeats," 130.

The Genealogy of Noah's Sons (10:1–32)

Political history is not in view in chapters 1–9, it opens up in chapter 10 only. In chapters 10–11 we see nations and tribes.[483] The narrator's attention is still on the whole of humanity, hence the segmented genealogy of chapter 10. Such a universal interest in the common ancestry of humankind is virtually unknown in ANE.[484] Mesopotamian genealogies may be concerned with the common ancestor of the tribe or ethnic group but never with that of the whole human race.

Levin has noticed that the genealogy in Genesis 10–11 specifies the place of the nation of Israel. The genealogy progresses from the nations through Shem's descendants to Abraham's sons. It is Abraham whose progeny Israel is. In the genealogy, it is always the last member, the most significant of the lineage, who carries on the line. Of Noah's three sons, Shem is the oldest (6:10; 9:18), his descendants, however, are listed last in 10:21–31. The same holds for the grandfather of Eber (eponym of the "Hebrews;" 11:10–14), Arpachshad.[485]

This might be explained by the narrator's concern to avoid any sign of superiority characteristic of Mesopotamian genealogies. The narrative's universal outlook is underlined by the fact that Israel is not mentioned in the genealogies and the genealogy of Noah's sons lists seventy names, a number of totality.[486] It is the human race en bloc that is in the purview of the narrator. This is the reason he lists the common ancestry of different nations.[487] The genealogy in chapter 10 demonstrates the fulfillment of God's command and blessing (9:1; cf. 1:28).[488] At the same time, Israel's story is being introduced.

The structure of the two chapters can be outlined in two different ways. Chapter 10 contains the genealogy of Noah's sons, while chapter 11 that of Shem between the story of Babylon and Terah's genealogy introducing Abraham's story. The foci of the genealogies are getting sharper: smaller and smaller ethnic units are listed. This, however, holds true for the genealogies only and not for the narratives, these being Nimrod's and Babylon's stories.

---

483. Baumgart, *Die Umkehr des Schöpfergottes*, 13–14. For a historical discussion, see Day, *From Creation to Abraham*, 163–87.

484. See Levin, "Understanding Biblical Genealogies," 34.

485. Levin, 34.

486. Waltke, *Genesis*, 161; Walton, "Genesis," 55.

487. See Malamat, "King Lists," 164.

488. Clines, "Theme in Genesis," 494.

Here, a reverse process is taking place. Nimrod's story remembers one of the descendants of Ham, while the tower of Babylon is constructed by the entire human populace. It is not just one nation doing this – each group represented in the genealogies of chapter 10 is involved in building the city and its tower.

Chapter 10	Genealogy of Noah's sons (*ʾēlleh tôlǝdôt*) + Nimrod narrative
Chapter 11	Babylon narrative + Genealogy of Shem (*ʾēlleh tôlǝdôt*; 11:10)

As for the second outline, Nimrod's story interrupts Ham's genealogy – his narrative becomes the structural centerpiece of chapter 10, just as the Babylon story does by interrupting Shem's genealogy.[489]

    A Japheth (10:1–5)
        B Ham (10:6–7)
            C Nimrod, founder of Babylon (10:8–12)
        B' Ham (10:13–20)
    A' Shem (10:21–32)
            C' The founding of Babylon (11:1–9)
    A" Shem (11:10–26)

Japheth is eliminated from the story, and Abram-Abraham will take the scene in chapter 12. Ham's offspring founds Babylon as well as disrupts Shem's genealogy, causing trouble. The two centerpieces of this structure are the narratives C and C' wedged between genealogies, making them the climaxes. Babylon's climaxing role is in sharp contrast to what Shem's genealogy points at. While we hear of Babylon no more, Shem's offspring is going to have a story – quite a significant one at that.

A further element shared by both chapters is Shem's genealogies (10:21–31 and 11:10–26). Whereas the genealogy in 10:21–26 lists all the descendants of Shem's every son – meaning it is reminiscent of WSL – 11:10–26 lists only the descendants of Arphaxad to Abram, thus resembling MKL, with one important qualification: Shem's genealogy is no king list. Genesis 11:26 lists the three sons of Terah thus providing a transition to Terah's genealogy, a WSL list again (11:27–32, starting with the phrase *ʾēlleh tôlǝdôt*). At the same time,

---

    489. I do not find the chiasm by Bailey compelling (Bailey, "Literary and Grammatical Aspects," 274). Genesis 10:1, comprising the first half of the chiasm (A-B-C), is disproportionate when compared to 10:2–31 (A'-B'-C').

this introduces the Abraham story commencing in chapter 12. In other words, Shem's first genealogy is more universal, the second more specific, tracing merely one bloodline. The first is significant for the whole of humanity, as chapter 10 is concerned with the origin and spread of humanity, while the second in chapter 11 is with Abraham.[490]

Between 10:8–12 and 11:1–9, another two connections can be observed: similarities in wording and style.[491] First, both narratives report the *beginning* of something.[492] Nimrod is said "to begin [*hēḥēl*] to become a mighty warrior on the earth" (10:8 AT). Regarding the Babylon story, Yahweh grows concerned, "If as one people speaking the same language they have begun [*haḥillām*] to do this, then nothing they plan to do will be impossible for them" (11:6).

Second, in both narratives we find an aetiology, introduced by "that is why" (*'al-kēn*).

> *That is why* it is said, "Like Nimrod, a mighty hunter before the LORD." (10:9)

> *That is why* it was called Babylon – because there the LORD confused the language of the whole world. From there the LORD scattered them over the face of the whole earth. (11:9 AT)

Both are followed by a saying related to Nimrod and the naming of his city respectively. And uniquely, as the topographic designation occurs only in 10:10 and 11:2, both take place "in the land of Shinar."[493]

Though the syntax of 10:11 makes it difficult to determine the subject of the sentence, 10:8–12 seems to suggest that it was Nimrod who founded Babylon, Erek, Akkad, and Calneh.[494] And it was he who founded Nineveh, Rehoboth Ir, Kalah, Resen. These were royal cities. Nimrod "is the first warrior

---

490. Cf. Baumgart, *Die Umkehr des Schöpfergottes*, 21. Genesis 12:3, by its application of *mišpāḥâ*, is clearly related to ch. 10 where the same is a keyword; Baumgart, 23.

491. Cf. Hom, "Mighty Hunter," 67–68.

492. Genesis is keen on telling beginnings. A third passage is 4:26.

493. Chs. 10–11 might be viewed as what Gordon calls the "Buildup and Climax," i.e. first reporting the whole with big brush strokes, then some aspects in detail, cf. Gen 1–2 (Gordon, "'This Time,'" 47, cf. Blenkinsopp, "P and J in Genesis," 11; and "Post-exilic Lay Source," 58). Nimrod's story thus has an introductory function to 11:1–9. Blenkinsopp, *Creation, Un-Creation*, 168–69, too reads it in connection to the Babylon story.

494. For an overview of research, see Day, *From Creation to Abraham*, 188–206.

(10,8) – quite possibly, then, one of the nephilim – and the beginning of his kingdom, which includes Babel, is located in 'the land of Shinar' (v. 10), the very location of the tower (11,2)."[495] However, he is not called a "king," as that is as good as a taboo term in PH. Nimrod (not to mention Canaan) and, through him, Babylon and Akkad could not, of course, originate with Ham as they were centers of Semitic people. The narrator appears more concerned with empire than with putting his audience straight about ethnology.[496] The Shem section "looks like a travesty of a geographical distribution."[497] Genealogies were used for propaganda. For Mesopotamian kings, they served imperial political agenda. The Hebrew narrator is turning the tables on Babylon in an apparently innocuous way by dissociating Babylon, and other imperial centers, from the Shemite family and associating it with cursed Ham. By this move, Babylon's wrong done to Noah-Israel in 9:22 gets a further facet. Even Assyria has its limited place in Shem's line but not Babylon – Babylon is being disowned.[498] This is buttressed by the recognition that the genealogy maps the different ethnic groups in their perceived proximity to Israel and each other.[499]

Nimrod attempts to establish centers of power with Babylon as the prime city among them, thereby hijacking the universal plan and trying to make it into a national Mesopotamian story.[500] Shem's genealogy, by both concluding PH and starting that of Abram,[501] demonstrates, however, that it is not a

---

495. Kawashima, "*Homo Faber*," 494.

496. Identity "moves between two poles of ethnic fission and ethnic fusion," McEntire, and Park, "Ethnic Fission," 34, observe. They add of Israelite ethnicity, which I think holds also of a broader Semitic identity regarding Akkad and Babylon, "This strategy was especially important in times of close contact, competition, and conflict with other groups. The contraction of the lineage served as a justification for tightening ethnic formations in response to current social and political circumstances." They claim later on that it is not modern genetics that underpins "nations" in Gen 10 (McEntire and Park, 35).

497. Simons, "'Table of Nations,'" 237.

498. Sasson, "Tower of Babel," 212n3, seems to suggest that there are three different Cushs in ch. 10. I do not think, however, that the author or compiler was trying to solve "the problem of homonymous Cush" by different listings of his/their offspring, ingenious though Sasson's solution sounds.

499. See Levin, "Understanding Biblical Genealogies," 22.

500. Cf. Blenkinsopp, *Abraham*, 19. Blenkinsopp relates the origin of the *gibbōrîm* (6:1–4) to the first of them, "Nimrud, founder of the first great empire in Mesopotamia, the prototype of Babylon (Gen 10:8–11) and therefore of the Neo-Babylonian empire" (Blenkinsopp, "Post-exilic Lay Source," 55; cf. Schüle, *Prolog*, 401). He also associates Nimrod with Cain by virtue of their being city builders (Blenkinsopp, "Post-exilic Lay Source," 58–59).

501. Steinberg, "Genealogical Framework," 48.

king list that emerges out of this but a list of commoners – a Mesopotamian-turned-West Semitic list.

As for the four cities founded by Nimrod, Babylon was the capital city of Babylonia. Erech (Uruk) was the dominant Sumerian city around 2700 ruled by Gilgamesh. Akkad was the capital of Sargon the Great who extended his empire from Elam in the North of the Persian Gulf to the Mediterranean in the twenty-third century. We know nothing of Calneh. Along with Nimrod's depiction as a mighty hunter, "the twice-occurring motif of four cities (vv. 10–12a) suggests imperialist notions along the lines of the 'four corners of the earth.'"[502]

Genesis 10:11 refers to Asshur known also as a descendant of Shem (10:22) and the eponym of the Assyrian capital city. Setting up their headquarters now here and now there, Assyrian kings made Nineveh and Calah (or Nimrud, named after the big hunter) their capital cities. Nineveh surpassed Asshur or Calah in significance. The exact location of Rehoboth Ir (meaning "town square")[503] and Resen, along with Calneh[504] in 10:10, is unknown. Apparently these cities, founded by Nimrod and Asshur, are significant because they are associated with conquest and oppression. This might be hinted at by the reference to Nimrod who "grew to be a mighty warrior on the earth. He was a mighty hunter before the Lord; that is why it is said, 'Like Nimrod, a mighty hunter before the Lord'" (10:8–9).

This sounds positive of Nimrod. Having founded these cities, however, Nimrod has become the mythic prototype of empire founders. This might be buttressed by the association of hunting and conquest.[505] If this is a critique, it is expressed in a low-key way. At the same time, Nimrod is Ham's descendant which, after his deed in chapter 9, raises the question, Can anyone good come from Ham?

---

502. Hom, "Mighty Hunter,'" 68. "The overall effect indicates a response on the part of the text to Assyrian ideology – whereas a Babylonian or Assyrian monarch typically presumed to be king of the world, 'before YHWH' makes clear that YHWH is actually king of the world," Hom concludes (Hom, 68). While I wholeheartedly agree with the first part of her assertion, I fail to see how the phrase makes clear what she claims it does.

503. Cf. Donald Wiseman's suggestion who thinks that Rehoboth Ir stands for Asshur since in Sumerian *ash* means "square" and *ur* "city" (Wiseman, "Genesis 10," 20–21).

504. Although William Albright's emendation of Calneh to *kullānâ*, "all of them," referring to Mesopotamian cities, has been widely accepted, it destroys the reference to four cities (Albright, "End of 'Calneh in Shinar,'" 254–55).

505. See Walton, "Genesis," 57.

Several ambiguities of the two verses have been noticed by Levin: "began to be mighty" makes hardly any sense in the context; *gibbōr* could mean "giant," "hero," "mighty man," "champion," "man of power" or "potentate"; *bā'āreṣ* can be rendered as "on earth" or "in the land"; the subject of *yāṣā'*, "go out," could be Nimrod as well as Asshur; the "great city" can be either Resen or Nineveh.[506] Finally, Nimrod's origin as stemming from Cush, the eponymous father of Ethiopia, raises the question, what on earth is a Cushite doing in Mesopotamia?[507] Levin sees in Nimrod no "total counterpart of any one historical character. He is rather the composite Hebrew equivalent of the Sargonid dynasty: the first, mighty king to rule after the flood."[508] Ingenious though this proposal sounds it is too conjectural.[509] Levin is to be commended for parting company with the search expedition, futile as it has been, for a historical equivalent of Nimrod.[510] With such ambiguities, Nimrod does not represent the Sargonid dynasty, I think, but rather Mesopotamian kingship. The narrative uses soft polemic to critique kingship.

As often observed, the chapter does not mention Israel. Unlike Babylon, Israel cannot boast of an origin in primordial times. Indeed, it has no territory of its own in chapters 10–11, Abraham will have to live in Canaan with no land of his own.[511] Yet, Israel will have a particular place in world history by election.[512] Hanson, followed by Hallo, claims that beginning an ethnic history in primeval times was widespread.[513] The more striking thing is that Israel "renders account of the past to itself" by providing extensive lists of

---

506. Levin, "Nimrod the Mighty," 351–52.

507. Speiser, "In Search of Nimrod," 32, has argued for "Cush" being a reference to "Kassite." But, in the OT, it normally denotes the Upper Nile valley; cf. Stordalen, *Echoes of Eden*, 280.

508. Levin, "Nimrod the Mighty," 366.

509. This is visible in the number of "may," "might," and "could" wordings; Levin, "Nimrod the Mighty," 364–65. He also surmises that ancient Hebrews "probably had their own version of the 'bringing down' of kingship after the Flood" (Levin, 364). If they did it was omitted from Genesis.

510. E.g. Speiser, "In Search of Nimrod," 32–36; Gispen, "Who Was Nimrod?" 207–14.

511. Baumgart, *Umkehr des Schöpfergottes*, 24–25.

512. Cf. Schüle, *Prolog*, 378.

513. Hanson, "Rebellion in Heaven," 196n4; Hallo, "Biblical History," 17.

nations and minimizing its own primordial role.[514] By the end of chapter 10, humankind has spread over the face of the earth, thus recreating it after the flood (cf. 8:17; 9:1).[515]

As for the transition note, there is none. Instead, several notes hint at a major motif of chapter 11 which is the scattering by Yahweh of the people (see 11:4, 8–9) who, as opposed to the nations and tribes of chapter 10, do not want to spread. Their refusal to do so triggers both the people's building project and Yahweh's intervention. As mentioned earlier, the references to the dispersion in chapter 10 are spread out, as are the descendants of Noah. Three verbs are used to denote the dispersion: *pārad* (10:5, 32), *pûṣ* (10:18), and *pālag* (10:25). This all happened "after the flood," as underlined twice by the time adjuncts enveloping the chapter (10:1, 32). The other references to the dispersion are also accompanied with time references: "in his time the earth was divided" (10:25), and more gratuitously, "Later the Canaanite clans scattered" (10:18). It is emphatic that these dispersions happened after the flood, so fulfilling the Creator's order (1:28; 9:1).

In chapter 11, the verb *pûṣ* (11:4, 8–9) is used. Here, the people's resistance to their dispersion (11:4) is introduced by the time reference, "When people set out from the East" (11:2 AT). The third use of the verb, stating the *fait accompli*, is introduced by a place adjunct, "From there the LORD scattered them" (11:9). These all concern the dispersion of humankind. However, Nimrod moves in the opposite direction. This is, once again, highlighted by a sort of time reference, "He began as a mighty warrior in the country" (10:8 AT).[516] While other people spread around founding countries, Nimrod founds kingdoms the prime example of which is Babylon. This city is the scene of the next story.

Things Gone Awry: Babylon and Shem (11:1–26)

Chapter 11, consisting of a story about the empire's capital and a genealogy of Shem, is the last section rounding off PH and providing a transition to

---

514. I am referring to Huizinga's famous definition of history as "the intellectual form in which a civilization renders account to itself of its past" (Huizinga, "Definition of the Concept of History," 9).

515. Galambush, *Reading Genesis*, 50.

516. Following a translation of *bāāreṣ* suggested by Levin, "Nimrod the Mighty," 351–52.

the Abraham story. How does the chapter do this double duty? The story in 11:1–9 along with the genealogy following it is probably PH's shrewdest and sharpest criticism of Babylon.

Challenging Imperial Royal Politics: The City of Babylon (11:1–9)[517]

Winston Churchill once famously remarked that Russia was a riddle wrapped in a mystery inside an enigma. The same can be claimed of the story of Babylon (11:1–9). The story itself is no mean riddle. It is not at all clear why it is wrapped in genealogies, nor what its role in and contribution to PH/Genesis are. Churchill's statement is relevant to our discussion of the Babylon story not just because of the story's enigmatic features and puzzling subject matter defying interpretation, but also because it concerns an empire. In what follows, I will study this riddle along with its wrapping in the hope that, by the end of this enterprise, we will see how both wrapping and the wrapped thing contribute to a concerted attack on the empire.

The story of the city of Babylon is conventionally interpreted in terms of human arrogance followed by divine judgment: by building a "sky scraper" humankind aspires to reach heaven and challenges God.[518] This interpretation has recently been contested by a number of scholars, most of them reading the story synchronically and in terms of a horizontal, rather than vertical, sin – a sin committed against creation and humankind.[519] Indeed, Croatto and Míguez see an attempt at building an empire.[520] Sympathetic as I am to this approach, what has troubled me is the lack of any clear reference to empire or creation. The author could have easily mentioned that the people in 11:3 began their endeavor under the leadership of some king, or after the construction of the city and tower, they decided to elect one – but there is

---

517. Since the original audience did not make the distinction between Babel and Babylon, I will consistently refer to Babylon. In this chapter, I will use my former papers; Czövek, "Babilon és Genezis," 184–207, and "Diversity vs. Uniformity," 275–82.

518. E.g. Wenham, *Genesis 1–15*, 239–45; Hamilton, *Book of Genesis*, 356; Lim, *Grace in the Midst*, 185; McKeown, *Genesis*, 71, Jubilees is the first attested interpretation in this vein; see Simon, "'Ha az égbe hág is fel Babilon,'" 12.

519. E.g. van Wolde, *Genesis*, 168–69; Croatto, "Reading of the Story," 203–23; Míguez, "Comparative Bible Study," 152–65; Hiebert, "Tower of Babel," 29–58; Măcelaru, "Babel from Text to Symbol," 51–58.

520. Harland, "Vertical or Horizontal," 515–33, provides a helpful summary of different approaches.

nothing of this sort. This lack of reference, however, is telling. The silence, along with more loquacious features of the story, if correctly interpreted, may work as a password that opens the gate to the tower of Babylon.

The introduction to the story (11:1–2) describes the initial situation that is bound to change by the end of the narrative. It is introduced by *wayəhî* that regularly links what follows to the preceding (e.g. 4:2–3; 12:10; 13:7; 14:1; 15:17; 17:1; 21:20, 22; 23:1; 25:20; 26:1). The conventional rendering would rather call for a nominal clause. Hence, it seems more appropriate to render 11:1, "And the whole earth became one tongue and one language." What the Babylon story connects to cannot be Shem's table just before it, since that is a genealogy, but must be the Nimrod story. The implication is that, through Nimrod's efforts to found empires, people became a political unity (more anon), a process which inevitably leads to empires. To be sure, "In contrast to the many differences among peoples set forth in chapter 10, chapter 11 begins by imagining the opposite – uniformity of speech."[521]

The initial circumstances of the plot consist of a common language[522] and "the whole world," humanity *en bloc* (cf. 11:5).[523] As for the "one language," Uehlinger states that "From the perspective of rulers, it is as normal that the subjects do 'one mouth' and 'one speech' respectively, i.e. are united – unless this unity is directed against the rulers."[524] In an inscription in Dur-Sharrukin, Sargon II claims,

> By order of Ashur, my lord, and the power of my sceptre, I deported the people of the four parts of the world, speaking a foreign and incomprehensible language, dwellers of mountains

---

521. O'Connor, *Genesis 1–25A*, 174.

522. Uehlinger, *Weltreich*, 576, notices both the tension between the "many languages" (10:5, 20, 31) and "one lip" (11:1, 6–7, 9) and the common theme, i.e. the state of the great variety of people (ch. 10) as a result of God's intervention (11:1–9). Schüle, *Prolog*, 391–92, takes the first phrase to mean "understanding each other" while the second "the same words" which is the lexicon, the vocabulary of the speakers. Similarly to my approach, Schüle (and Uehlinger) sees the transgression of humankind on a horizontal level. Still, he thinks humankind's plan threatens God (Schüle, 392) whereas I think God's creation and humanity are threatened forcing God to intervene.

523. Importantly, Nebuchadnezzar II boasted of employing every nation in his empire to build Etemenanki (Jensen, "Babylonischer Turm," 385) with the workforce probably consisting of Jews as well; Van Seters, *Prologue to History*, 183. Giorgetti, "'Mock Building Account,'" 7, considers "the whole world" equivalent to the Akkadian phrases *šar kullat kibrāt arba'i*, "king of all the four regions (of the earth)" and *šar kiššati*, "king of the universe."

524. Uehlinger, *Weltreich*, 438.

and plains, all subjects of the light of the gods and lord of everything. I turned them into a sole language and put them there. I assigned them some Assyrians as scribes and overseers, who were able to teach them the fear of god and king.[525]

In this text, the "one mouth" of the deported "appears as a correction of the ideologically disturbing fact of being multilingual";[526] foreign languages were seen as barbaric, incomprehensible, and as such violating harmony, world order.[527] "One language and a common speech" thus connotes political unity.[528] The protagonists of our story act as a group politically united. The focus of the plot shifts from "the whole world" to "East" to "a plain in Shinar" (11:1–2). The verb "move," *nāsaʻ*, usually denotes the breaking up of tents and setting out of nomadic people (e.g. 12:9; 13:11; 20:1; 33:17) – stock breeding nomads go to settle, *yāšab*, in the city. The plot is set into motion by their plan: "Come, let's make bricks and bake them thoroughly. . . . Come, let us build ourselves a city, with a tower that reaches to the heavens, so that we may make a name for ourselves; otherwise we will be scattered over the face of the whole earth" (11:3–4). As opposed to the Mesopotamian view, present in BCS (Tablet VI), here, Babylon is built on human initiative, not by gods.

Hurowitz has studied ANE building accounts and observed six permanent components.[529] Giorgetti has applied Hurowitz's observations to the Babylon story by seeing it as a "mock building account" made up of a similar scenario (11:1–2 are the setting for the narrative).[530] The application of Hurowitz's model by Giorgetti may seem a bit strained, particularly the correspondence

---

525. Fuchs, *Inschriften Sargons II*, 296.

526. Uehlinger, *Weltreich*, 509.

527. Uehlinger, 509–12. Batto, "Paradise Reexamined," 49–50, however, has challenged the view that foreign languages were seen as barbaric.

528. Uehlinger, *Weltreich*, 344–513. "Significantly, the language of 'one mouth' (*pû ištēn*) is often found in the annalistic accounts ending in a building account or associated with the populating of a city. The language of 'one mouth' represents the subjugation of the various peoples to the authority of these kings, who saw themselves as kings of 'all the world'" (Giorgetti, "'Mock Building Account,'" 6).

529. Hurowitz, *I have Built You an Exalted House*.

530. Giorgetti, "'Mock Building Account.'"

of numbers 4–6.⁵³¹ Still, by positing a specific setting, it provides a compelling anti-empire interpretation.⁵³²

Hurowitz	Giorgetti
(1) Circumstances of the project and decision to build	(1) Circumstances of the project and decision to build 11:3–4
(2) Preparations: gathering workers and material	(2) Preparations for building 11:3–4
(3) Description of the building	(3) Details of the construction 11:3–4
(4) Dedication rites and festivities	(4) "Dedication" festivities and participation of deity 11:5
(5) Blessing or prayer of the king	(5) Divine decrees and curses for the builders 11:6–7
(6) Blessings and curses for future generations	(6) Curses for the project and future generations of kings 11:8–9

Using brick and tar (11:3) is often mentioned in Mesopotamian construction inscriptions. Making a name was linked to building projects in Mesopotamia too.⁵³³ In the first millennium, naming a city is a widely attested custom of reigning kings. Building the city and naming it also seem closely linked.⁵³⁴ Indeed, the builders' intention is twofold, "so that we may make a

---

531. But see Giorgetti, 15n53.

532. Hurowitz, *I have Built You an Exalted House*, 64; Giorgetti, "'Mock Building Account,'" 5.

533. O'Connor, *Genesis 1–25A*, 176, notes that making a name
    is to acquire the honor, respect, and status needed to gain resources and community connections for the sake of the survival and well-being of one's family or tribal group. In the case of nations and peoples, to make a name is to acquire honor and influence among other peoples and nations. Such influence aids in keeping relationships smooth and secure, always needed for safety and prosperity.
Strong suggests that name making was related to royal victory stelae (Strong, "Shattering the Image of God," 625–34). Giorgetti correctly objects that the story "does not specifically reflect the victory stelae or their images" (Giorgetti, "'Mock Building Account,'" 19n74).

534. Uehlinger, *Weltreich*, 386–96. Witte, *Die biblische Urgeschichte*, 321, claims, ignoring Uehlinger's linguistic-historical evidence that making a name refers to the praxis of Alexander the Great to found cities and name them after himself. Rolf Rendtorff observes in another context:
    I am always amazed by the sureness, not to say boldness, of some scholars, who feel able to date with precision all kinds of texts within this period, even

name for ourselves; otherwise we will be scattered over the face of the whole earth" (11:4). Giorgetti observes, "Completely lacking from the account is the divine revelation and consent for the project, which is an essential part of the Mesopotamian accounts.... In particular, the construction of and boasting about an entirely new city is viewed as an act of hubris."[535] The city's building lacks divine participation and approval.

Much of the discussion has focused on whether the building of the city and, particularly, tower connotes a good or evil endeavor. The discussion seems futile. For first-millennium Mesopotamians, including people living in sixth-century Babylonia, "a city with a tower that reaches to the heavens" was an idiomatic reference to a city with its citadel, characteristic of Mesopotamian royal cities and connoting imperial interests.[536] "At that time my lord Marduk told me in regard to E-temen-anki, the ziqqurrat of Babylon, which before my day was (already) very weak and badly buckled, to ground its bottom on the breast of the netherworld, to make its top vie with the heavens," Nabupolassar claims in the late seventh century.[537] Even if the story originates in some particular historico-political event and is thus intended as "a politically relevant parable" its particularity is transposed to a level of "paradigmatic reflection on the problem of world empire."[538]

Clearly, then, the story about building a city with its tower/citadel is about political unity and power: the linguistic evidence points in this direction. By building the city and the tower, the people strive for power, their endeavor is an empire. Uehlinger claims that, semantically, *migdāl* does not stand for "ziggurat" and can only be interpreted in this way if the text cannot be made sense of with conventional means of semantics.[539] His stance is understandable as his concern lies with the original meaning and setting of the story, which he considers an anti-Sargonide tale. "The language of 'raising the head'

---

within specific decades. It is even more amazing when certain historical events are mentioned in texts that, according to their interpreters, were written much later.(Rendtorff, "Paradigm is Changing," 49).

I wonder whether ignoring the explicit reference to Babylon in the story is among those that amazes Rendtorff.

535. Giorgetti, "'Mock Building Account,'" 9–10.
536. Uehlinger, *Weltreich*, 201–53.
537. George, "Tower of Babel," 83.
538. Uehlinger, *Weltreich*, 535.
539. Uehlinger, 231–36.

high into the sky/heavens is utilized by various Mesopotamian kings and refers to all different kinds of structures . . . in addition to ziggurats," Giorgetti notes.[540] Since, however, in its present form the tale is undoubtedly Babylonian in its outlook, I will interpret it accordingly. The "ziggurat" seems to enrich our understanding of the story – it opens up a new vista with its "coded" message. Indeed, "a tower that reaches to the heavens" (11:4) is reminiscent of the language in connection with ziggurats. After all, sixth-century Jews living in Babylonia may not have been acquainted with the precise referent "city and tower" but may have taken it literally.

Ziggurats were not erected for people to reach heaven but for gods to descend on earth.[541] "The ziggurat was the architectural focus of the temple complex, which in turn functioned as the central organ in the economic, political, and cultural spheres of early communities in Mesopotamia."[542] Building the city and its ziggurat (see SFS) was a divine or a divinely authorized human enterprise in Mesopotamia, "the responsibility of gods and rulers."[543] As we saw above, kingship and capital cities were intimately interrelated, just as they are, by implication, in our story. By building the city and the tower, the people want to achieve fame in the Mesopotamian way.[544] That is what one frequently finds in Mesopotamian hymns and myths related to building projects. What is needed for unity is leadership. And if it is leadership, it can only be the one – kingship.

Building the city and the ziggurat[545] is the beginning of their plan, the crown of which is a kingdom. As soon as they are done, people familiar with Mesopotamian myths and royal ideology would expect kingship to be lowered from heaven. It is not kingship, however, that descends from heaven nor is it

---

540. Giorgetti, "'Mock Building Account,'" 14.

541. Contra LaCoque, "Whatever Happened in the Valley," 36.

542. Walton, "Mesopotamian Background," 165.

543. Miller, "Eridu, Dunnu, and Babel," 239.

544. My approach here is similar to that of Holloway to the ark. He states, "the question left begging by the literal reading is the semantics of the text and the cultural milieu in which it was composed" (Holloway, "Shape of Utnapishtim's Ark," 618).

545. With a square base of ninety-one meters on each side (see George, "Tower of Babel") and a ninety-one-meter height, the Etemenanki belonged to the biggest ziggurats; cf. Baumgart, *Umkehr des Schöpfergottes*, 515–17. "The verticality of the ziggurat was its dominant visual feature" (Van de Mieroop, "Reading Babylon," 264–65). No wonder that it impressed people of various ethnic and social backgrounds. It can be expected that the ziggurat did not leave Babylonian Jews untouched; Baumgart, *Umkehr des Schöpfergottes*, 557.

Marduk, but Yahweh, whose coming down prevents kingship's descent. The ziggurat constructed to aid the gods in their travel to earth to be worshipped becomes the staircase – for Yahweh to come down![546]

On descending, Yahweh finds that it is one nation with one language – a homogeneous culture that does not allow for diversity (11:6–7).[547] Giorgetti sees in Yahweh's descent (11:5) the festive procession culminating in the divinity's entering the city temple or, alternatively, the "divine invitee on his way to see the dedication festivities for a building within the city such as a royal palace."[548] In 11:6–7, Yahweh relates to the heavenly council what he has seen so that the council can decree a cursing instead of a blessing.[549] Thus Yahweh suggests to confuse, *năbĕlāh*, their language. The verb is very reminiscent of *nĕbālāh*, "folly."[550]

Yahweh did not descend to authorize state religion, some royal city, or dynasty, because Yahweh is interested in the welfare of the whole of humankind and not just in that of some privileged cities, nations, classes, or individuals. That is the reason we, though accustomed to their absence by now, do not find a king list or stories about kings, which could be expected, at the end of the Babylon story. Instead, the genealogy of Shem is told, followed by the Abraham story. Moreover, "to place the name" was a standard formula for building projects in Mesopotamia.[551] The people wanted to make a name, *šēm*, for themselves, but it is Yahweh who will make a name to a descendant of Shem, another commoner: "I will make you into a great nation and I will bless you; I will make your name great, and you will be a blessing" (12:2).[552]

Jacob Wright argues that name making, often related to martial valor, was, in their best interest, encouraged by ancient states, whereas the OT books,

---

546. Cf. Walton, "Genesis," 62–63, 65.

547. Thus, it is not just "linguistic and anthropological diversification" that the multiplication of humankind inevitably brings about; see Swiggers, "Babel and the Confusion," 186.

548. Giorgetti, "'Mock Building Account,'" 15.

549. Giorgetti, 14–17.

550. Also noticed by Wenham, "Genesis 1–11 as Protohistory," 95.

551. Giorgetti, "'Mock Building Account,'" 17.

552. Also noticed by Jenkins, "Great Name," 46; Sailhamer, *Pentateuch as Narrative*, 133; Hess, *Studies in the Personal Names*, 118; Baumgart, *Umkehr des Schöpfergottes*, 27. By focusing on the words *šēm* and *šām*, the pun is sometimes missed by commentators like Kikawada, "Shape of Genesis," 25, and Fokkelman, *Narrative Art in Genesis*, 16–18; or dismissed by others on account of terminological difference; e.g. Gertz, "Babel im Rücken," 31.

edited after the collapse of Judahite statehood, emphasized procreation.[553] The people's attempt at making a name at Babylon may be linked to warfare. This should not surprise us – Babylon's might was based on military power. Yahweh, however, outlines the alternative for Abraham and his descendants: instead of conquests they will be a great nation by procreation and by leaving the empire.

But back to the story. Walton correctly states that Yahweh is not opposed to architecture or urbanization as such. He goes on to claim that nothing "was wrong with towers or with cities."[554] Generally speaking, that is true. Regarding Mesopotamia and in the light of the previous discussion, however, this seems to miss one crucial point of the story and the general picture – "cities with towers" were intrinsically related to imperial efforts.[555] Yahweh's judgment "represents a reversal of the imperialistic project (dominion of 'the four quarters of the earth') and an 'overthrowing' of the royal prerogative."[556]

The subtle use of the WSL pattern as well as the shrewd manipulation of the MKL pattern may reflect, once again, a critique of the arrogant superiority of city and kingship to tribal societies. As opposed to MKL, the genealogies in Genesis 10–11 list nations descended from Noah. They do not mention kings: their focus is universal. The next chapter relates how Babylon and Abram-Abraham came to be.[557]

Uehlinger sees in the fame motif a back-reference to 6:4: the builders want to achieve the status of glory possessed by the heroes killed by the flood.[558] There are several links between 6:1–4 and 11:1–9 in addition to this. Genesis 6:1–4 is about actions of "the daughters of humankind/sons of God" while 11:1–9 is about actions of the "sons of humankind" (11:5). Both relate

---

553. Wright, "Making a Name," 131–62.

554. Walton, "Mesopotamian Background," 169.

555. Whereas Walton, 169, sees "the act of religious hubris, making God in the image of man," i.e. religion, as the point of criticism, I see the imperial tendency of Mesopotamian city states, i.e. politics.

556. Giorgetti, "'Mock Building Account,'" 19.

557. Ch. 10 is the background to 11:1–9, just as the genealogies in chs. 10–11 are the background to Abraham.

558. Uehlinger, Weltreich, 570.

events about some beginnings (6:1; 11:6) that apparently concern the whole of humankind (6:1; 11:1–2, 5, 8–9).[559]

The above interpretation may shed some light on the Nimrod episode.[560] I have claimed that the Babylon story is the elaboration of 10:10 that refers to Babylon, Uruk, Akkad, and Calneh as the "prime" or "head cities" of Nimrod's kingdom. As opposed, however, to the relative unanimity of the Mesopotamian tradition of five antediluvian cities,[561] Genesis 10:10 and 10:11–12 come one short of this tradition. Indeed, 10:11 manages to do this by making Asshur into a person, a historical curiosity – and a theological tour de force. Note also that these cities were founded by one postdiluvian man without any divine involvement.

On account of his being a hero, *gibbôr*, Nimrod is linked to the heroes of old in 6:4. Reading his short story, we learn what one of them achieved. Nimrod founded capital cities of empires and began to behave as a hero. What a hero was like to people living in sixth-century Babylonia, we could imagine by thinking of, for instance, Gilgamesh who performed heroic deeds but who, at the same time, was dreaded for his tyrannical rule. Genesis 10 is just as ambiguous toward Nimrod. The beneficiaries definitely held such a king and conqueror in high esteem just as those subjected to his rule moaned about him. In other words, I am suggesting that, along with several references in Genesis 1–11 to mythical figures and events in Mesopotamian mythology, this one too is a double entendre playing on their equivocal assessment. Certainly, Nimrod became famous (10:9), just as the people in 11:4 (cf. 6:4) aspired to become. But the fame of these royal cities and empires he built was achieved with the blood of subjects. Once again and importantly and ironically, no kingship descended on any of those cities.

Nimrod "began to be a mighty hero on the earth" (10:8 AT) that materialized in founding capital cities (10:10–12) which, again, was only the beginning of what they were doing (11:6).[562] The narrator could have stated Nimrod was a big bully but this would have raised eyebrows, to say the least. To avoid this, he said, Nimrod was a great hunter. This is a sarcastic pun applying "hunter"

---

559. Cf. Sasson, "'Tower of Babel.'" For more thematic correspondences, see Carr, "Βίβλος γενέσεως Revisited (Part Two)," 332–33.

560. Cf. Kooij, "Story of Genesis," 38.

561. See Hallo, "Antediluvian Cities," 63.

562. *gibbôr ṣayid* may be a pun on *gibbôr ḥayil*.

as a metonymy. Mesopotamian kings prided themselves on their hunting feats. But in countries subdued by them they were not remembered by those hunts but by their brutal conquests.[563] The narrator does not stop there but does his best to be as adulatory as possible. To disperse all suspicion, he adds, "before Yahweh," which has as good as no semantic content, unless *lipnê* has the meaning "against," as possibly in 6:11.[564]

The protagonists wanted more geographical and linguistic unity (homogeneity) meant to be achieved by political unity, as opposed to Yahweh, whose main concern was heterogeneity, not one language but many, not one culture but a variety and in various places.[565] To this end, Yahweh confuses human language and scatters humankind all over the face of the earth.[566] Thus, the sin is horizontal, directed not against God but rather against creation, nations, languages, and ethnic groups. This focus on God's creation accords well with PH's stress. Filling the earth is God's purpose from the very beginning. If humankind is intent on sticking together, Yahweh feels compelled to intervene and resort to "force."[567]

BCS is normally studied with reference to Genesis' creation account. Some motifs, as well as the sequence of events on Tablet VI, however, when compared with the Babylon story, may aid our interpretation of 11:1–9. Even though humankind has been created to relieve the gods from labor, in the epic, it is the gods who volunteer to build Esagila for Marduk. This, of course, was essential for the claim of Marduk's supremacy and Babylon's primacy the epic is putting forward. This also serves as the gods' resting place.

---

563. Cf. Goldingay, *Old Testament Theology*, 187–88.

564. See Clark, "Flood," 184.

565. Contra Hiebert, "Tower of Babel," who sees the story directed against cultural homogeneity only, whose supporting pillar has always been imperial politics.

566. Cf. deClaissé-Walford, "God Came Down," 413–14.

567. Brueggemann, "Kerygma of the Priestly Writers," 397–414, studies P and finds the blessing in 1:28 as its quintessential formulation, recurring at certain points in Genesis and Exodus. The five terms of blessing are "be fruitful" as opposed to no more barrenness; "multiply" as opposed to no more lack of heirs; "fill the earth" as opposed to no more being crowded out; "subdue" as opposed to no more subservience; "have dominion" as opposed to no more being dominated (Brueggemann, 401). For the exilic community poised to reenter the land, it was definitely encouraging.

> Now, Lord, you who have liberated us,
> What courtesy may we do you?
> We will make a shrine, whose name will be a byword,
> Your chamber that shall be our stopping place, we shall find rest therein.
> We shall lay out the shrine, let us set up its emplacement,
> When we come (to visit you), we shall find rest therein.

Unsurprisingly, the plan meets Marduk's hearty approval,

> Then make Babylon the task that you requested,
> Let its brickwork be formed, build high the shrine.

The gods set out to do the job, they make bricks and raise the head of Esagila plus their own shrines. With the work accomplished, Marduk proclaims,

> This is Babylon, your place of dwelling.
> Take your pleasure there, seat yourselves in its delights!

Babylon, the capital of the kingdom has been established. Everything is in place: Babylon and Esagila (along with Etemenanki), city and shrine erected,[568] tutelary god ritually inaugurated – what else is needed? Only one thing needs to be done: kingship lowered. Even if it is not explicitly referred to, the obvious purpose of both the Babylonian epic and the New Year festival was to buttress Babylon's kingship and claim to political supremacy.[569]

In the Genesis story, we see the same focus of the builders on city and its ziggurat. No deity is mentioned but, in these endeavors, they are clearly implied. Nor is kingship mentioned but this is what would obviously follow and what is assumed all along as the very purpose of the whole undertaking. And that is what makes Yahweh concerned – this is just the beginning of what they intend, and nothing will be impossible for them (11:6). So, Yahweh puts an end to the endeavor.

On archaeological and historical grounds, Kraeling correctly claims that the cessation of the building can apply only to the tower, not the residential

---

568. George, "Tower of Babel," 87, argues that the reference in BCS VI.63 is to the Etemenanki.

569. Cf. Uehlinger, *Weltreich*, 504.

sections of the city.⁵⁷⁰ Still, 11:8 refers to the halt of the building of the "city."⁵⁷¹ This is important. Ziggurat stands for religion whereas city for kingship; they metonymically denote the endeavor. Yahweh's concern is not merely religion but politics – they go hand in hand. It is kingship that Yahweh's descent forestalls; the city is stymied from being finished and kingship from being established. "Creator God and world empire do not correspond to each other."⁵⁷² Humankind's sin, in short, is not a failure to execute God's command to fill the earth but a misinterpretation of the command to subdue the earth in that, by their imperialistic endeavor, they would have ended up subduing each other in total denial of the Creator's original plan.⁵⁷³

The name of the city where Yahweh confused, *bālal*, languages is Babylon. Giorgetti sees Yahweh as carrying out the curses on the people for failure of invoking divine help in the building of the city by scattering them from their center of power. Yahweh's scattering "represents a reversal of the imperialistic project (dominion of 'the four quarters of the earth') and an 'overthrowing' of the royal prerogative."⁵⁷⁴

The failure of the building of the tower and city is to be understood as a sarcastic and hopeful critique by the oppressed exiles of the oppressor who "gathered" the conquered nations of the empire thus attempting to build a strong and permanent Babylonia. The necessary concomitant of "gathering" was the destruction of the culture of those exiled. Homogeneity and heterogeneity are in antagonistic relation.

Indeed, Mesopotamian city ideology, present also here, linked the city's preeminence with creation. This superiority is based on and is evident in three areas: military force, divine favor, and cultural achievements.⁵⁷⁵ BCS was related to and fostered Babylonian nationalism.⁵⁷⁶ Mesopotamian city states vied with each other all the time trying to assert themselves – at the cost of others (see SKL). Thus, it is not just an "ambitious urban project of

---

570. Kraeling, "Tower of Babel," 276; cf. von Soden, "Etemenanki vor Asarhaddon," 263.
571. But see the Samaritan and LXX texts adding "and the tower."
572. Schüle, *Prolog*, 383.
573. See Turner, *Announcements of Plot*, 31–32.
574. Giorgetti, "'Mock Building Account,'" 18–19.
575. Vanstiphout, "Introduction," 8.
576. See Foster, *Before the Muses*, 436.

the Babylonians"[577] but an ambitious imperial project – the beginning of kingship and empire.

The similarities between the Babylon and Exodus stories have been recognized. One can find motifs in common with both stories: brickwork, explicit or implicit references to primeval times, and kingship.[578] In support of the anti-empire interpretation of the Babylon story, Schüle discusses Genesis 11:1–9 in relation to Exodus. In Exodus 1:10, 14, as in Genesis 11:3, the words *hābâ, ləbēnîm, ḥōmer* are used. Because of the similarity of terminology between Babylon's and Egypt's construction materials and project, Schüle sees here the monumental architecture epitomized. "Brick" and "tar" in Exodus 1:14 symbolize forced labor, indeed, slavery. The correspondence climaxes in the notion of empire: If people start to gather in one place this has the taste of self-enslavement, as opposed to the free unfolding of human life intended in creation.

Further intertextual correspondences are identified by Schüle between the Genesis and the Exodus stories. The Egyptians' speech in Exodus 1:10 is couched in a syntax and words reminiscent of Genesis 11:3–4. Most importantly, in both cases we see people acting in the interest of holding the empire together. Finally, the action of the Egyptians in Exodus 3:8, parallel to that in Genesis 11:7, makes God intervene. The agreement in terminology (*yārad*) and theme is impressive once again – God leaves his heavenly abode and takes the earthly scene of human activities. To sum up, Egypt the evil empire is modeled on motifs known from the Babylon story.[579]

By scattering humankind, Yahweh wishes to achieve what Yahweh planned in the beginning – a diverse world. Scattering is not an end in itself but a means to create a heterogeneous culture and society. The narrator sees humankind's strength in being "scattered" – that is, not gathered in exile.[580] Atrahasis offers birth control as the solution to overcrowding. PH offers

---

577. So Kikawada, "Shape of Genesis," 29.

578. For more "echoes" of Gen 11:1–9 in Exod 1–2, see Kikawada and Quinn, *Before Abraham Was*, 112–17. See also Gerhard's thesis that the Moses figure is a critique of Neo-Babylonian kingship; Gerhard, *Aussetzungsgeschichte des Mose*.

579. Schüle, *Prolog*, 406–10; cf. Keiter, "Outsmarting God," 200–204.

580. Cf. Kooij, "Story of Genesis," 38; LaCocque, "Whatever Happened in the Valley," 31. I wonder whether this is an oblique reference to the Cyrus edict when the exiled nations of Babylon were "scattered" to their homelands "all over the earth."

dispersion, filling the earth (see 1:28; 9:1) to this as well as to exile.[581] Babylon promotes a homogenous empire, PH a heterogeneous creation. Civilizations and cultures can only exist by retaining their inherent diversity, which is totally at loggerheads with the intention and function of Mesopotamian empires based on and aiming at homogeneity.

Universal religion is often an OT perspective (e.g. Isa 2:1–5; 19:19–25) – not here though. The reason is simple. In the empire, the common religion cannot be but the one, that of the state. Babylonian state religion would not tolerate any alternative. The story's critique is all the more poignant as the name "Babylon" means "the gate of gods." "You Babylonians may boast that you live in the gate of God, but we could as well say that yours is the place where God confused the languages of men and whence they were scattered over the earth."[582] In the Genesis narrative, Babylon is not a city that descent from heaven is destined for world rule, but one the language and imperialistic plans of which Yahweh confuses.

Speiser notes that in Akkadian construction records the verb *balālu*, a cognate of Hebrew *bālal*, is used with reference to "sprinkling" with a compound of fragrant oils and essences before laying the foundation. This pun "could have served to undermine all of the Tower of Babel."[583] Speiser goes on to suggest another potential world play. The name *bab-ili* could be associated with the verb *babālum*, "to carry," the participle of which is *bābilum*.

> In fact, we have direct evidence of such punning in a bilingual poem in praise of the city, where *Bābilu* is spoken of as *bibil libbišu* "his wish fulfillment." A rival of Babylon, say in some Kassite center or in the entourage of Tukulti-Ninurta I, could have seized on the same wordplay for less friendly purposes. He could have gone on from *babālum* to its cognate *šutābulum*, which includes among its connotations that of "to drive out." Then, mindful of the idiom *šutābulum šaptā* "to move the lips," he might even have hit on the paranomasia of "to scatter speech."[584]

---

581. Kikawada and Quinn, *Before Abraham Was*, 51.
582. Hallo, "Scurrilous Etymologies," 770.
583. Speiser, "Word Plays," 322.
584. Speiser, 323.

Seen in the light of Mesopotamian worldview, even if it is soft, the polemic against the city as the gate to heaven is audible. Indeed, without such a polemic, the story would not be complete, as recognized by most interpreters. Blenkinsopp states, "It is difficult to avoid the conclusion that the author has composed a satire directed at human pretensions in the political sphere exemplified by the Neo-Babylonian empire in both its civic (the city) and religious aspects (the tower or ziggurat)."[585] Babylon's demise has of course theological relevance. "The connection between god and city was thought to have been so close that the decline of a city was usually blamed on its abandonment by the patron deity."[586]

As is well-known, the main ziggurat of Babylon, restored by Nebuchadnezzar II, was called Etemenanki meaning "House which is the Foundation of Heaven and Earth." The name of the most significant temple, next to Etemenanki, was Esagila, "The House of Raised Head." Both of them were dedicated to Babylon's chief deity, Marduk. The story of the building of the tower might be taken as a critique of the temple allegedly linking heaven and earth.

Finally, another Genesis story springs to mind, seemingly relevant to our discussion. In Genesis 28, headed for Paddan Aram, Jacob goes to sleep on his last night before leaving Canaan: "He had a dream in which he saw a stairway [*sullām*] resting on the earth, with its top reaching to heaven, and the angels of God were ascending and descending on it" (28:12). The word *sullām*, considered a cognate with Akkadian *simmiltu*,[587] may refer not so much to an ordinary stairway but rather to that of a Mesopotamian ziggurat.[588] For Babylonian religion, cities with temples and priests were not merely important – they were essential institutions and instruments in religion. If it is a ziggurat to which the narrative alludes, the story of Jacob's vision is polemical: God is not accessible or revealed in Babylonian ziggurats.[589] Indeed, God

---

585. Blenkinsopp, "Post-exilic Lay Source," 58; similarly Carr, *Formation*, 245; contra Uehlinger, *Weltreich*, 549.

586. Van de Mieroop, *Ancient Mesopotamian City*, 47.

587. Millard, "Celestial Ladder," 86.

588. Cf. Walton, "Mesopotamian Background," 161n20, and "Genesis," 62, 146n264. Uehlinger, *Weltreich*, 233–34, by not understanding how *sullām* here could con/denote a ziggurat, fails to see this import of the story.

589. Cf. Matthews, and Benjamin, *Social World of Ancient Israel*. Houtman, "What Did Jacob See," 350–51, also notices the link between Gen 11 and 28 but does not relate *sullām* to a ziggurat.

may be accessible in a distant, seemingly God-forsaken province without temples, cities, and kings. This polemic gets an even sharper wording in Jacob's realization:

> When Jacob awoke from his sleep, he thought, "Surely the LORD is in this place, and I was not aware of it." He was afraid and said, "How awesome is this place! This is none other than the house of God; this is the gate of heaven." Early the next morning Jacob took the stone he had placed under his head and set it up as a pillar and poured oil on top of it. He called that place Bethel, though the city used to be called Luz. (28:16–19)

Indeed, as opposed to a number of Mesopotamian stories in which gods approve/order the construction of temples Jacob is told nothing of this – sanctuaries are, after all, not all-important in religion. Again, there is no king, no city, no temple, no priest in this story – a commoner meets Yahweh. Israel's God is not defeated. Mediation of blessing does not depend on buildings and institutions.[590]

Shem's Genealogy (11:10–26)

Both the Nimrod and Babylon stories are implicitly or explicitly linked to Ham. When, however, no kingship materializes, when kingship does not deliver, the focus shifts to Shem's descendants, to one line and individual in particular.

In Shem's genealogy, ten generations lead up to Abraham just as there are ten generations from Adam to Noah in chapter 5. And as the tenth generation in chapter 5 ends with a father begetting three sons, the same happens to the tenth member of Shem's genealogy: Terah too begets three sons.[591] The linear genealogy in chapter 5 demonstrated the realization of God's blessing (1:28) and, by leading up to Noah, prepared the story of destruction and re-creation. Similarly, Shem's linear genealogy in chapter 11 serves to highlight the fulfillment of God's blessing[592] and the need of and, by leading up to Abram, preparation for a new beginning.

---

590. Hieke, *Genealogien der Genesis*, 257.
591. Alter, *Genesis*, 48.
592. Smith, "Structure and Purpose," 312; Turner, *Announcements of Plot*, 32.

The genealogy demonstrates much similarity to the genealogy in chapter 5 which follows the formula: And N lived x years and fathered O. And N lived, after fathering O, y years, and fathered sons and daughters. And the total years of N was z, and he died. The genealogy in chapter 10 is in turn patterned: And N lived x years and fathered O. And N turned, after fathering O, y years, and fathered sons and daughters. The genealogy in chapter 11 differs by omitting the references to N's total years and his death. Moreover, "The shortening of lives suggests a literary movement from the mythic world of primeval history (chs. 1–11) toward a reality where humans might live less than a century, rather than nine centuries as in the case with Methuselah (5:25) and others in Adam's genealogy."[593] It is true that Israel is not mentioned in the genealogies. By the remarkable similarity, however, Shem's line appears the direct continuation of that of Seth, which provides Israel with a genealogy reaching back to primeval times.

> The material of Genesis 1–11 does not fit together in a random way. As a whole, it has momentum that drives toward the emigration of Abram and his family from Mesopotamia to Canaan on instruction from God. The means used to structure the movement of the text in this direction is the insertion of genealogies.[594]

We have seen how Babylon's story is the climax of PH's criticism of the empire. Shem's genealogy is an organic part of the old world, as it provides an exit from the empire judged by God and come to an end. With Abram's birth (11:26), a new story has been introduced.

---

593. O'Connor, *Genesis 1–25A*, 181.
594. Van Wijk-Bos, *Making Wise the Simple*, 95.

CHAPTER 3

Prospects:
A New Genealogy and Beyond

Though not part of my study, a look at how the narrative unfolds may be helpful.

Terah's Genealogy (11:27–32)

With Terah's genealogy (11:27–32), a new narrative begins, that of Abraham. Even though with the Abraham narrative a new section begins in the Pentateuch, as several scholars, among them David Clines, have recognized, it is significant that the precise end of the previous material and so the beginning of the Abraham story is not clear-cut.[1]

In chapters 10–11, tribes and nations spread throughout the earth. Baumgart has observed that it is against this background that Terah and Abraham leave their original place. By moving westward, the journey of Terah, and later Abram, reenacts the journey started by the whole earth in 11:2.[2] Like the people, on arriving at Shinar, "settled there" (11:2), so do Terah and family in Haran (11:32).[3] In this vein, Awabdy claims, "Following this analysis, it would not be beyond the narrative trajectory to read Terah–Abram's westward migration–settlement–migration–entrance (11.31–12.9) as an intentional plot

---

1. Clines, "Theme in Genesis 1–11," 503.
2. Baumgart, *Die Umkehr des Schöpfergottes*, 25–26.
3. Awabdy, "Babel," 18–19; differently LaCocque, "Whatever Happened in the Valley," 33.

contrast to the כל־הארץ westward migration–settlement–scattering (11.1–9)."[4] The contiguous genealogies do not obscure this connection. The rearranged birth order (10:1–31; 11:27–30) and the vertical genealogy of Shem (11:10–26) are meant to guide readers from the Tower of Babylon story to Terah, smoothly leading up to the narrative of Terah's children (11:27–25:11).[5]

Terah's *toledot* is a remarkable genealogy. It is obvious at first glance that it is not really a genealogy, given that Terah's offspring were listed in 11:26. Therefore, nearly all the genealogical information is immaterial. That, however, does not hold for the non-genealogical references. That is to say, for a genealogy, the section is rather eventful. We learn Abram's and Nahor's wives' names (11:29), that Abram's wife was barren (11:30), and that Lot was part of the travel company to Haran (11:31) – all essential for the subsequent narrative and enclosed by the two *wayyiqqah* references (11:29–31). As for Terah's third son, references to Haran envelope the section. While Terah's son Haran dies in Ur of the Chaldeans, Terah and family arrive at Haran (11:28 and 31).

Terah set out to Canaan (11:31), like Abram will do in the next chapter. Since the reason is not told, the reader wonders why they only got to Haran. I suggest that, Ur of the Chaldeans being at the Eastern end and Haran at the Western end of the Babylonian empire, these locales, two sin centers, serve as metonymic or meristic references as if to exhort exilic Jewry, Terah tried to leave the empire but did not succeed – follow in Abraham's footsteps.[6]

Abraham's Story: Genesis 12:1 and Beyond

Moving on, the Abraham story is set against the backdrop of PH. For instance, we see conspicuous differences from 11:1–9:

---

4. Awabdy, "Babel," 22.
5. Awabdy, 28.
6. Is this a hint at the composition date of this section under Nabunaid who favored the Sin cult (cf. Hendel, "Historical Context," 61–63)? For a different interpretation, see Blenkinsopp, *Abraham*, 31.

1. The people want to make a name for themselves so that they are not spread out while Yahweh makes a name for Abraham who will be the father of nations;[7]
2. the people in Babylon are opposed by Yahweh while Abraham has him on his side;
3. the people's endeavor fails while Abraham's move from Haran to Canaan is the blessed beginning of promises;[8]
4. and, as opposed to the tribes and nations that own their land by inheritance (in a natural way) in chapter 10, Abraham is called to have his own land by God.[9]

But it is not only the Babylon story and the nations' list in chapter 10 against which that of Abraham is to be read. Commenting on the genealogies in chapters 5 and 11, Bailey observes that "as a climax, it is the tenth descendant in both passages who marks a significant change in the development of the narrative (Noah in chapter 5, and Abraham in 11)."[10] Like his forefather, Abraham is the vehicle of Yahweh's saving commitment to creation. Indeed, Abraham's blessing (12:1–3) reverses the curse of the serpent in chapter 3 and "heralds the triumph of the seed of the woman over the seed of the serpent. The blessing is not only for Israel, but for all the families of the earth."[11]

As early as 1969, Terrence Fretheim noticed the crucial narratological function of Genesis 12:1–3. He considered it a key passage providing a cornerstone for the entire structure of J by speaking of "all the families of the earth" (12:3) and so linking the genealogies with Abraham's story; by listing promises to Abraham in five verbs the subject of which is God (12:2–3); and by specifying "all the families of the earth" (12:3) as the target group of the blessings of the promises. The concerns of the narrative are Israel as a great

---

7. Baumgart speaks of "one nation" only but Abraham becomes the father of several. Warning, "Terminologische Verknüpfungen," 386–90, has offered a brief study to point out linguistic links between PH and the Abraham story.

8. Baumgart, *Umkehr des Schöpfergottes*, 27.

9. Uehlinger, *Weltreich*, 578.

10. Bailey, "Literary and Grammatical Aspects," 279. On more similarities between Noah and Abraham, see Carr, "Βίβλος γενέσεως Revisited (Part Two)," 334–36. On the Abrahamic promise rooted in PH and fulfilled in Genesis, see Wright, *Climax of the Covenant*, 21–23.

11. Hamilton, *Book of Genesis*, 273–74.

nation and Israel's relationship to the rest of humankind. In short, Israel exists to be a blessing for the nations.[12] Again, Abraham's call prepares just that.

In Abraham's story, *toledot* formulas multiply just as his offspring do (25:12, 19; 36:1, 9; 37:2). Notice this sequence: *toledot* of heaven and earth (2:4) > *toledot* of Adam (5:1) > *toledot* of Noah (6:9) > *toledot* of Noah's sons (10:1, 32) > *toledot* of Shem (11:10) > *toledot* of Terah (11:27) > story of Abraham (12:1–25:11) > *toledot* of Ishmael (25:12, 19) – *toledot* of Isaac (25:19) – *toledot* of Esau (36:1/9) – *toledot* of Jacob (37:2). The first six *toledot* narrow down the story, the next six extend it "horizontally." The latter six have no common offspring but a common ancestor.[13] In other words, as opposed to MKL, the Genesis *toledot* are not primarily backward but forward looking. "The king lists consistently suggest a backward movement in time, while the biblical genealogies move forward in time. This would suggest a different purpose for the two forms of literature."[14] This is a radical departure from the genealogy genre but, at the same time, this is what one should expect from an alternative vision: instead of looking into the past, looking forward. The use of WSL and the adoption of a modified form of MKL are also in the service of this alternative vision in Genesis 1–11 pointing ahead to the Abraham story. Indeed, this is the function of the *toledot*: to assist the new beginning by Abraham.[15] Note also that Terah's *toledot* (11:27), introducing the Abraham story, is the seventh, meaning it is a central one in Genesis,[16] marking the transition from primeval to patriarchal history.[17] "Primeval history derives from primeval event."[18]

Genealogies are more universal in character in Genesis than in Mesopotamia: the universe as well as the whole of humankind and its different clans and tribes have their genealogies – the good, the bad, and the

---

12. Fretheim, *Creation, Fall, and Flood*, 13–17. Fretheim makes his observations with a tenth-century J in mind. However, his interpretation holds also for a sixth-century context.

13. Ziemer, *Abram*, 367.

14. Hess, "Genealogies of Genesis," 253.

15. Cf. Awabdy, "Babel," 12–13.

16. Kessler and Deurloo, *Commentary on Genesis*, 6.

17. Note Carr's helpful and cautious observations regarding both synchronic and diachronic aspects of the *toledot*; "Βίβλος γενέσεως Revisited (Part One)."

18. Westermann, *Genesis 1–11*, 64. Elsewhere Westermann states "What is peculiar to the biblical primeval story is that it links the account of the primeval period with history" (Westermann, 65).

indifferent. Abraham's story bursts the *toledot* scheme because its theological import points beyond an isolated stage between creation and exodus.[19] Conspicuously, Abraham is without a *toledot* – Israel's forefather has none, it is a totally different story. "Why and for what purpose was Abraham chosen to become a great and mighty nation, and to be a blessing to all the nations of the earth?" Heschel asks. "Not because he knew how to build pyramids, altars, and temples, but 'in order that he may charge his children and his household after him to keep the way of the Lord by doing righteousness and justice' (Gen. 18:18–19)."[20]

Speiser claims that Israel's "purpose was not so much to tell the story of a nation or of nations, as to give the history of a society embarked on a particular quest, the quest for an enduring way of life, a way of life that had *universal* validity."[21] It is noteworthy in this context that military aspects in the patriarchal narrative are suppressed. Abraham and the patriarchs are depicted as royal figures nonetheless.[22]

Seen in this way, PH provides a foundation for Clines' threefold theme:

- Progeny: Adam's/Noah's/Shem's/Terah's/Abraham's offspring are multiplied.
- Land: though first cursed (3:17), after the flood, the curse is lifted (8:21), so preparing for Israel's gift.
- Covenant: foreshadowed by the Noahite covenant, the Abrahamic covenant to be added later.

It is significant that the first programmatic announcement of Pentateuch's theme is, as one should expect, right after PH and at the beginning of the patriarchal narrative, in 12:1–3. This theme, touched upon in PH, is elaborated on by subsequent sections of the Pentateuch.

---

19. Ziemer, *Abram*, 369.
20. Heschel, *Prophets*, 210.
21. Speiser, "Biblical Idea of History," 208, my italics. Van Seters, *Prologue to History*, 1, asserts right at the outset of his study that "the beginning of a national tradition by an account of the primeval origins of peoples and nations, as we have it in Genesis, is rather exceptional in Near Eastern historiography."
22. See Muffs, "Abraham the Noble," 81–107; Matthews and Benjamin, *Social World of Ancient Israel*, 205–10. Alexander too claims that "there are strong grounds for believing that the main line of descent in Genesis is viewed as a royal lineage" (Alexander, "Genealogies," 267).

It is also fascinating to see in what way the Moses story is the sequel to its antecedent. In a nutshell, the Sargon legend is generally considered a Neo-Assyrian work designed to establish the legitimacy of Sargon II. The Moses story may originally have been a subversive alternative to that legend. The circumstances surrounding their births make the similarities apparent. Both challenge and then destroy royal authority.[23] Whereas Sargon goes on to found a new empire with a new capital city, Moses, however, founds a nation without kingship and city. And the shrine is built in the wilderness and not in a city.

---

23. Cf. Carr, *Formation*, 313–14.

CHAPTER 4

Conclusions

General

Two general remarks seem in order. First, Lambert gives expression to the scholarly consensus, "The authors of ancient cosmologies were essentially compilers. Their originality was expressed in new combinations of old themes, and in new twists to old ideas. Sheer invention was not part of their craft."[1] This holds true of PH with the qualification that its combinations of old themes amount to ingenious invention. Moreover, PH is the introduction to not only Genesis but the Pentateuch by introducing themes and motifs that are revisited in later parts of the Pentateuch.[2] The decisive themes and motifs are, I have argued, city, kingship, and shrine. In PH, city is replaced by land, kings by commoners and their offspring, and a shrine centered religion by righteousness.

These themes and motifs had already been around in Mesopotamia. Israel used them to tell a new story and, by doing so, replace the Mesopotamian narrative. Israel was aware that it was a latecomer in ANE, and, in addition, that Mesopotamian culture and civilization were older and more prestigious. This awareness, however, does not appear to have caused in Israel an inferiority complex. Indeed, in contrast to these archaic cultures, Israel defined its cultural identity as a new beginning. Similarly to the OT narrative motif of

---

1. Lambert, "New Look," 297.
2. See Carr, "Βίβλος γενέσεως Revisited (Part Two)."

the youngest brother elevated to primacy, Israel saw itself as a younger culture chosen by God for preeminence.[3]

Second, there was a time in OT scholarship when creation and anything related to it were seen as a late and secondary development in Israel's faith. Consequently, Genesis in general and PH in particular were not considered to be sources for OT theology.[4] In the last fifty years or so, this has definitely changed; both creation and PH have gained a new lease of life. This study is a result of this reevaluation.

We have seen that the narratives and genealogies in PH are more universal in character than those in Mesopotamia. PH's creation is not told to promote a city and its stories have an egalitarian outlook – the universe and the whole of humankind, along with its different clans and tribes, have their genealogies.

In what follows, I will make concluding observations with not only PH but the subsequent narrative in mind.

City

The founding of cities appears rather marginal in the plot of PH.[5] We read of the first city construction by Cain (4:17). Then, there is the reference to Nimrod's imperial endeavor to found capital cities (10:10–12). Finally, there is the Babylon story of a failed construction project (11:1–9). All in all, cities have a rare and questionable appearance in PH.

There might have been parodies of the city theology, of which we know one at least.[6] But the author of The Rulers of Lagaš could not break the mold of patriotism – the high view of kingship and city is not challenged. No wonder, then, that PH, intent on a fresh start, transfers the benefits of city to land. Whereas cities in Mesopotamia were proud centers of power and oppression, privilege and superiority, land was needed more by the masses and available more widely to them. Thus, PH divests the city of its privileges and transfers God's blessing of land to human beings. "This blessing is expressed by God's

---

3. Hendel, "Genesis 1–11," 24.

4. See von Rad, "Theological Problem," 131–43; cf. Barr, *Concept of Biblical Theology*, 473.

5. In Israel, as opposed to Mesopotamia, there was only the occasional myth about founding cities; Hallo, "Urban Origins," 567. Cities were not attributed the high prestige of divine and mythic status as in Mesopotamia.

6. See Sollberger, "Rulers of Lagaš," 279.

presence, by fertile progeny, by rich landholding and in dominion. Without fertile progeny, ownership of landholding and dominion are worth nothing, without land, finally, royal dominion is itself worth nothing."[7]

Kingship

By linking kingship to the beginnings, SKL's claim is that kingship is authoritative. By linking Abraham to Adam through the genealogies, Genesis' claim is similarly to go back to primordial times but, by reference to the defining story impacting both Israel and humankind, it is an egalitarian world. Moreover, by presenting these figures as human beings who beget and finally die implies no ancestral cult. The lack of any reference to a common office makes these genealogies very dissimilar to functions of royal cults and offices. Also, if ANE king lists and genealogies wanted their readers to find the ideal in the past, PH did not list its genealogies to present ideals. The narrative passages tell of as much, if not more, failure as they reveal success. Thus, the genealogies guide us forward in history and we may recognize what we can learn from the past as well as make sure that past failures should not be repeated. Last but not least, the table of nations in Genesis 10 emphasizes the common humanity of all nations who likewise share in both the failures and hopes of their ancestors just as in a common creation in God's image.[8]

In other words, it is not local heroes, kings, or demigods that are the founders of culture and civilization or the bulwarks of society, as in SKL and MKL, but commoners and everyday people from all tribes, languages, and races.[9] Also, whereas, in Mesopotamia, the source of the law was the king, in the Pentateuch, it is God directly.[10] All in all, PH presents an egalitarian world.

In his 1968 essay, Brueggemann's conclusion, based on a remarkable similarity between the plots of PH and the reigns of David and Solomon, was

---

7. Ziemer, *Abram*, 317.
8. Hess, "Genealogies of Genesis," 250.
9. Kikawada and Quinn, *Before Abraham Was*, 128, state, "The author of Genesis 1–11 is willing – indeed, seems to be insisting – that we reject civilization and all its works rather than be implicated in the crimes that are necessary to its foundation and continuance." This judgment is one-sided. We have seen both the positive and negative sides of culture.
10. See Heger, "Source of Law," 324–42.

that the Genesis account was secondary, its author in this way celebrated the Davidic monarchy. In the light of PH's general attitude to kingship, it is hard to believe that PH came to such an assessment. Kikawada and Quinn rightly claim "that the author's view of the monarchy was far from flattering."[11]

Diffey concludes his study of three royal promise texts in Genesis by claiming "that the concept of kingship is much more than a passing idea within the Genesis narrative. Instead it appears to be a central feature to the patriarchal promises."[12] If my argument holds, kingship cannot be a central feature but rather a hidden torrent coming to the surface every now and then. In PH, it is only alluded to (e.g. 1:26), with further references in the patriarchal narrative becoming clearer.[13]

After referring to the Mesopotamian concept of the king being the image of the deity and the royal and divine cults' equation, Hallo observes,

> In Israel, by contrast, earthly kingship was regarded with suspicion, as an accommodation to alien polities and a perversion of the theocratic ideal. The king could not be worshipped like a god, and the deity could be described as a king only in incorporeal terms, not in terms of the usual physical trappings of kingship.[14]

In his famous comparison of Homeric and biblical literature, Auerbach astutely observes "that in the Homeric poems life is enacted only among the ruling class – others appear only in the role of servants to that class."[15] I will quote at length Auerbach's conclusion who sees OT narratives as distinct from Homer in that

> the great and sublime events in the Homeric poems take place far more exclusively and unmistakably among the members of a ruling class; and these are far more untouched in their heroic elevation than are the Old Testament figures, who can

---

11. Kikawada and Quinn, *Before Abraham Was*, 110. They see monarchy and civilization as dangers to a sedentary way of life (111). Again, I think it is too simplistic a critique.

12. Diffey, "Royal Promise," 316.

13. Cf. Alexander, *From Paradise*, 134–45, who, however, assigns too much significance to the undercurrent of kingship in Genesis.

14. Hallo, "Text, Statues and the Cult," 64.

15. Auerbach, *Mimesis*, 21.

fall much lower in dignity (consider, for example, Adam, Noah, David, Job); and finally, domestic realism, the representation of daily life, remains in Homer in the peaceful realm of the idyllic, whereas, from the very first, in the Old Testament stories, the sublime, tragic, and problematic take shape precisely in the domestic and commonplace: scenes such as those between Cain and Abel, between Noah and his sons, between Abraham, Sarah, and Hagar, between Rebekah, Jacob, and Esau, and so on, are inconceivable in the Homeric style. The entirely different ways of developing conflicts are enough to account for this. In the Old Testament stories the peace of daily life in the house, in the fields, and among the flocks, is undermined by jealousy over election and the promise of a blessing, and complications arise which would be utterly incomprehensible to the Homeric heroes. The latter must have palpable and clearly expressible reasons for their conflicts and enmities, and these work themselves out in free battles; whereas, with the former, the perpetually smoldering jealousy and the connection between the domestic and the spiritual, between the paternal blessing and the divine blessing, lead to daily life being permeated with the stuff of conflict, often with poison. The sublime influence of God here reaches so deeply into the everyday that the two realms of the sublime and the everyday are not only actually unseparated but basically inseparable.[16]

By and large, this description fits PH's world, void of rulers, as opposed to ANE literature.

Finally, Noah and Abraham are royal and priestly figures but commoners. It is thus the more startling that, despite growing up in Pharaoh's house, Moses is not a king but a prophet who, by leading the people, makes history. Indeed, "no genealogical line leads to Moses."[17] Whereas, for ANE people, it was the king who embodied the desire for continuity,[18] for Israel, it was humankind created in God's image. In this way, royal ideology is replaced by

---

16. Auerbach, 22–23.
17. Schüle, *Prolog*, 55.
18. See Oppenheim, *Ancient Mesopotamia*, 79.

prophecy and law is given directly by God without the mediation of a king. This is the radical alternative of Israel's exilic vision of society and culture.

Shrine

The startling fact is that, defying Mesopotamian expectations, there is no reference to organized religion in PH (although there are religious activities; see 4:3–5, 28; 8:20). Importantly, religious order is not founded at creation.

With the narrative unfolding, Abraham, without organized cult, is recognized as God's blessed one by Melchizedek, the universal example of the righteous priest and king.[19] There is, of course, the shrine in Exodus but it is a rather late development in Israel's narrated history, not inherent in the created order. Even there, there are no unqualified divine benefits attributed to the shrine. Cross draws attention to two passages (Exod 29:45–46; Lev 26:11–13) and emphasizes that it is the word *miškan/škn* applied here instead of *yšb* and derivates – "to tabernacle" instead of "to dwell."[20]

> The Priestly source wholly eschewed the literal term *yšb*, "to dwell" of the divine presence or "nearness in his earthly shrine. Those who have translated *miškān* as "Dwelling," and imputed a doctrine of the concrete abode of Yahweh in his shrine to the Priestly school could not be further from understanding the Priestly, self-conscious, technical usage.[21]

Shrine here is not a privileged institution of king and deity. Indeed, in PH, God is not bound to any institution. It is therefore noteworthy that the only explicit reference to sacrifice is in 8:20 – there is no shrine, no cult, and no sacrifice before the flood.[22] The garden and land replace the city, a covenant-based egalitarian religion replaces the temple-based hierocracy, progeny replaces ancestor worship as do commoners kings – a good world without kings, cities, and temples.

---

19. Ziemer, *Abram*, 162. Note that Melchizedek takes the scene as a king – without a genealogy.
20. Cross, *Canaanite Myth*, 298–99.
21. Cross, 299.
22. Note the terminology of 4:3–4 where Cain and Abel are not said to offer sacrifices.

A Universal Vision and Politics

The above discussion has, I hope, made clear that PH differs from its ANE counterparts not just in minor details but in its underlying socio-political agenda and values. These are at loggerheads with those sustaining Babylon and so thoroughgoing and subversive that a very discrete vision of politics and society, culture, and religion is imagined. In what follows, I will outline this vision.

In Mesopotamia, creation is the foundation for organizing society and religion. In PH, creation plays a similar role with important differences. Carr is correct in his claim,

> Instead of having the cult and other aspects of human culture established at creation or in a time span extending from Creation to Flood, the Priestly writing describes the cult and other human potentialities as being established over a stretch of cosmic history extending up through Moses. Moreover, these potentialities are not the simple outgrowth of the original creative impulse, but instead are outgrowths of God's indestructible, covenantal responses to human history.[23]

Whereas, throughout the ANE world, institutionalized religion played a crucial role for society and politics, PH's narrative without organized religion offers quite a different outlook. For organized religion, righteousness becomes the standard by which individuals, nations, and events are measured. Indeed, it is an underlying agenda, and, without this ethical aspect, PH cannot really be understood. The foundation of this aspect was already laid with the image of God concept at creation. Not just the king, but all humankind bears the Creator's image; PH's world is egalitarian and not hierarchical as ANE kingdoms were. What is also emphatic is righteousness. In chapter 4, Cain is reproached for killing his brother. Noah is saved for his righteousness while humankind has become violent. Yahweh, the God of Israel, the creator God is no tribal-national deity supporting the cause of his nation only but concerned with the welfare of the whole creation.[24]

---

23. Carr, *Reading the Fractures*, 132.

24. Of course, later on, there will be priests, sacrifices, rituals, laws, sanctuary – an organized religion. Still, Israel's religion is based on righteousness, i.e. love, the right attitude toward God and the neighbor.

In his treatment of Neo-Assyrian political propaganda, Holloway claims that "empires must maintain the fiction of invincibility at their peril."[25] Indeed, it is the empire's vested interest to maintain this fiction; but history teaches us that it cannot be done for good. Even the most powerful and brutal empire terminates when Yahweh descends.

For Gordon McConville, "the Old Testament's political theology can be viewed as a critical dialogue with the dominant powers in ancient Israel's world."[26] If anywhere, in PH, we witness this dialogue. With PH as its introduction, Genesis "establishes a relationship between Israel and creation, and between Israel and other nations."[27] PH, however, has a different view of what constitutes a good world, thus challenging Mesopotamia. "The argument with Mesopotamian politics is at the same time an argument with its religion, each political vision being founded ultimately on a concept of God and creation."[28] This concept has universal values and is not restricted to primeval times but effects politics and society, present and future. Though the trajectory of this agenda will lead to spectacular divine deliverances, the exodus is but one manifestation of Yahweh's commitment to righteousness. McConville claims: "The story of Israel leads out of tyranny and into freedom, in a vision that is universal."[29] This holds good as much for Israel in Exodus as for humanity in PH. In PH, Israel's universal vision of the world is sketched.

We have seen that, in Mesopotamia, creation served political ends; after creation, political institutions, first and foremost kingship and religion, were established. In PH, the world's story, and, within it, that of Israel, begins with the creation of humankind. At this point, there is no shrine, no city, no king – no representatives of ethno-national interests. Indeed, in PH, shrine and king are never mentioned and city plays only a marginal role. Creation is not narrated to vindicate political institutions.[30] A world founded on creation and originated by a benevolent creator who faces no opposition has of course universal relevance.

---

25. Holloway, *Aššur is King!*, 81.
26. McConville, *God and Earthly Power*, 30.
27. McConville, 30.
28. McConville, 172.
29. McConville, 168.
30. Cf. McConville, 170.

Second, in the exile, Judah came to see where her own nationalistic theology of holy city, sacrosanct temple, and chosen dynasty leads. She also came to see at her own expense what devastation and oppression Mesopotamian royal ideology is capable of. No wonder that exclusivist ethnic claims are countered in PH by universalism. That is one reason genealogies are included in PH. Though interrupting the narrative flow, they advocate universalistic values. PH leads to the genealogy of Israel's ancestor but without nationalistic zeal. In this vein, McConville asserts

> that Genesis–Kings is not merely oblique evidence of an ancient dispute over primordial or universal conceptions of nationhood, but rather that it constitutes an argument for the latter. Israel, in its laws and in its self-understanding according to its own literature, testifies to what it might mean to be a people that lives in obedience to norms of justice-righteousness that transcend its own life and become universal.[31]

If I have argued cogently, PH is to be seen as the preface to, indeed grounding document of, this epic argument. This in turn affects how to relate to the world outlined in PH.

Third, regarding McConville's concept of justice, I have argued that God's concern is with ethics in general and an egalitarian society, driven by a politics of diversity, in particular. In this way, ethics and universalism are closely related. Despite the *ṣdq* root's rare occurrence, justice figures prominently in PH.[32] It does so, however, in a somewhat oblique way, with the root hardly applied. The creation narratives' references to the divine image concept democratize the concept, attributing high significance to each individual. This entails a view of an egalitarian society. McConville claims that "the effect of beginning with creation is that justice-righteousness is located prior to history, in the character of God, thence inscribed on the creation."[33] Ethics and, more specifically, human life are also accorded priority in that violence and homicide are not tolerated. Explicitly or implicitly, they are crimes committed

---

31. McConville, 170.
32. Cf. McConville, 42.
33. McConville, 170–71.

against God's image, hence God himself (see 4:10–11, 23–24; 6:5–13; 9:6).[34] PH's world is not hierarchic and unaware of privileged classes.

PH's political criticism and vision are at their shrewdest as well as sharpest when they reach their climax in 11:1–9 where the narrator launches its most sustained attack on Babylon. Indirectly, here, city, shrine, and kingship are all assaulted. The building of the city and its ziggurat is abandoned and kingship fails to descend from heaven.

As has become clear by now, PH is not just politically relevant but is by definition a political treatise. By pitting Yahweh and Yahwistic values against Marduk and his values, it envisions an alternative world with a different society and politics from that of Babylon. PH's Yahwism is critical and liberating of the oppressive and exploitative politics of Babylon. In addition to its political import, PH can also be read as a parable of Israel's trauma.

The Primeval History as a Parable: Israel's Trauma

Robert Polzin has read the early stories in Samuel as "a kind of parabolic introduction to the Deuteronomic history of kingship."[35] Barbara Green has followed him by reading the Saul narrative as a parable of the monarchy.[36] Thus, I suggest that PH is Israel's parable about, and attempt at, coming to terms with the loss of country, temple, and kingship, brought about by the Babylonian empire. Society, culture, and religion were destroyed in an instant. Israel was forced to re-evaluate the basis of her existence, which it did in the exile.[37] I have argued that PH is to be read as Israel's counter-narrative offering an alternative to the Babylonian empire's royal-imperial ideology. So, let us read PH's sections as episodes of this parable.

The land God gave to Israel was good, indeed, very good – just like the world God created. "Called into existence by its God in the no-man's-land of the wilderness,"[38] God put Israel in this "garden"[39] so that Israel could

---

34. Cf. McConville, 42.
35. Polzin, *Samuel and the Deuteronomist*, 44.
36. Green, *King Saul's Asking*.
37. For a similar interpretation of the Yahwist, see Van Seters, *Prologue to History*, 128–29; of Gen 2–3, see Enns, *Evolution of Adam*, 65–66, 88–91; Smith, *Genesis of Good and Evil*, 45–48.
38. Blenkinsopp, *Creation, Un-Creation*, 8.
39. See LaCocque, *Trial of Innocence*, 64–66.

rule over and subdue it (see 1:28). Yahweh also made a covenant with her people, the terms of which were clear. Israel, however, did not obey Yahweh's command and was thus misled, into exile, by serpent-Babylon. Hence, Israel's labor and the ground-country were cursed alike, and Israel expelled from the "garden."[40] Regarding Babylon's role in "leading Israel astray," it first takes the scene as the serpent. For this, it is duly punished by God. As a matter of fact, of the three culprits, serpent-Babylon alone is cursed (3:14).

In chapter 4, Babylon is cast in the role of Cain who slays his brother.[41] Curiously, Israel did not disown Babylon by saying Cain never belonged to the family. Indeed, it is Cain who does not treat Abel as his brother.[42] But in this way, Babylon's sin is the more outrageous. This is implied by her curse. "You are more cursed than the ground" (4:11 AT), that is Israel's land. I argued above that this curse surpasses that of Adam (see 3:17), "Cursed is the ground because of you; through painful toil you will eat of it all the days of your life." Concerning Israel and Babylon, the respective curses take on new meanings. In chapter 3, it was because of Adam-Israel's disobedience that God cursed the ground. In chapter 4, it is because of Cain-Babylon's sin (see also 4:7) that God curses – this time not the ground but the offender himself. Those perpetrating fratricide-genocide are more cursed than the ground. While the ground is cursed to produce "unfruit," Cain-Babylon is cursed to unsettled life, an anathema to Babylonian society.[43]

Conspicuously, the fratricide is set in a story frame of offering. Whereas Abel's offering is accepted, Cain's is rejected (4:4–5). Importantly, Cain is not

---

40. See Wright, *Resurrection of the Son*, 92. Only after becoming like God and being expelled from Eden, humankind's creative capacities and activities begin to unfold. Israel's exilic theological-literary activity seems similar to that.

41. This interpretation is strengthened by God's partial treatment of the brothers, a crux for interpreters: "elect" Abel-Israel is preferred for no particular reason; cf. Goldingay, *Old Testament Theology*, 150; cf. Deut 7:7–8. By denying that he is his brother's keeper, Cain "acknowledges that no proper difference in status exists between himself and his brother to warrant killing him, as a shepherd might a sheep" (Carmichael, "Paradise Myth," 57). Note that "shepherd" was used of ANE kings.

42. Van Wolde, "Story of Cain," 33–35. Abel is seven times referred to as Cain's brother; Simon, *A ki nem mondott*, 52.

43. See Fox, "Can Genesis Be," 37. Notice, however, that it is Cain-Babylon who becomes the cultural inventor in 4:17–24, an acknowledgement of Babylon's socio-cultural achievement. Fox's interesting study about the younger brother motif could be applied to Babylon; Fox, "Stalking the Younger Brother," 45–68.

judged because of his improper offering but for his improper behavior toward his brother – ethics seems more relevant than cult.

To add insult to injury, it is not just that Babylon murders her younger brother but it even boasts of it (4:23–24). In this reading, the bragging of Lamech, or, through a metathesis, Melech, "King,"[44] may imply Babylon's inherent and incurable inclination to violence. Right after the reference to Lamech's violence, Adam's grandson Enosh is mentioned as the representative of a generation of Yahwistic worship. With Abel-Israel slain, a new Israel is born in the exile to call on Yahweh's name.

The most dramatic depiction of Israel's national disaster is of course the flood story. The flood destroyed everything of old Israel, it is true, and the effect is pictured in vivid terms. Only a remnant survived. Still, it is not so much backward but rather forward looking by an emphasis on the re-creation motif. The new start is hinted at already in the statement of Lamech, or, again, king (a hoped-for Davidic offspring?), this time from another, Israelite genealogy, "He will comfort us in the labor and painful toil of our hands caused by the ground the LORD has cursed" (5:29).

Despite Yahweh's punishment of Israel and the abrupt end of Judahite kingship, there is hope for a better future in the person of Noah, the new Israel. The devastation was due to Israel's violence – the social injustice and wickedness. It was executed by Babylon, which was severe, indeed, out of proportion.[45] This also explains why the flood story uniquely stresses the clean animals brought into the ark (7:2–3, 8) as well as the covenant with Noah (6:18). The narrator is intent on dispersing the doubts of exilic Israel: Yahweh has not terminated the covenant but is ready to start over.[46] To make his commitment to Israel unmistakable, Yahweh makes a unilateral covenant with his creation-Israel (9:8–17). In the after-flood scene, Noah-Israel is once again seen as humiliated and denied human status by Ham-Babylon who is

---

44. Radday, "Humor in Names," 78, has suggested that Lamech is a palindrome for *melek*, thus non-king. Note that there is no *lmk* root in Hebrew. If this metathesis is implied this is the only reference to kingship in chs. 1–9. For a synchronic attempt at making sense of the two Lamechs of the two genealogies, see Hess, "Lamech in the Genealogies," 24.

45. See Dobbs-Allsopp, "Tragedy, Tradition, and Theology," 36. A number of OT passages complain about or hint at God's harsh judgment at 586 (e.g. Lamentations; Pss 74; 89; Isa 40:1–2).

46. Studying the Eridu Genesis, Jacobsen, "Eridu Genesis," 527, argues that the flood served as a metaphor for surviving a socio-political catastrophe and starting all over again.

subsequently cursed just as the serpent was in chapter 3.[47] PH ends in Babylon (11:1–9) as Israel's story did.[48]

Genesis 1–11 also suggests that Israel not only learned her lesson but abandoned her nationalistic theology that partly led to the national disaster, and adopted a more universalistic approach to religion and worship. The author could have easily written a story with real or fictional Israelite kings and heroes as a counter-narrative to the Babylonian metanarrative. Of course, it would have amounted to casting out demons with the help of Belial. PH drew up the outlines of a world where worship of the true God is not a matter of ethnicity or social rank.

After the loss of Abel, Eve bears another son, Seth, reminiscent of Shem, the ancestor of Israel, who fathers Enosh, "man/humankind." In his time, "men began to call on the name of the LORD" (4:26). With the flood over and despite the fact that hardly anything has changed, God renews the covenant with Israel,[49] "Never again will I curse the ground because of man, even though every inclination of his heart is evil from childhood. And never again will I destroy all living creatures, as I have done" (8:21; see 9:9–17). The covenant, however, is universal, embracing all living creatures and all nations, stressed by God.

Babylon's violence is obliquely referred to at the end of the flood story. The reference to bloodshed takes on new content in this reading, as Yahweh seems to have the moral significance in mind, "Whoever sheds the blood of man, by man shall his blood be shed; for in the image of God has God made man" (9:6). Genocide and bloodshed through subjugation of one people by another is strictly prohibited.

In 11:1–9, Babylon is the place where people from all over the world converge – as in exile. (Israel is included, so the story that began with the expulsion from the garden reaches its climax in Babylon.) They are supposed to build a homogeneous empire only to make Yahweh descend and confuse the language of the empire, thus dissolving it.

---

47. That is why Nimrod, founder of Babylon (10:10) is Ham's offspring.

48. Blenkinsopp, *Creation, Un-Creation*, 8.

49. Note that whereas, by the proclamation of Marduk's power, BCS was employed as a "magic formula" to guard against evil spirits during and after the restoration of the temple in Babylon (Heidel, *Babylonian Genesis*, 65), the Genesis account, by the proclamation of God's might, declares God's power visible in the created order.

The Theme of the Primeval History

I have now reached the stage where I can put forward my view of what PH is all about. Clines has suggested that it is through trial and error that theme can be ascertained.[50] This seems unsatisfactory to me. I have argued that the absence of kingship, city, and shrine, constituting themes in Mesopotamia as they were, make PH an anti-Babylonian writing. In my view, PH's theme is an alternative vision to that of Mesopotamia, of humankind created in God's image, capable of doing good and bad, with no kingship, city, and shrine. If Clines' proposal of the Pentateuch's theme as the partial fulfillment of the promise of land, progeny, and covenant holds, my thesis definitely holds it up. However, I did not come to this conclusion by trial and error but by studying PH and relevant Mesopotamian texts.

"P did not intend to write an alternative primeval history in relation to the Mesopotamian ones. He definitely wanted to provide his own version, not simply to fill in an already existing tradition. In this respect, P functions as a counter story," Kvanvig claims.[51] His statement of P, however, holds of PH in general, in my view. PH wanted to provide its own version of the beginnings of the world and humankind, culture and civilization, society and politics as well as the new start after the flood. PH sketched how the new start went awry with Babylon. PH functions as a counter story to that of Babylon and sets the scene to the new beginning by Abram – without city, king, and shrine. PH's view is that human life, whether society, politics, or culture, is possible without these institutions.

I have claimed that each major unit of Genesis 1–11, including the flood story that may look ill-fitting,[52] is necessary to contribute to PH's theme. What Clines generally states holds in this case too: I have done a good job if this study convinces the reader that PH "is a literary work, and not a rag-bag or a scissors-and-paste job."[53] I have suggested that PH could be seen as

---

50. Clines, "Theme in Genesis 1–11," 486, and *Theme of the Pentateuch*, 23.

51. Kvanvig, *Primeval History*, 258. Both Kvanvig and I posit a Babylonian origin to PH; both of us concern ourselves with the socio-political and theological import of the narrative. The main difference between Kvanvig and me is that he studies P and non-P separately whereas I do the final text. After all, no source but only the final text has been canonical.

52. Contra Fritz, "'Solange die Erde steht,'" 611.

53. Clines, "Theme in Genesis 1–11," 504.

the introduction to Genesis/Pentateuch by inaugurating their themes. How exactly PH does this requires further research.

Relevance and Implications

If I have argued cogently and presented a compelling case for reading PH against a Neo-Babylonian background, further study, be it synchronic, diachronic, or comparative, seems necessary on subsequent units of the Pentateuch as well as the whole of the Pentateuch from the perspective of kingship-city-shrine.

PH is often used for purposes of apologetics. This is the wrong perspective when read in scientific terms like geology, paleontology etc. By drawing on ANE myths, Gilgamesh, Atrahasis, and BCS among and foremost of them, Genesis defeats myth on its own turf by countering myth by myth. This seems the only feasible way. Reading Genesis on its own terms makes an interpretation that takes myth into account mandatory.

This study is particularly relevant in my estimation to people and communities living in a similar context to that of exilic Israel. I have first of all the persecuted church in mind that, unlike the Western church, lives in a predominantly non-Christian society or community that is hostile to the Christian worldview and values. I am sure that the way PH views and discusses questions of society, politics, and culture (e.g. social hierarchy and equality; homogeneity vs. heterogeneity in politics and culture; the value of humankind) from a theological vantage point can be helpful for those who live in an inimical environment. Seeing and learning the ways PH polemicizes with the tenets of Mesopotamian ideology/theology should be beneficial for persecuted Christians. Wherever persecution and oppression are harsher, the soft polemic may be something to study and use. More generally, Christians, not only of the persecuted church but those in a minority position, may find this study useful. As a matter of fact, if we faithfully follow Christ, we will inevitably find ourselves in a minority position most of the time.

This exposition of PH might be helpful once its socio-political relevance is realized. PH was formulated in the shadow of the Neo-Babylonian empire whose narrative and attitudes induced exilic Jews to present their Yahwistic view of society, politics, and culture after their country, capital city, and temple were destroyed. Even though Babylonia has been long gone today's world is not void of empires. (Today, there are three of them: the US, Russia, and China.) Today's empires, by various means, maintain their version of empire. They feel obliged and entitled to topple democratically elected governments, invade independent countries, and repress their own minorities. All this is accomplished by virtue of the ruling ideology and in the name of the empire, be it Western democracy, the concept of the untouchable, "divine" emperor or sacrosanct state. Though not always, but interestingly, empires go hand in hand with centralization, a rather autocratic governance, and homogeneity, that is to say self-governance, different voices, and diversity are not tolerated. Equality, a core value for PH, is not striven for.

Recently, there has been a trend to abandon traditional democratic values and redefine democracy by states, whether or not belonging to Western democracies, that do not qualify as empires. Authoritarian governments seem to flourish in countries that had apparently turned their back on dictatorship and authoritarian forms of governments. Populist politicians are not only popular in countries hitherto democratic but are intent on building centralized, homogeneous states that favor and prefer economic and political success and progress over a society of equality and justice. For these politicians, state control, lack of transparency, and social inequality are the necessary price a government must pay for the sake of its own success and that of its subjects. In these "illiberal democracies," a contradiction in terms, state control is high, they are centralized and autocratic where populist propaganda and nationalistic tendencies play a major role, corruption is rampant, human rights and democratic values are ignored. The economic and political agenda trumps considerations of environment, human rights, justice, and employment. Political success and economic progress are preferred to the welfare of both the individual and community.

The trouble with Christians, often, is that we may be critical of some manifestations of empire, be it left-wing or right-wing, but not with the concept of empire itself. PH, and much of biblical literature for that matter, was different – PH does not trust *the* empire. At the root of this distrust lies PH's basic conviction of God's sovereign rule, a good creation, and humankind created in the image of the Creator, concepts empires habitually oppose. It is these very values that are not upheld; indeed, they are threatened by the empire which acts as a cruel and inhumane machine.

Even in secular post-Christendom, the Bible is a favorite read and Genesis is one of the best-known books of the Bible. As ever, Christianity is anxious about a fast-changing society and culture seeking the right way to face new challenges. PH's strategy can equip God's alternative community with some important tools to present an alternative vision of society, politics, and culture. Clearly, this alternative community is to demonstrate, indeed embody, before the eyes of the world the Creator's love to his creation as well as the righteousness needed for a responsible socio-political and ecological engagement. In this endeavor, the concept of righteousness as discussed by Gordon McConville comes to our help. He asks,

> Can there be a recipe for mature political life, nurturing the creation intention to bless humanity, the dignity of humanity as such, and the divine will to righteousness in the world? In what way can *Israel* fulfil the divine intention that righteousness should be realized concretely on earth? Must it not succumb to dangers of nationalism and power itself?[54]

And in what way can righteousness be realized on earth? McConville's response is,

> The Old Testament's story from creation to politics differs from the ANE precisely in this respect, that its interpretation of origins is at the service neither of the idea of one nation's intrinsic right to predominate, nor of a given political *status quo*. There was a positive side to the story in that it illustrated Yahweh's readiness to allow his rule to find correspondences in a variety of actual political forms. However, it ends in an absence of institutions, and only eschatological pointers.[55]

In other words, there is no kingship lowered from heaven, no shrine or city founded at creation. These institutions are no absolutes but subjects to God's sovereign authority and righteousness.[56]

---

54. McConville, *God and Earthly Power*, 171, his italics.
55. McConville, 174.
56. On the other hand, God adapts to ever-new political formations. Cf. Miller, "Eridu, Dunnu, and Babel," 243:
> The theme of the city does not, of course, disappear from the biblical tradition. With the monarchy the cities, and one particular city especially, rise to

God accommodated to new realities in Israel, to the Davidic monarchy, Jerusalem as the capital city, the temple. However, the 586 disaster made the failure of these institutions as well as Yahweh's ultimate authority yet more manifest. The tension between socio-political institutions and God's will had various facets, but the relativization of human institutions was stated right at the beginning: when God created humankind, he created them in his image male and female, equal he created them. PH is but a long elaboration of this principle. By this elaboration, PH issues a challenge and outlines an alternative to the empire.

---

prominence, but the Primeval History of Genesis does not project this back to the beginning. For Israel, in some sense the city was as viable and as ambiguous as kingship, as capable of fulfilling the destiny of God for the human community (Isa 1:26; Zech 8:3–5) as kingship was (e.g., Isa 11:1–9), and as capable of subverting that divine intention as was kingship (Isa 1:21–23; Mic 3:9–12).

Bibliography

Albenda, Pauline. "Of Gods, Men and Monsters on Assyrian Seals." *Biblical Archaeologist* 41, no. 1 (1978): 17–22.

Albertz, Rainer. "Die Kulturarbeit im Atramḫasīs im Vergleich zur biblischen Urgeschichte." In *Werden und Wirken des Alten Testaments. Festschrift für Claus Westermann zum 70. Geburtstag*, edited by Rainter Albertz, Hans-Peter Müller, Hans W. Wolff, and Walther Zimmerli, 38–57. Göttingen: Vandenhoeck & Ruprecht, Neukirchener Verlag, 1980.

———. "Das Motiv für die Sintflut im Atramḫasīs-Epos." In *Mythos im Alten Testament und seiner Umwelt. Festschrift für Hans-Peter Müller zum 65. Geburtstag*, BZAW 278, edited by Armin Lange, Hermann, Lichtenberger, and Diethard Römheld, 3–16. Berlin: de Gruyter, 1999.

Albright, W. F. "The End of 'Calneh in Shinar.'" *Journal of Near Eastern Studies* 3, no. 4 (1944): 254–55.

———. Review of *The Two Sources of the Predeuteronomic History (JE) in Gen. 1–11*, by S. Mowinckel. *Journal of Biblical Literature* 57, no. 2 (1938): 230–31.

Alexander, T. D.*From Paradise to the Promised Land: An Introduction to the Pentateuch*. Grand Rapids: Baker Academic, 2012.

———. "Genealogies, Seed and the Compositional Unity of Genesis." *Tyndale Bulletin* 44, no. 2 (1993): 255–70.

Alster, Bendt. "An Aspect of 'Enmerkar and the Lord of Aratta.'" *Revue d'Assyriologie et d'Archéologie Orientale* 67, no. 2 (1973): 101–10.

———. "Dilmun, Bahrain, and the Alleged Paradise in Sumerian Myth and Literature." In *Dilmun: New Studies in the Archaeology and Early History of Bahrain*, edited by Daniel T. Potts, BBVO 2, 39–74. Berlin: Reimer, 1983.

Alter, R. *The Art of Biblical Narrative*. New York: Basic Books, 1981.

———. *Genesis: Translation and Commentary*. New York: Norton, 1996.

———. *The Pleasures of Reading in an Ideological Age*. New York: Simon & Schuster, 1989.

Amit, Y. *Reading Biblical Narratives: Literary Criticism and the Hebrew Bible*. Minneapolis: Fortress Press, 2001.

Anderson, Bernard W. "From Analysis to Synthesis: The Interpretation of Gen 1–11." *Journal of Biblical Literature* 97, no. 1 (1978): 23–39.

Arneth, M. *Durch Adams Fall ist ganz verderbt . . . Studien zur Entstehung der alttestamentlichen Urgeschichte*. FRLANT 217. Göttingen: Vandenhoeck & Ruprecht, 2007.

Auerbach, E. *Mimesis: The Representation of Reality in Western Literature*. Princeton: Princeton University Press, 1953.

Awabdy, M. A. "Babel, Suspense, and the Introduction to the Terah-Abram Narrative." *Journal for the Study of the Old Testament* 35, no. 1 (2010): 3–29.

Baden, Joel S. "The Tower of Babel: A Case Study in the Competing Methods of Historical and Modern Literary Criticism." *Journal of Biblical Literature* 128, no. 2 (2009): 209–24.

Bailey, John A. "Initiation and the Primal Woman in Gilgamesh and Genesis 2–3." *Journal of Biblical Literature* 89, no. 2 (1970): 137–50.

Bailey, Nicholas A. "Some Literary and Grammatical Aspects of Genealogies in Genesis." In *Biblical Hebrew and Discourse Linguistics*, edited by Robert D. Bergen, 267–82. Winona Lake: Eisenbrauns, 1994.

Bailkey, Nels. "Early Mesopotamian Constitutional Development." *American Historical Review* 72, no. 4 (1967): 1211–36.

Baker, D. W. "Diversity and Unity in the Literary Structure of Genesis." In *Essays on the Patriarchal Narrative*, edited by A. R. Millard and D. J. Wiseman, 189–205. Leicester: IVP, 1980.

Barr, James. *The Concept of Biblical Theology: An Old Testament Perspective*. London: SCM, 1999.

———. *The Garden of Eden and the Hope of Immortality: The Read-Tuckwell Lectures for 1990*. London: SCM, 1992.

Bartelmus, R. *Heroentum in Israel und seiner Umwelt*. ATANT 65. Zurich: Theologischer Verlag, 1979.

Batto, Bernard F. "The Covenant of Peace: A Neglected Ancient Near Eastern Motif." *Catholic Biblical Quarterly* 49, no. 2 (1987): 187–211.

———. "The Divine Sovereign: The Image of God in the Priestly Creation Account." In *David and Zion: Biblical Studies in Honor of J. J. M. Roberts*, edited by B. F. Batto and K. L. Roberts, 143–86. Winona Lake: Eisenbrauns, 2004.

———. "The Institution of Marriage in Genesis 2 and in *Atrahasis*." *Catholic Biblical Quarterly* 62, no. 4 (2000): 621–31.

———. "The Malevolent Deity in Mesopotamian Myth." In *In the Beginning: Essays on Creation Motifs in the Ancient Near East and the Bible*, 199–228. Siphrut 9. Winona Lake: Eisenbrauns, 2013.

———. "Paradise Reexamined." In *The Biblical Canon in Comparative Perspective: Scripture in Context IV*, ANETS 11, edited by K. L. Younger, Jr., W. W. Hallo, B. F. Batto, 33–66. Lewiston: Edwin Mellen, 1991.

———. *Slaying the Dragon: Mythmaking in the Biblical Tradition*. Louisville: Westminster John Knox, 1992.

———. "The Sleeping God: An Ancient Near Eastern Motif of Divine Sovereignty." *Biblica* 68, no. 2 (1987): 153–77.

Bauckham, Richard. *Living with Other Creatures: Green Exegesis and Theology*. Waco: Baylor University Press, 2011.

Baumgart, N. C. *Die Umkehr des Schöpfergottes. Zu Komposition und religionsgeschichtlichem Hintergrund von Gen 5–9*. HBS 22. Freiburg: Herder, 1999.

Beattie, D. R. G. "*Peshat* and *Derash* in the Garden of Eden." *Irish Biblical Studies* 7, no. 2 (1985): 62–75.

Beauchamp, P. "מִין *mîn*." *Theological Dictionary of the Old Testament*. Vol. 8, edited by G. J. Botterweck, H. Riggren, H. J. Fabry, 288–91. Grand Rapids: Eerdmans, 1997.

Berlejung, A. *Die Theologie der Bilder. Herstellung und Einweihung von Kultbildern in Mesopotamien und die alttestamentliche Bilderpolemik*. OBO 162. Freiburg–Göttingen: Universitätsverlag–Vandenhoeck & Ruprecht, 1998.

Bidmead, Julye. *The Akītu Festival: Religious Continuity and Royal Legitimation in Mesopotamia*. Gorgias Dissertations, Near Eastern Studies 2. Piscataway: Gorgias, 2002.

Bird, Phyllis A. "'Male and Female He Created Them': Gen 1:27b in the Context of the Priestly Account of Creation." *Harvard Theological Review* 74, no. 2 (1981): 129–59.

Black, J. A. "The New Year Ceremonies in Ancient Babylon: 'Taking Bel by the Hand' and a Cultic Picnic." *Religion* 11, no. 1 (1981): 39–59.

Black, Jeremy A., Graham Cunningham, Eleanor Robson, and Gábor Zólyomi. *The Literature of Ancient Sumer*. Oxford: Oxford University Press, 2004.

Blenkinsopp, J. *Abraham: The Story of a Life*. Grand Rapids: Eerdmans, 2015.

———. *Creation, Un-Creation, Re-Creation: A Discursive Commentary on Genesis 1–11*. London: T&T Clark, 2011.

———. "P and J in Genesis 1–11: An Alternative Hypothesis." In *Fortunate the Eyes that See: Essays in Honor of David Noel Freedman in Celebration of His Seventieth Birthday*, edited by Astrid B. Beck, Andrew H. Bartlet, Paul R. Raabe, Chris A. Franke, 1–15. Grand Rapids: Eerdmans, 1995.

———. *The Pentateuch: An Introduction to the First Five Books of the Bible*. New York: Doubleday, 1992.

———. "A Post-exilic Lay Source in Genesis 1–11." In *Abschied vom Jahwisten. Die Komposition des Hexateuch in der jüngsten Diskussion*, edited by Jan Christian Gertz, Konrad Schmid, and Markus Witte, 49–61. BZAW 315. Berlin: de Gruyter, 2002.

———. "The Structure of P." *Catholic Biblical Quarterly* 38, no. 3 (1976): 275–92.

———. "Uncreation: The Great Flood: Gen 6:5–9:17." In *The Pentateuch*, edited by L. Bright. Chicago: ACTA, 1971.

Boomershine, Thomas E. "The Structure of Narrative Rhetoric in Genesis 2–3." *Semeia* 18 (1980): 113–29.

Borger, R. "Gen. iv 1." *Vetus Testamentum* 9, no. 1 (1959): 85–86.

Borgman, Paul. *Genesis: The Story We Haven't Heard*. Downers Gove: IVP Academic, 2001.

Bosserman, Christina. "Seeing Double: An Iconographic Reading of Genesis 2–3." In *Distinctions with a Difference: Essays on Myth, History, and Scripture in Honor of John N. Oswalt*, edited by Bill T. Arnold and Lawson G. Stone, 39–61. Wilmore: First Fruits, 2017.

Bray, Gerald. "The Significance of God's Image in Man." *Tyndale Bulletin* 42, no. 2 (1991): 195–225.

Brodie, Thomas L. *Genesis as Dialogue: A Literary, Historical, and Theological Commentary*. New York: Oxford University Press, 2001.

Brown, William P. *The Seven Pillars of Creation: The Bible, Science, and the Ecology of Wonder*. Oxford: Oxford University Press, 2010.

Brueggemann, Walter. "David and His Theologian." *Catholic Biblical Quarterly* 30, no. 2 (1968): 156–81.

———. "From Dust to Kingship." *ZAW* 84 (1972): 1–18.

———. *Genesis*. Interpretation: A Bible Commentary for Teaching and Preaching. Atlanta: John Knox, 1982.

———. "The Kerygma of the Priestly Writers." *ZAW* 84 (1972): 397–414.

Bührer, W. "Göttersöhne und Menschentöchter: Gen 6,1–4 als innerbiblische Schriftauslegung." *ZAW* 123 (2011): 495–515.

Calvin, J. *Genesis*. Edinburgh: Calvin Translation Society, 1847.

Carmichael, Calum M. "The Paradise Myth: Interpreting without Jewish and Christian Spectacles." In *A Walk in the Garden: Biblical, Iconographical and Literary Images of Eden*, edited by Paul Morris and Deborah Sawyer, 47–63. JSOTSup 136. Sheffield: Sheffield Academic Press, 1992.

Carr, David M. *The Formation of the Hebrew Bible: A New Reconstruction*. Oxford: Oxford University Press, 2011.

———. *The Hebrew Bible: A Contemporary Introduction to the Christian Old Testament and the Jewish Tanakh*. Hoboken: Wiley-Blackwell, 2021.

———. *An Introduction to the Old Testament: Sacred Texts and Imperial Contexts of the Hebrew Bible*. Chichester: Wiley-Blackwell, 2010.

———. *Reading the Fractures of Genesis: Historical and Literary Approaches*. Louisville: Westminster John Knox, 1996.

———. "The Politics of Textual Subversion: A Diachronic Perspective on the Garden of Eden Story." *Journal of Biblical Literature* 112, no. 4 (1993): 577–95.

———. "Βίβλος γενέσεως Revisited: A Synchronic Analysis of Patterns in Genesis as Part of the Torah (Part One)." *ZAW* 110 (1998): 159–72.

———. "Βίβλος γενέσεως Revisited: A Synchronic Analysis of Patterns in Genesis as Part of the Torah (Part Two)." *ZAW* 110 (1998): 327–47.

Cassuto, U. *A Commentary on the Book of Genesis*. Part 1, *From Adam to Noah: Genesis 1—VI 8*. Jerusalem: Magnes, 1989.

———. "The Episode of the Sons of God and the Daughters of Man (Genesis 6:1–4)." In *Biblical and Oriental Studies*. Vol. 1: *Bible*, 17–28. Jerusalem: Magnes, 1973.

Castellino, G. "The Origins of Civilization according to Biblical and Cuneiform Texts." In *"I Studied Inscriptions from before the Flood:" Ancient Near Eastern, Literary, and Linguistic Approaches to Genesis 1–11*, edited by Richard S. Hess and David Toshio Tsumura, 75–95. SBTS 4. Winona Lake: Eisenbrauns, 1994.

Chapman, Cynthia R. "The Breath of Life: Speech, Gender, and Authority in the Garden of Eden." *Journal of Biblical Literature* 138, no. 2 (2019): 242–62.

Charlesworth, James H. *The Good and Evil Serpent: How a Universal Symbol Became Christianized*. The Anchor Yale Bible Reference Library. New Haven: Yale University Press, 2010.

Clark, W. Malcolm. "The Flood and the Structure of the Pre-patriarchal History." *ZAW* 83 (1971): 184–211.

———. "A Legal Background to the Yahwist's Use of 'Good and Evil' in Genesis 2–3." *Journal of Biblical Literature* 88, no. 3 (1969): 266–78.

Clifford, Richard J. *Creation Accounts in the Ancient Near East and in the Bible*. CBQMS 26. Washington, DC: Catholic Biblical Association, 1994.

———. "The Hebrew Scriptures and the Theology of Creation." *Theological Studies* 46, no. 3 (1985): 507–23.

Clines, David J. A. "The Failure of the Flood." In *Making a Difference: Essays on the Hebrew Bible and Judaism in Honor of Tamara Cohn Eskenazi*, edited by David J. A. Clines, Kent Harold Richards, Jacob L. Wright, 74–84. HBM 49. Sheffield: Sheffield Phoenix Press, 2012.

———. "Noah's Flood: The Theology of the Flood Narrative." *Faith and Thought* 100, no. 2 (1972–73): 128–42.

———. "The Significance of the 'Sons of God' Episode (Genesis 6:1–4) in the Context of the 'Primeval History' (Genesis 1–11)." *Journal for the Study of the Old Testament* 13, no. 4 (1979): 33–46.

———. "Theme in Genesis 1–11." *Catholic Biblical Quarterly* 38, no. 4 (1976): 483–507.

———. *The Theme of the Pentateuch*. JSOTSup 10. Sheffield: JSOT Press, 1978.

Cohn, Robert L. "Narrative Structure and Canonical Perspective in Genesis." *Journal for the Study of the Old Testament* 8, no. 25 (1983): 3–16.

Cotter, D. W. *Genesis*. Berit Olam: Studies in Hebrew Narrative and Poetry. Collegeville: Liturgical Press, 2003.

Crites, S. "Unfinished Figure: On Theology and Imagination." In *Unfinished..: Essays in Honor of Ray Hart*, edited by Mark C. Taylor, 155–84. JAARTS. Chico: Scholars Press, 1981.

Croatto, J. Severino. "A Reading of the Story of the Tower of Babel from the Perspective of Non-Identity: Gen 11:1–9 in the Context of Its Production." In *Teaching the Bible: The Discourse and Politics of Biblical Pedagogy*, edited by Fernando F. Segovia and Mary Ann Tolbert, 203–23. Maryknoll: Orbis, 1998.

———. "Reading the Pentateuch as a Counter-Text: A New Interpretation of Genesis 1:14–19." In *Congress Volume Leiden 2004*, VTSup 109, edited by A. Lemaire, 383–400. Leiden: Brill, 2006.

Cross, Frank Moore. *Canaanite Myth and Hebrew Epic: Essays in the History of the Religion of Israel*. Cambridge: Harvard University Press, 1973.

Crouch, C. L. "חטאת as Interpolative Gloss. A Solution to Gen 4,7." *ZAW* 123 (2011): 250–58.

Crüsemann, F. "Autonomie und Sünde. Gen 4,7 und die 'jahwistische' Urgeschichte." In *Traditionen der Befreiung*. Vol. 1: *Methodische Zugänge*, edited by Willy Schottroff and Wolfgang Stegemann, 60–77. Munich: Kaiser, 1980.

———. "Die Eigenständigkeit der Urgeschichte. Ein Beitrag zur Diskussion um den 'Jahwisten.'" In *Die Botschaft und die Boten. Festschrift für Hans Walter Wolff zum 70. Geburtstag*, edited by J. Jeremias and L. Perlitt, 11–29. Neukirchen-Vluyn: Neukirchener Verlag, 1981.

———. *The Torah: Theology and Social History of Old Testament Law*. Minneapolis: Fortress, 1996.

Curtis, E. M. "Images in Mesopotamia and the Bible: A Comparative Study." In *The Bible in the Light of Cuneiform Literature: Scripture in Context III*, edited by William W. Hallo, Bruce William Jones, Gerald L. Mattingly, 31–56. ANETS 8. Lewiston: Edwin Mellen, 1990.

Czövek T. "Diversity vs. Uniformity – Some Observations on Primeval History." In *Christian Values vs. Contemporary Values*, edited by C. Constantineanu, G. Raţă, P. Runcan, 275–82. Puturea de a fi altafel 2. Bukarest: EDP, 2014.

———. "Babilon és Genezis — Egy bibliai szakasz értelmezése 21. századi kitekintéssel." In *Vallási pluralizmus, vallásközi párbeszéd és kortárs ideológiák: Magyar protestáns teológiai kitekintése*, edited by Á. Kovács, 184–207. Budapest: Kálvin, 2013.

Dalley, Stephanie. *Myths from Mesopotamia*. Oxford: Oxford University Press, 2000.

Darshan, G. "Ruaḥ 'Elohim in Genesis 1:2 in Light of Phoenician Cosmogonies: A Tradition's History." *Journal of Northwest Semitic Languages* 45, no. 2 (2019): 51–78.
Dauphinais, Michael, and Matthew Levering. *Holy People, Holy Land: A Theological Introduction to the Bible*. Grand Rapids: Brazos, 2005.
Davila, James R. "The Flood Hero as King and Priest." *Journal of Near Eastern Studies* 54, no. 3 (1995): 199–214.
Day, John. *From Creation to Abraham: Further Studies in Genesis 1–11*. London: T&T Clark, 2022.
———. "The Flood and the Ten Antediluvian Figures in Berossus and in the Pirestly Source in Genesis." In *From Creation to Babel: Studies in Genesis 1–11*, 61–76. LHB/OTS 592. London: Bloomsbury, 2013.
———. "The Meaning and Background of the Priestly Creation Story (Genesis 1.1–2.4A)." In *From Creation to Babel: Studies in Genesis 1–11*, 1–23. LHB/OTS 592. London: Bloomsbury, 2013.
deClaissé-Walford, Nancy L. "God Came Down . . . and God Scattered: Acts of Punishment or Acts of Grace?" *Review and Expositor* 103, no. 2 (2006): 403–17.
Diffey, Daniel S. "The Royal Promise in Genesis: The Often Underestimated Importance of Genesis 17:6, 17:16 and 35:11." *Tyndale Bulletin* 62, no. 2 (2011): 313–16.
Dobbs-Allsopp, F. W. "Tragedy, Tradition, and Theology in the Book of Lamentations." *Journal for the Study of the Old Testament* 22, no. 74 (1997): 29–60.
Dohmen, Christoph. "Die Statue von Tell Fecherīje und die Gottebenbildlichkeit des Menschen. Ein Beitrag zur Bilderterminologie." *Biblische Notizen* 22 (1983): 91–106.
Dragga, Sam. "Genesis 2–3: A Story of Liberation." *Journal for the Study of the Old Testament* 17, no. 55 (1992): 3–13.
Ebeling, E. "Enki (Ea)." In *Reallexikon der Assyriologie und Vorderasiatischen Archäologie*. Vol. 2, *Ber–Ezur*, edited by E. Ebeling and B. Meissner, 374–79. Berlin: de Gruyter, 1938.
Eco, Umberto. *The Role of the Reader: Explorations in the Semiotics of Texts*. Advances in Semiotics Series. Bloomington: Indiana University Press, 1979.
Embry, Brad. "The 'Naked Narrative' from Noah to Leviticus: Reassessing Voyeurism in the Account of Noah's Nakedness in Genesis 9.22–24." *Journal for the Study of the Old Testament* 35, no. 4 (2011): 417–33.
Enns, Peter. *The Evolution of Adam: What the Bible Does and Doesn't Say about Human Origins*. Grand Rapids: Brazos, 2012.

Fauth, Wolfgang. "Der königliche Gärtner und Jäger im Paradeisos. Beobachtungen zur Rolle des Herrschers in der vorderasiatischen Hortikultur." *Persica* 8 (1979): 1–53.

Finkelstein, J. J. "The Antediluvian Kings: A University of California Tablet." *Journal of Cuneiform Studies* 17, no. 2 (1963): 39–51.

———. "The Genealogy of the Hammurapi Dynasty." *Journal of Cuneiform Studies* 20, no. 3/4 (1966): 95–118.

Firmage, Edwin. "Genesis 1 and the Priestly Agenda." *Journal for the Study of the Old Testament* 24, no. 82 (1999): 97–114.

Fisher, Eugene. "*Gilgamesh* and Genesis: The Flood Story in Context." *Catholic Biblical Quarterly* 32, no. 3 (1970): 392–403.

Fockner, Sven. "Reopening the Discussion: Another Contextual Look at the Sons of God." *Journal for the Study of the Old Testament* 32, no. 4 (2008): 435–56.

Foh, Susan T. "What is the Woman's Desire?" *Westminster Theological Journal* 37, no. 3 (1975): 376–83.

Fokkelman, J. P. *Narrative Art in Genesis: Specimens of Stylistic and Structural Analysis*. The Biblical Seminar 12. Eugene: Wipf & Stock, 1991.

Foster, Benjamin R. *Before the Muses: An Anthology of Akkadian Literature*. Bethesda: CDL Press, 2005.

Fox, E. "Can Genesis Be Read as a Book?" *Semeia* 46 (1989): 31–40.

———. "Stalking the Younger Brother: Some Models for Understanding a Biblical Motif." *Journal for the Study of the Old Testament* 18, no. 60 (1993): 45–68.

Frankel, David. "Noah's Drunkenness and the Curse of Canaan: A New Approach." *Journal of Biblical Literature* 140, no. 1 (2021): 49–68.

Frankfort, Henri. *Kingship and the Gods: A Study of Ancient Near Eastern Religion as the Integration of Society & Nature*. Chicago: University of Chicago Press, 1948.

Fretheim, Terence E. *Creation, Fall, and Flood: Studies in Genesis 1–11*. Minneapolis: Augsburg, 1969.

———. *God and World in the Old Testament: A Relational Theology of Creation*. Nashville: Abingdon, 2005.

Friedman, Richard E. *The Hidden Book in the Bible*. New York: HarperCollins, 1998.

Fritz, V. "'Solange die Erde steht' – Vom Sinn der jahwistischen Fluterzählung in Gen 6–8." *ZAW* 94 (1982): 599–614.

Frymer-Kensky, Tikva. "The Atrahasis Epic and Its Significance for Our Understanding of Genesis 1–9." *The Biblical Archaeologist* 40, no. 4 (1977): 147–55.

Fuchs, A. *Die Inschriften Sargons II. aus Khorsabad*. Göttingen: Cuvillier, 1993.

Galambush, Julie. *Reading Genesis: A Literary and Theological Commentary*. Reading the Old Testament. Macon: Smyth & Helwys, 2018.

Garr, W. Randall. *In His Own Image and Likeness: Humanity, Divinity, and Monotheism*. CHANE 15. Leiden: Brill, 2003.

George, A. R. *The Babylonian Gilgamesh Epic: Introduction, Critical Edition and Cuneiform Texts*. Vol. 1. Oxford: Oxford University Press, 2003.

———. *The Babylonian Gilgamesh Epic: Introduction, Critical Edition and Cuneiform Texts*. Vol. 2. Oxford: Oxford University Press, 2003.

———. *Babylonian Topographical Texts*. Orientalia Lovaniensia Analecta 40. Leuven: Peeters, 1992.

———. "The Gilgameš epic at Ugarit." *Aula Orientalis* 25, no. 2 (2007): 237–54.

———. *House Most High: The Temples of Ancient Mesopotamia*. Mesopotamian Civilizations 5. Winona Lake: Eisenbrauns, 1993.

———. "The Tower of Babel: Archaeology, History and Cuneiform Texts." *Archiv für Orientforschung* 51 (2005/2006): 75–95.

Gerhard, M. *Die Aussetzungsgeschichte des Mose. Literar- und traditionsgeschichtliche Untersuchungen zu einem Schlüsseltext des nichtpriesterschriftlichen Tetrateuch*. WMANT 109. Neukirchen-Vluyn: Neukirchener, 2006.

Gertz, Jan Christian. "Antibabylonische Polemik im priesterlichen Schöpfungsbericht?" *ZThK* 106 (2009): 137–55.

———. "Babel im Rücken und das Land vor Augen. Anmerkungen zum Abschluss der Urgeschichte und zum Anfang der Erzählungen von den Erzeltern Israels." In *Die Erzväter in der biblischen Tradition. Festschrift für Matthias Köckert*, edited by A. C. Hagedorn and H. Pfeiffer, 9–34. BZAW 400. Berlin: de Gruyter, 2009.

Gertz, Jan Christian, K. Schmid, and M. Witte, eds. *Abschied vom Jahwisten. Die Komposition des Hexateuch in der jüngsten Diskussion*. BZATW 315. Berlin: de Gruyter, 2002.

Gese, H. "Der bewachte Lebensbaum und die Heroen: zwei mythologische Erwägungen zur Urgeschichte der Quelle J." In *Wort und Geschichte. Festschrift für Karl Elliger zum 70. Geburtstag*, edited by H. Gese and P. Rüger, 77–85. AOAT 18. Neukirchen-Vluyn–Kevelaer: Neukirchener Verlag–Verlag Butzon & Bercker Kevelaer, 1973.

———. "Geschichtliches Denken im Alten Orient und im Alten Testament." *ZThK* 55, no. 2 (1958): 127–45.

Gevirtz, S. "Lamech's Song to His Wives (Genesis 4:23–24)." In *"I Studied Inscriptions from before the Flood:" Ancient Near Eastern, Literary, and Linguistic Approaches to Genesis 1–11*, edited by R. S. Hess and D. T. Tsumura, 405–15. SBTS 4. Winona Lake: Eisenbrauns, 1994.

Giorgetti, Andrew. "The 'Mock Building Account' of Genesis 11:1–9: Polemic against Mesopotamian Royal Ideology." *Vetus Testamentum* 64, no. 1 (2014): 1–20.

Gispen, W. H. "Who Was Nimrod?" In *The Law and the Prophets: Old Testament Studies Prepared in Honor of Oswald Thompson Allis*, edited by J. H. Skilton, 207–14. Nutley: Presbyterian and Reformed, 1974.

Gowan, Donald E. *Genesis 1–11: From Eden to Babel*. International Theological Commentary. Grand Rapids: Eerdmans, 1988.

Goldingay, John. *Models for Interpretation of Scripture*. Grand Rapids: Eerdmans, 1995.

———. *Old Testament Theology*. Vol. 1: *Israel's Gospel*. Downers Grove: InterVarsity Press, 2003.

———. "The Place of Ishmael." In *The World of Genesis: Persons, Places, Perspectives*, edited by Philip R. Davies and David J. A. Clines, 146–49. JSOTSup 257. Sheffield: Sheffield Academic Press, 1998.

———. "Postmodernizing Eve and Adam (Can I have my Appricot as well as Eating it?)." In *The World of Genesis: Persons, Places, Perspectives*, edited by Philip R. Davies and David J. A. Clines, 50–59. JSOTSup 257. Sheffield: Sheffield Academic Press, 1998.

Good, Edwin M. *Genesis 1–11: Tales of the Earliest World*. Stanford: Stanford University Press, 2011.

Gordon, Cyrus H. "'This Time' (Genesis 2:23)." In *Sha'arei Talmon: Studies in the Bible, Qumran, and the Ancient Near East Presented to Shemaryahu Talmon*, edited by Michael Fishbane, Emanuel Tov, and Weston W. Fields, 47–51. Winona Lake: Eisenbrauns, 1992.

Green, Barbara. *King Saul's Asking*. Interfaces. Collegeville: Liturgical Press: 2003.

Greenfield, J. C. "Apkallu." *Dictionary of Deities and Demons in the Bible*, edited by Karel van der Toorn, Bob Becking, Pieter W. van der Horst, 72–74. Grand Rapids: Eerdmans, 1999.

Gros Louis, K. R. R. "Genesis I–II." In *Literary Interpretations of Biblical Narratives*. Vol. I, edited by K. R. R. Gros Luis and J. Ackermann, 41–51. Nashville: Abingdon, 1974.

———. "Genesis 3–11." In *Literary Interpretations of Biblical Narratives*. Vol. II, edited by K. R. R. Gros Luis and J. Ackermann, 37–52. Nashville: Abingdon, 1982.

Gross, W. "Die Gottebenbildlichkeit des Menschen im Kontext der Priesterschrift." *Theologische Quartalschrift* 161 (1981): 244–64.

Gunkel, H. "The Influence of Babylonian Mythology Upon the Biblical Creation Story." In *Creation in the Old Testament*, edited by Bernhard W. Anderson, 25–52. Issues in Religion and Theology 6. Philadelphia: Fortress, 1984.

Hallo, William W. "Antediluvian Cities." *Journal of Cuneiform Studies* 23, no. 3 (1971): 57–67.

———. "Biblical History in its Near Eastern Setting: The Contextual Approach." In *Scripture in Context*. Vol. 1: *Essays on the Comparative Method*, edited by Carl D. Evans, William W. Hallo, and John B. White, 1–26. PTMS 34. Pittsburgh: Pickwick, 1980.

———. "The Birth of Kings." In *The World's Oldest Literature: Studies in Sumerian Belles-Lettres*, 223–38. Culture and History of the Ancient Near East 35. Leiden: Brill, 2010.

———. "Compare and Contrast: The Contextual Approach to Biblical Literature." In *The Bible in the Light of Cuneiform Literature: Scripture in Context III*, edited by William W. Hallo, Bruce William Jones, and Gerald L. Mattingly, 1–30. ANETS 8. Lewiston: Edwin Mellen, 1990.

———. "Royal Ancestor Worship in the Biblical World." In *Sha'arei Talmon: Studies in the Bible, Qumran, and the Ancient Near East Presented to Shemaryahu Talmon*, edited by Michael Fishbane, Emanuel Tov, Weston W. Fields, 381–401. Winona Lake: Eisenbrauns, 1992.

———. "Royal Hymns and Mesopotamian Unity." In *The World's Oldest Literature: Studies in Sumerian Belles-Lettres*, 175–86. Culture and History of the Ancient Near East 35. Leiden: Brill, 2010.

———. "Scurrilous Etymologies." In *Pomegranates and Golden Bells: Studies in Biblical, Jewish, and Near Eastern Ritual, Law, and Literature in Honor of Jacob Milgrom*, edited by David P. Wright, David Noel Freedman, Avi Hurwitz, 767–76. Winona Lake: Eisenbrauns, 1995.

———. "Sumerian Religion." In *The World's Oldest Literature: Studies in Sumerian Belles-Lettres*, 93–111. Culture and History of the Ancient Near East 35. Leiden: Brill, 2010.

———. "Text, Statues and the Cult of the Divine King." In *Congress Volume Jerusalem 1986*, edited by J. A. Emerton, 54–66. VTSup 40. Leiden: Brill, 1988.

———. "Urban Origins in Cuneiform and Biblical Sources (Founding Myths of Cities in the Ancient Near East: Mesopotamia and Israel)." In *The World's Oldest Literature: Studies in Sumerian Belles-Lettres*, 547–72. Culture and History of the Ancient Near East 35. Leiden: Brill, 2010.

Hallo, William W., and William Kelly Simpson. *The Ancient Near East: A History*. Fort Worth: Harcourt Brace College, 1998.

Hamilton, James M. "The Seed of the Woman and the Blessing of Abraham." *Tyndale Bulletin* 58, no. 2 (2007): 253–73.

Hamilton, Victor P. *The Book of Genesis: Chapters 1–17*. NICOT. Grand Rapids: Eerdmans, 1990.

Hanson, Paul D. "Jewish Apocalyptic Against Its Near Eastern Environment." *Revue Biblique* 78, no. 1 (1971): 31–58.

———. "Rebellion in Heaven, Azazel, and Euhemeristic Heroes in 1 Enoch 6–11." *Journal of Biblical Literature* 96, no. 2 (1977): 195–233.

Harland, P. J. "Vertical or Horizontal: The Sin of Babel." *Vetus Testamentum* 48, no. 4 (1998): 515–33.

Hartley, John E. *Genesis.* NIBC. Peabody: Hendrickson, 2000.

Hartman, Thomas C. "Some Thoughts on the Sumerian King List and Genesis 5 and 11b." *Journal of Biblical Literature* 91, no. 1 (1972): 25–32.

Hasel, Gerhard F. "The Significance of the Cosmology in Genesis I in Relation to Ancient Near Eastern Parallels." *Andrews University Seminary Studies* 10, no. 1 (1972): 1–20.

Hauser, Alan J. "Genesis 2–3: The Theme of Intimacy and Alienation." In *"I Studied Inscriptions from before the Flood:" Ancient Near Eastern, Literary, and Linguistic Approaches to Genesis 1–11*, edited by Richard S. Hess and David Toshio Tsumura, 383–98. SBTS 4. Winona Lake: Eisenbrauns, 1994.

———. "Linguistic and Thematic Links Between Genesis 4:1–16 and Genesis 2–3." *Journal of Evangelical Theological Society* 23, no. 4 (1980): 297–305.

Heger, Paul. "Source of Law in the Biblical and Mesopotamian Law Collections." *Biblica* 86, no. 3 (2005): 324–42.

Heidel, Alexander. *The Babylonian Genesis: The Story of the Creation.* Chicago: University of Chicago Press, 1951.

Heinzerling, R. "'Einweihung' durch Henoch? Die Bedeutung der Altersangaben in Gensis 5." *ZAW* 110 (1998): 581–89.

Hendel, Ronald S. "'Begetting' and 'Being Born' in the Pentateuch: Notes on Historical Linguistics and Source Criticism." *Vetus Testamentum* 50, no. 1 (2000): 38–46.

———. "Of Demigods and the Deluge: Toward an Interpretation of Genesis 6:1–4." *Journal of Biblical Literature* 106, no. 1 (1987): 13–26.

———. "Genesis 1–11 and Its Mesopotamian Problem." In *Cultural Borrowings and Ethnic Appropriations in Antiquity*, edited by Eric S. Gruen, 23–36. Stuttgart: Franz Steiner, 2005.

———. "Historical Context." In *The Book of Genesis: Composition, Reception, and Interpretation*, edited by Craig A. Evans, Joel N. Lohr, and David L. Petersen, 51–81. Leiden: Brill, 2012.

———. "Tangled Plots in Genesis." In *Fortunate the Eyes that See: Essays in Honor of David Noel Freedman in Celebration of His Seventieth Birthday*, edited by Astrid B. Beck, Andrew H. Bartlet, Paul R. Raabe, Chris A. Franke, 35–51. Grand Rapids: Eerdmans, 1995.

Herion, G. A. "Why God Rejected Cain's Offering: The Obvious Answer." In *Fortunate the Eyes that See: Essays in Honor of David Noel Freedman in Celebration of His Seventieth Birthday*, edited by Astrid B. Beck, Andrew H. Bartlet, Paul R. Raabe, Chris A. Franke, 52–65. Grand Rapids: Eerdmans, 1995.

Heschel, Abraham Joshua. *The Prophets: An Introduction.* Vol. 1. New York: Harper Torchbooks, 1962.

———. *The Sabbath: Its Meaning for Modern Man*. New York: Farrar, Straus and Giroux, 1951.
Hess, Richard S. "The Genealogies of Genesis 1–11 and Comparative Literature." *Biblica* 70, no. 2 (1989): 241–54.
———. "Lamech in the Genealogies of Genesis." *Bulletin for Biblical Research* 1, no. 1 (1991): 21–25.
———. *Studies in the Personal Names of Genesis 1–11*. AOAT 234. Kevelaer; Neukirchen-Vluyn: Butzon & Bercker Kevelaer; Neukirchener, 1993.
Hiebert, Theodore. "The Tower of Babel and the Origin of the World's Cultures." *Journal of Biblical Literature* 126, no. 1 (2007): 29–58.
Hieke, Thomas. *Die Genealogien der Genesis*. HBS 39. Freiburg: Herder, 2003.
Hill, Carol A. "Making Sense of the Numbers of Genesis." *Perspectives on Science and Christian Faith* 55, no. 4 (2003): 239–51.
Hoffmeier, James K. "Genesis 1–11 as History and Theology." In *Genesis: History, Fiction, or Neither? Three Views on the Bible's Earliest Chapters*, edited by Charles Halton and Stanley N. Gundry, 23–58. Grand Rapids: Zondervan, 2015.
Holloway, Steven W. *Aššur is King! Aššur is King! Religion in the Exercise of Power in the Neo-Assyrian Empire*. CHANE 10. Leiden: Brill, 2002.
———. "The Shape of Utnapishtim's Ark: A Rejoinder." *ZAW* 110 (1998): 617–26.
———. "What Ship Goes There: The Flood Narratives in the Gilgamesh Epic and Genesis. Consideration in Light of Ancient Near Eastern Temple Ideology." *ZAW* 103 (1991): 328–55.
Hom, Mary Katherine Y. H. "'. . . A Mighty Hunter before YHWH': Genesis 10:9 and the Moral-Theological Evaluation of Nimrod." *Vetus Testamentum* 60, no. 1 (2010): 63–68.
Hoopen, Robin B ten. "Genesis 5 and the Formation of the Primeval History: A Redactional Historical Case Study." *ZAW* 129 (2017): 177–93.
———. "Where Are You, Enoch? Why Can't I Find You? Genesis 5:21–24 Reconsidered." *Journal of Hebrew Scriptures* 18 (2018): 1–23.
Houtman, C. "What Did Jacob See in His Dream at Bethel? Some Remarks on xxviii 10–22." *Vetus Testamentum* 27, no. 3 (1977): 337–51.
Huizinga, J. "A Definition of the Concept of History." In *Philosophy and History: Essays Presented to Ernst Cassirer*, edited by Raymond Klibansky and H. J. Paton, 1–10. Oxford: Clarendon, 1936.
Hulst, A. R. "בנה, bnh, bauen." In *Theologisches Handwörterbuch zum Alten Testament*. Vol. 1, edited by Ernst Jenni and Claus Westermann, 325–27. Munich; Zurich: Kaiser; Theologischer Verlag, 1971.
Hurowitz, Victor. *I have Built You an Exalted House: Temple Building in the Bible in the Light of Mesopotamian and Northwest Semitic Writings*. JSOTSup 115. Sheffield: Sheffield Academic Press, 1992.

Hutzli, Jürg. "The Procreation of Seth by Adam in Gen 5:3 and the Composition of Gen 5." *Semitica* 54 (2012): 147–62.

Isaac, J. R. "Here Comes This Dreamer." In *From Babel to Babylon: Essays on Biblical History and Literature in Honor of Brian Peckham*, edited by Joyce Rilett Wood, John E. Harvey, and Mark Leuchter, 237–52. The Library of Hebrew Bible/Old Testament Studies 455. New York: T&T Clark, 2006.

Jacob, Benno. *Das erste Buch der Tora: Genesis*. Berlin: Schocken, 1934.

———. *The First Book of the Bible: Genesis*. New York: KTAV, 1974.

Jacobsen, Thorkild. "The Battle between Marduk and Tiamat." *Journal of the American Oriental Society* 88, no. 1 (1968): 104–8.

———. "Early Political Development in Mesopotamia." *Zeitschrift für Assyriologie* 52 (1957): 91–140.

———. "The Eridu Genesis." *Journal of Biblical Literature* 100, no. 4 (1981): 513–29.

———. "Lugalbanda and Ninsuna." *Journal of Cuneiform Studies* 41, no. 1 (1989): 69–86.

———. "Primitive Democracy in Ancient Mesopotamia." *Journal of Near Eastern Studies* 2, no. 3 (1943): 159–72.

———. "Political Institutions, Literature, and Religion." In *City Invincible: A Symposium on Urbanization and Cultural Development in the Ancient Near East*, edited by Carl H. Kraeling and Robert McC Adams, 61–94. Chicago: University of Chicago Press, 1960.

———. *The Sumerian King List*. Assyriological Studies 11. Chicago: University of Chicago Press, 1939.

Janowski, Bernd. "Die lebendige Statue Gottes. Zur Anthropologie der priesterlichen Urgeschichte." In *Die Welt als Schöpfung, 140–71*. BThAT 4. Neukirchen-Vluyn: Neukirchener, 2008.

Jenkins, Allan K. "A Great Name: Genesis 12:2 and the Editing of the Pentateuch." *Journal for the Study of the Old Testament* 4, no. 10 (1979): 41–57.

Jensen, P. "Babylonischer Turm." In *Reallexikon der Assyriologie und Vorderasiatischen Archäologie*. Vol. 1, edited by E. Ebeling and B. Meissner, 384–86. Berlin; Leipzig: de Gruyter, 1928.

Johnson, Richard. "Patriarchal Ages in Genesis." *Perspectives on Science and Christian Faith* 56, no. 2 (2004): 152–53.

Joines, K. R. "The Serpent in Gen 3." *ZAW* 87 (1975): 1–11.

Jónsson, Gunnlaugur A. *The Image of God: Genesis 1:26–28 in a Century of Old Testament Research*. CBOTS 26. Lund: Almquist & Wiksell International, 1988.

Kaminski, Carol M. "Beautiful Women or 'False Judgment'? Interpreting Genesis 6.2 in the Context of the Primeval History." *Journal for the Study of the Old Testament* 32, no. 4 (2008): 457–73.

Kawashima, Robert S. "*Homo Faber* in J's Primeval History." *ZAW* 116 (2004): 483–501.

———. "Violence and the City: On the Yahwist's Leviathan." *Near Eastern Archaeology* 78, no. 4 (2015): 264–72.

Kearney, P. J. "Creation and Liturgy: The P Redaction of Ex 25–40." *ZAW* 89 (1977): 375–87.

Keil, Carl Friedrich. *Biblical Commentary on the Old Testament*. Vol. 1: *The Pentateuch*. Grand Rapids: Eerdmans, 1949.

Keiter, Sheila Tuller. "Outsmarting God: Egyptian Slavery and the Tower of Babel." *Jewish Biblical Quarterly* 41, no. 2 (2013): 200–204.

Kessler, Martin. "Rhetorical Criticism of Gen 7." In *Rhetorical Criticism: Essays in Honor of James Muilenburg*, edited by Jared Judd Jackson and Martin Kessler, 1–17. Pittsburgh Theological Monograph Series 1. Pittsburgh: Pickwick, 1974.

Kessler, Martin, and Karel Deurloo. *A Commentary on Genesis: The Book of Beginnings*. Mahwah: Paulist, 2004.

Kikawada, Isaac M. "The Double Creation of Mankind in *Enki and Ninmah*, *Atrahasis* I 1–351, and *Genesis* 1–2." *Iraq* 45, no. 1 (1983): 43–45.

———. "Genesis on Three Levels." *Annual of the Japanese Biblical Institute* 7 (1981): 3–15.

———. "Literary Convention of the Primeval History." *Annual of the Japanese Biblical Institute* 1 (1975): 3–21.

———. "The Shape of Genesis 11:1–9." In *Rhetorical Criticism: Essays in Honor of James Muilenburg*, edited by Jared Judd Jackson and Martin Kessler, 18–32. Pittsburgh Theological Monograph Series 1. Pittsburgh: Pickwick, 1974.

———. "Two Notes on Eve." *Journal of Biblical Literature* 91, no. 1 (1972): 33–37.

Kikawada, Isaac M., and Arthur Quinn. *Before Abraham Was: The Unity of Genesis 1–11*. Nashville: Abingdon, 1985.

Kilmer, Anne Draffkorn. "The Mesopotamian Concept of Overpopulation and its Solution as Reflected in the Mythology." *Orientalia* 41, no. 2 (1972): 160–77.

———. "The Mesopotamian Counterparts of the Biblical *Nĕpīlîm*." In *Perspectives on Language and Text: Essays and Poems in Honor of Francis I. Andersen's Sixtieth Birthday July 28, 1985*, edited by Edgar W. Conrad and Edawrd G. Newing, 39–43. Winona Lake: Eisenbrauns, 1987.

King, L. W. *Babylonian Boundary-Stones and Memorial-Tablets in the British Museum*. London: British Museum, 1912.

Kline, Meredith G. "Divine Kingship and Genesis 6:1–4." *Westminster Theological Journal* 24, no. 2 (1962): 187–204.

Knierim, Rolf P. *The Task of Old Testament Theology: Substance, Method, and Cases*. Grand Rapids: Eerdmans, 1995.

Kooij, A. van der. "The Story of Genesis 11:1–9 and the Culture of Ancient Mesopotamia." *Bibliotheca Orientalis* 53 (1996): 28–38.

Kraeling, E. G. H. "The Earliest Hebrew Flood Story." *Journal of Biblical Literature* 66, no. 3 (1947): 279–93.

———. "The Significance and Origin of Gen. 6:1–4." *Journal of Near Eastern Studies* 6, no. 4 (1947): 193–208.

———. "The Tower of Babel." *Journal of the American Oriental Society* 40 (1920): 276–81.

Kramer, S. N. *History Begins at Sumer: Thirty-Nine Firsts in Man's Recorded History.* Philadelphia: University of Pennsylvania Press, 1981.

———. "Man's Golden Age: A Sumerian Parallel to Genesis XI. 1." *Journal of the American Oriental Society* 63, no. 3 (1943): 191–94.

Kraus, F. R. "Zur Liste der älteren Könige von Babylonien." *Zeitschrift für Assyriologie und Vorderasiatische Archäologie* 50 (1952): 29–60.

Kreuzer, S. "Saul – not always – at War: A New Perspective on the Rise of Kingship in Israel." In *Saul in Story and Tradition*, edited by Carl S. Ehrlich and Marsha C. White, 39–58. FAT 47. Tübingen: Mohr Siebeck, 2006.

Kvanvig, Helge S. "Gen 6,1–4 as an Antediluvian Event." *Scandinavian Journal of the Old Testament* 16, no. 1 (2002): 79–112.

———. *Primeval History: Babylonian, Biblical, and Enochic: An Intertextual Reading.* JSJSup 149. Leiden: Brill, 2011.

LaCocque, André. *The Trial of Innocence: Adam, Eve, and the Yahwist.* Eugene: Cascade, 2006.

———. "Whatever Happened in the Valley of Shinar? A Response to Theodore Hiebert." *Journal of Biblical Literature* 128, no. 1 (2009): 29–41.

Lambert, W. G. "Another Look at Hammurabi's Ancestors." *Journal of Cuneiform Studies* 22, no. 1 (1968): 1–2.

———. "The Great Battle of the Mesopotamian Religious Year: The Conflict in the Akītu House." *Iraq* 25, no. 2 (1963): 189–90.

———. "The History of the muš-ḫuš in Ancient Mesopotamia." In *L'animal, l'homme, le dieu dans le Proche-Orient ancien: Actes du Colloque de Cartigny 1981*, edited by Philippe Borgeaud, Yves Christe, and Ivanka Urio, 87–94. Les Cahiers du CEPOA 2. Leuven: Peeters, 1985.

———. "Myth and Ritual as Conceived by the Babylonians." *Journal of Semitic Studies* 13, no. 1 (1968): 104–12.

———. "A New Fragment from a List of Antediluvian Kings and Marduk's Chariot." In *Symbolae Biblicae et Mesopotamicae Francisco Mario Theodoro De Liagre Böhl dedicatae*, edited by M. A. Beek, A. A. Kampman, C. Nijland, J. Ryckmans, 271–80. Leiden: Brill, 1973.

———. "A New Look at the Babylonian Background of Genesis." *Journal of Theological Studies* 16, no. 2 (1965): 287–300.

Lambert, W. G., and A. R. Millard. *Atra-Ḥasis: The Babylonian Story of the Flood.* Oxford: Clarendon, 1969.

Langdon, S. *Building Inscriptions of the Neo-Babylonian Empire*. Paris: Leroux, 1905.
Larsson, Gerhard. "Chronological Parallels between the Creation and the Flood." *Vetus Testamentum* 27, no. 4 (1977): 490–92.
Leichty, E. "The Colophon." In *Studies Presented to A. Leo Oppenheim, June 7, 1964*, edited by Robert D. Biggs and John A. Brinkman, 147–54. Chicago: University of Chicago Press, 1964.
Levenson, Jon D. *Creation and the Persistence of Evil: The Jewish Drama of Divine Omnipotence*. Princeton: Princeton University Press, 1988.
Levin, Y. "Nimrod the Mighty, King of Kish, King of Sumer and Akkad." *Vetus Testamentum* 52, no. 3 (2002): 350–66.
———. "Understanding Biblical Genealogies." *Currents in Research: Biblical Studies* 9 (2001): 11–46.
Lewis, Theodore J. "CT 13.33–34 and Ezekiel 32: Lion-Dragon Myths." *Journal of the American Oriental Society* 116, no. 1 (1996): 28–47.
Lim, Johnson T. K. *Grace in the Midst of Judgement: Grappling with Genesis 1–11*. BZAW 314. Berlin: de Gruyter, 2002.
Liverani, M. "Adapa, Guest of the Gods." In *Myth and Politics in Ancient Near Eastern Historiography*, edited by Zainab Bahrani and Marc Van de Mieroop, 3–23. Studies in Egyptology and the Ancient Near East. London: Equinox, 2004.
Lohr, J. N. "Sexual Desire? Eve, Genesis 3:16, and תשוקה." *Journal of Biblical Literature* 130, no. 2 (2011): 227–46.
Loewenstamm, Samuel E. "The Flood." In *Comparative Studies in Biblical and Ancient Oriental Literature*, 93–121. AOAT 204. Kevelaer; Neukirchen-Vluyn: Butzon & Bercker; Neukirchener Verlag, 1980.
Longacre, Robert E. "The Discourse Structure of the Flood Narrative." *Journal of the American Academy of Religion* 47, no. 1 (1979): 89–133.
Longman, Tremper, III. *Genesis*. The Story of God Bible Commentary. Grand Rapids: Zondervan, 2016.
Lowery, Daniel D. *Toward a Poetics of Genesis 1–11: Reading Genesis 4:17–22 in Its Near Eastern Context*. BBRSup 7. Winona Lake: Eisenbrauns, 2013.
Măcelaru, Marcel V. "Babel from Text to Symbol: Possibilities of Reconciliation in the Hebrew Bible." In *Reconciliation: The Way of Healing and Growth*, edited by Janez Juhant and Bojan Žalec, 51–58. Theologie Ost-West: Europäische Perspektiven 16. Berlin: LIT, 2012.
Machinist, P. "How Gods Die, Biblically and Otherwise. A Problem of Cosmic Restructuring." In *Reconsidering the Concept of Revolutionary Monotheism*, edited by Beate Pongratz-Leisten 187–239.Winona Lake: Eisenbrauns, 2011.
Malamat, Abraham. "The Arameans." In *Peoples of Old Testament Times*, edited by D. J. Wiseman, 134–55. Oxford: Clarendon, 1973.

———. "King Lists of the Old Babylonian Period and Biblical Genealogies." *Journal of the American Oriental Society* 88, no. 1 (1968): 163–73.
Mallowan, M. E. L. "Noah's Flood Reconsidered." *Iraq* 26, no. 2 (1964): 62–82.
Matthews, Victor H., and Don C. Benjamin. *Social World of Ancient Israel 1250–587 BCE*. Peabody: Hendrickson, 1993.
McConville, J. G. *God and Earthly Power: An Old Testament Political Theology: Genesis–Kings*. LHBOTS 454. New York: T&T Clark, 2006.
McDowell, Catherine L. *The Image of God in the Garden of Eden: The Creation of Humankind in Genesis 2:5—3:24 in Light of* mīs pî pīt pî *and* wpt-r *Rituals of Mesopotamia and Ancient Egypt*. Siphrut 15. Winona Lake: Eisenbrauns: 2015.
McEntire, Mark, and Wongi Park. "Ethnic Fission and Fusion in Biblical Genealogies." *Journal of Biblical Literature* 140, no. 1 (2021): 31–47.
McKeown, James. *Genesis*. The Two Horizons OT Commentary. Grand Rapids: Eerdmans, 2008.
Melvin, David P. "Divine Mediation and the Rise of Civilization in Mesopotamian Literature and in Genesis 1–11." *Journal of Hebrew Scriptures* 10 (2010): 2–15.
Meyers, Carol L. *The Tabernacle Menorah*. Missoula: Scholars Press, 1976.
Middleton, J. Richard. "The Liberating Image? Interpreting the Imago Dei in Context." *Christian Scholars Review* 24, no. 1 (1994): 8–25.
Míguez, N. O. "A Comparative Bible Study of Genesis 10–11: 9: An Approach from the Argentine." In *Scripture, Community, and Mission: Essays in Honor of D. Preman Niles*, edited by Philip Lauri Wickeri, 152–65. Hong Kong: CCA, 2002.
Miles, Jack. *God: A Biography*. London: Touchstone, 1995.
Millard, A. R. "The Celestial Ladder and the Gate of Heaven (Genesis xxviii. 12, 17)." *Expository Times* 78 (1966): 86–87.
———. "A New Babylonian 'Genesis' Story." *Tyndale Bulletin* 18, no. 1 (1967): 3–18.
Miller, Patrick D., Jr. "Eridu, Dunnu, and Babel: A Study in Comparative Mythology." *Hebrew Annual Review* 9 (1985): 227–51.
Miller, Robert. "What the Old Testament Can Contribute to an Understanding of Divine Creation." *Heythrop Journal* 60 (2019): 29–40.
Miscall, Peter D. "Jacques Derrida in the Garden of Eden." *Union Seminary Quarterly Review* 44 (1990): 1–9.
Moberly, R. W. L. *The Old Testament of the Old Testament: Patriarchal Narratives and Mosaic Yahwism*. Eugene: Wipf and Stock, 1992.
———. *The Theology of the Book of Genesis*. Old Testament Theology. Cambridge: Cambridge University Press, 2009.
———. "Why Did Noah Send out a Raven?" *Vetus Testamentum* 50, no. 3 (2000): 345–56.

Mobley, Gregory. "The Wild Man in the Bible and the Ancient Near East." *Journal of Biblical Literature* 116, no. 2 (1997): 217–33.

Mowinckel, Sigmund. *The Two Sources of the Predeuteronomic History (JE) in Gen. 1–11*. AUNVAOHFK 2. Oslo: Dybwad, 1937.

Moye, Richard H. "In the Beginning: Myth and History in Genesis and Exodus." *Journal of Biblical Literature* 109, no. 4 (1990): 577–98.

Muffs, Yochanan. "Abraham the Noble Warrior: Patriarchal Politics and Laws of War in Ancient Israel." *Journal of Jewish Studies* 33, nos. 1–2 (1982): 81–107.

Müller, Hans Peter. "Das Motiv für die Sintflut: Die hermeneutische Funktion des Mythos und seiner Analyse." *ZAW* 97 (1985): 295–316.

———. "Neue Parallelen zu Gen 2,7: Zur Bedeutung der Religionsgeschichte für die Exegese des Alten Testaments." In *Immigration and Emigration within the Ancient Near East: Festschrift E. Lipiński*, edited by K. van Lerberghe and A. Schoors, 195–204. OLA 65. Leuven: Peeters, 1995.

Neville, Richard. "Differentiation in Genesis 1: An Exegetical Creation *ex nihilo*." *Journal of Biblical Literature* 130, no. 2 (2011): 209–26.

Niehr, H. "In Search of Yhwh's Cult Statue in the First Temple." In *The Image and the Book: Iconic Cults, Aniconism, and the Rise of Book Religion in Israel and the Ancient Near East*, edited by K. van der Toorn, 73–95. Leuven: Peeters, 1997.

Nielsen, Eduard. "Creation and the Fall of Man: A Cross-Disciplinary Investigation." *Hebrew Union College Annual* 43 (1972): 1–22.

Niskanen, Paul. "The Poetics of Adam: The Creation of אדם in the Image of אלהים." *Journal of Biblical Literature* 128, no. 3 (2009): 417–36.

Nissinen, Martti. *Homoeroticism in the Biblical World: A Historical Perspective*. Minneapolis: Fortress, 1998.

Nötscher, F. "Enlil." *Reallexikon der Assyriologie und Vorderasiatischen Archäologie*. Vol. 2, *Ber–Ezur*, edited by E. Ebeling and B. Meissner, 382–87. Berlin: de Gruyter, 1938.

O'Connor, Kathleen M. *Genesis 1–25A*. Macon: Smyth & Helwys, 2018.

Oden, R. A. "Divine Aspirations in Atrahasis and in Genesis 1–11." *ZAW* 93 (1981): 197–216.

Oppenheim, A. Leo. *Ancient Mesopotamia*. Chicago: University of Chicago Press, 1964.

Orlinsky, Harry M. "Enigmatic Bible Passages: The Plain Meaning of Genesis 1:1–3." *Biblical Archaeologist* 46, no. 4 (1983): 207–9.

Otto, E. "Die Geburt des Mose. Die Mose-Figur als Gegenentwurf zur neuassyrischen Königsideologie im 7. Jh. v. Chr." In *Mose. Ägypten und das Alte Testament*, edited by E. Otto, 43–83. SBS 189. Stuttgart: Katholisches Bibelwerk, 2000.

———. "Die narrative Logik des Wechsels der Gottesnamen in der Genesis zur Differenzierung zwischen Erzählzeit und erzählter Zeit in Genesis." In *Die Tora. Studien zum Pentateuch. Gesammelte Schriften*, 587–600. BZAR 9. Wiesbaden: Harrassowitz, 2009.

———. "Die Paradieserzählung Genesis 2–3: Eine nachpriesterschriftliche Lehrerzählung in ihrem Religionsgeschichtlichen Kontext." In *"Jedes Ding hat seine Zeit . . ." Studien zur israelitischen und altorientalischen Weisheit. Diethelm Michel zum 65. Geburtstag*, edited by Anja A. Diesel et al, 167–92. BZAW 241. Berlin: de Gruyter, 1996.

Ottosson, M. "Eden and the Land of Promise." In *Congress Volume Jerusalem 1986*, edited by J. A. Emerton, 177–88. VTSup 40. Leiden: Brill, 1988.

Perdue, Leo G. *The Collapse of History: Reconstructing Old Testament Theology*. Overtures to Biblical Theology. Minneapolis: Augsburg Fortress, 1994.

Petersen, David L. "Genesis 6:1–4, Yahweh and the Organization of the Cosmos." *Journal for the Study of the Old Testament* 4, no. 13 (1979): 47–64.

———. "The Yahwist on the Flood." *Vetus Testamentum* 26, no. 4 (1976): 438–46.

Pettinato, G. "Die Bestrafung des Menschengeschlechts durch die Sintflut." *Orientalia* 37, no. 2 (1968): 165–200.

Phillips, Elaine A. "Serpent Intertexts: Tantalizing Twists in the Tales." *Bulletin for Biblical Research* 10, no. 2 (2000): 233–45.

Pola, Thomas. *Die ursprüngliche Priesterschrift. Beobachtungen zur Literaturkritik und Traditionsgeschichte von Pg*. WMANT 70. Neukirchen-Vluyn: Neukirchener, 1995.

Polzin, Robert. *Samuel and the Deuteronomist: A Literary Study of the Deuteronomic History: Part Two, 1 Samuel*. Bloomington: Indiana University Press, 1989.

Pongratz-Leisten, Beate. *Ina šulmi īrub: Die kult-topographie und ideologische Programmatik der akitu-Prozession in Babylonien und Assyrien im I. Jahrtausend v. Chr*. Baghdader Forschungen 16. Mainz: Philipp von Zabern, 1994.

Radday, Yehuda Thomas. "Humor in Names." In *On Humour and the Comic in the Hebrew Bible*, edited by Yehuda Thomas Radday and Athalya Brenner, 59–98. JSOTSup 92. Sheffield: Almond, 1990.

Rashi. *Kommentar zum Pentateuch*. Basel: Goldschmidt, 1994.

Reicke, B. "The Knowledge Hidden in the Tree of Paradise." *Journal of Semitic Studies* 1, no. 3 (1956): 193–201.

Reiner, Erica. "The Etiological Myth of the 'Seven Sages.'" *Orientalia* 30, no. 1 (1961): 1–11.

Rendtorff, R. "Gen 8,21 und die Urgeschichte des Jahwisten." *Kerygma und Dogma* 7 (1961): 69–78.

———. "Hermeneutische Probleme der biblischen Urgeschichte." In *Festschrift für Friedrich Smend zum 70. Geburtstag dargebracht von Freunden und Schülern*, 19–29. Berlin: Merseburger, 1963.

———. "The Paradigm is Changing: Hopes—and Fears." *Biblical Interpretation* 1, no. 1 (1993): 34–53.

Roberts, J. J. M. Review of *Slaying the Dragon: Mythmaking in the Biblical Tradition* by Bernard F. Batto. *Journal of Religion* 75, no. 1 (1995): 102.

Robinson, Robert B. "Literary Functions of the Genealogies of Genesis." *Catholic Biblical Quarterly* 48, no. 4 (1986): 595–608.

Ross, A. P. "The Curse of Canaan." *Bibliotheca Sacra* 137 (1980): 223–40.

Routledge, Robin. "Did God Create Chaos? Unresolved Tension in Genesis 1:1–2." *Tyndale Bulletin* 61, no. 1 (2010): 69–88.

Römer, Thomas. "The Origin and the Status of Evil According to the Hebrew Bible." In *Die Wurzel allen Übels: Vorstellungen über die Herkunft des Bösen und Schlechten in der Philosophie und Religion des 1.–4. Jahrhunderts*, edited by F. Jourdan and R. Hirsch-Luipold, 53–66. Ratio Religionis Studien 3. Tübingen: Mohr Siebeck, 2014.

Ruppert, Lothar. "Der alte Mensch aus der Sicht des Alten Testaments." *Trierer Theologische Zeitschrift* 85 (1976): 270–85.

Sailhamer, John H. "Exegetical Notes: Genesis 1:1–2:4a." *Trinity Journal* 5 (1984): 73–82.

———. *The Pentateuch as Narrative: A Biblical-Theological Commentary*. Grand Rapids: Zondervan, 1992.

Sandmel, Samuel. "Parallelomania." *Journal of Biblical Literature* 81, no. 1 (1962): 1–13.

Sarna, Nahum M. *Genesis*. JPS Torah Commentary. Philadelphia: Jewish Publication Society, 1989.

———. *Understanding Genesis*. New York: Jewish Theological Seminary of America, 1966.

Sasson, J. M. "The 'Tower of Babel' as a Clue to the Redactional Structuring of the Primeval History [Gen. 1–11:9]." In *The Bible World: Essays in Honor of Cyrus H. Gordon*, edited by Gary A. Rendsburg, R. Adler, Milton Arfa, and N. H. Winter, 211–19. New York: KTAV Publishing, 1980.

Sawyer, J. F. A. "The Image of God, the Wisdom of Serpents and the Knowledge of Good and Evil." In *Walk in the Garden: Biblical, Iconographical and Literary Images of Eden*, edited by Paul Morris and Deborah Sawyer, 64–73. JSOTSup 136. Sheffield: JSOT Press, 1992.

Scharlemann, R. P. "Transcendental and Poietic Imagination." In *Morphologies of Faith*, edited by Mary Gerhart and Anthony C. Yu, 109–22. AARSR 59. Atlanta: Scholars Press, 1990.

Schaudig, H. "Cult Centralization in the Ancient Near East? Conception of the Ideal Capital in the Ancient Near East." *One God – One Cult – One Nation: Archaeological and Biblical Perspectives*, eds. Reinhard Gregor Kratz and Hermann Spiekkermann, 145–68. BZAW 405. Berlin: de Gruyter, 2010.

Schlimm, M. R. "At Sin's Entryway (Gen 4,7): A Reply to C. L. Crouch." ZAW 124 (2012): 409–15.

Schmid, K. "Loss of Immortality? Hermeneutical Aspects of Genesis 2–3 and Its Early Receptions." In *Beyond Eden: The Biblical Story of Paradise (Genesis 2–3) and Its Reception History*, edited by Konrad Schmid and Christoph Riedweg, 58–78. FAT 2. Reihe 34. Tübingen: Mohr Siebeck, 2008.

———. "Die Unteilbarkeit der Weisheit. Überlegungen zur sogenannten Paradieserzählung Gen 2f. und ihrer theologischen Tendenz." ZAW 114 (2002): 21–39.

Schmidt, Werner H. "Anthropologische Begriffe im AT. Anmerkungen zum Hebräischen Denken." *Evangelische Theologie* 24, no. 7 (1964): 374–88.

Schüle, A. "The Divine-Human Marriages (Genesis 6:1–4) and the Greek Framing of the Primeval History." *Theologische Zeitschrift* 65, no. 2 (2009): 116–28.

———. "Made in the 'Image of God': The Concepts of Divine Images in Gen 1–3." ZAW 117 (2005): 1–20.

———. *Der Prolog der hebräischen Bibel. Der literar- und theologiegeschichtliche Diskurs der Urgeschichte (Genesis 1–11)*. AThANT 86. Zurich: Theologischer Verlag Zurich, 2006.

———. "The Reluctant Image: Theology and Anthropology in Gen 1–3." In *Theology from the Beginning: Essays on the Primeval History and its Canonical Context*, 27–44. FAT 113. Tübingen: Mohr Siebeck, 2017.

Sefati, Yitzhak. *Love Songs in Sumerian Literature: Critical Edition of the Dumuzi-Inanna Songs*. Bar-Ilan Studies in Near Eastern Languages and Culture. Ramat Gan: Bar-Ilan University Press, 1998.

Simon T. L. "'Ha az égbe hág is fel Babilon.' Identitáskeresés világbirodalmak árnyékában: adalékok a Ter 11,1–9 értelmezéséhez." *Pannonhalmi Szemle* 20 (2012): 6–28.

———. *A ki nem mondott és az el nem mondható: Bibliai példák az elhallgatás kommunikációs szerepéről*. LD 23. Budapest; Bakonybél: L'Harmattan; Szent Mauríciusz Monostor, 2020.

Simons, J. "The 'Table of Nations' (Genesis 10): Its General Structure and Meaning." In *"I Studied Inscriptions from before the Flood:" Ancient Near Eastern, Literary, and Linguistic Approaches to Genesis 1–11*, edited by Richard S. Hess and David Toshio Tsumura, 234–53. SBTS 4. Winona Lake: Eisenbrauns, 1994.

Simoons-Vermeer, Ruth E. "The Mesopotamian Flood Stories: A Comparison and Interpretation." *Numen* 21, no. 1 (1974): 17–34.

Sjöberg, Åke W. "Eve and the Chameleon." In *In the Shelter of Elyon: Essays on Ancient Palestinian Life and Literature in Honor of G. W. Ahlström*, edited by W. B. Barrick and J. R. Spencer, 217–25. Sheffield: JSOT Press, 1984.

———. "Die Göttliche Abstammung der sumerisch-babylonischen Herrscher." *Orientalia Suecana* 21 (1972): 87–112.

Ska, Jean-Louis. "Genesis 2–3: Some Fundamental Questions." In *Beyond Eden: The Biblical Story of Paradise (Genesis 2–3) and Its Reception History*, edited by Konrad Schmid and Christoph Riedweg, 1–27. FAT 2. Reihe 34. Tübingen: Mohr Siebeck, 2008.

———. *Introduction to Reading the Pentateuch*. Winona Lake: Eisenbrauns, 2006.

Skinner, John. *A Critical and Exegetical Commentary on Genesis*. ICC. Edinburgh: T&T Clark, 1930.

Slivniak, Dmitri M. "The Garden of Double Messages: Deconstructing Hierarchical Oppositions in the Garden Story." *Journal for the Study of the Old Testament* 27, no. 4 (2003): 439–60.

Smith, Gary V. "Structure and Purpose in Genesis 1–11." *Journal for the Evangelical Theological Society* 20, no. 4 (1977): 307–19.

Smith, George. "The Chaldean Account of the Deluge." *Transactions of the Society of Biblical Archaeology* 2 (1873): 213–34.

Smith, Mark S. *The Genesis of Good and Evil: The Fall(out) and Original Sin the Bible*. Louisville: Westminster John Knox, 2019.

———. *The Priestly Vision of Genesis 1*. Minneapolis: Fortress, 2010.

Sollberger, Edmond. "The Rulers of Lagaš." *Journal of Cuneiform Studies* 21 (1967): 279–91.

Sommer, Benjamin D. "The Babylonian Akitu Festival: Rectifying the King or Renewing the Cosmos?" *Journal of the Ancient Near Eastern Society* 27, no. 1 (2000): 81–95.

———. *A Prophet Reads Scripture: Allusion in Isaiah 40–66*. Stanford: Stanford University Press, 1998.

Sommerfeld, W. "Marduk. A. Philologisch. I. In Mesopotamien." In *Reallexikon der Assyriologie und Vorderasiatischen Archäologie*. Vol. 7: *Libanukšabaš — Medizin*, edited by D. O. Edzard, 360–70. Berlin: de Gruyter, 1987–90.

Sparks, Kenton L. "*Enūma elish* and Priestly Mimesis: Elite Emulation in Nascent Judaism." *Journal of Biblical Literature* 126, no. 4 (2007): 625–48.

Speiser, E. A. "Ancient Mesopotamia." In *The Idea of History in the Ancient Near East*, edited by R. C. Dentan, 35–76. New Haven: Yale University Press, 1955.

———. "The Biblical Idea of History in Its Common Near Eastern Setting." *Israel Exploration Journal* 7, no. 4 (1957): 201–16.

———. *Genesis*. Anchor Bible Series 1. Garden City: Doubleday, 1964.

———. "In Search of Nimrod." *Eretz Israel* 5 (1958): 32–36.

———. "Word Plays on the Creation Epic's Version of the Founding of Babylon." *Orientalia* 25, no. 4 (1956): 317–23.
Spieckermann, Hermann. "God and His People: The Concept of Kingship and Cult in the Ancient Near East." In *One God – One Cult – One Nation: Archaeological and Biblical Perspectives*, edited by Reinhard Gregor Kratz and Hermann Spiekkermann, 341–56. BZAW 405. Berlin: de Gruyter, 2010.
Spina, Frank Anthony. "The 'Ground' for Cain's Rejection (Gen. 4): *'adāmāh* in the Context of Gen. 1–11." *ZAW* 104 (1992): 319–32.
Spoelstra, Joshua J. "The Literary Shapes of the Primeval History: A Case for Chiasm in Genesis 1–11." *Journal of Northwest Semitic Languages* 48, no. 1 (2022): 43–60.
Steinberg, Naomi. "The Genealogical Framework of the Family Stories in Genesis." *Semeia* 46 (1989): 41–50.
Steinmetz, Devora. "Vineyard, Farm, and Garden: The Drunkenness of Noah in the Context of Primeval History." *Journal of Biblical Literature* 113, no. 2 (1994): 193–207.
Stoebe, H. J. "*ḥāmās*, Gewalttat." In *Theologisches Handwörterbuch zum Alten Testament*, edited by Ernst Jenni and Claus Westermann, 583–87. Vol. 1. Munich; Zurich: Kaiser; Theologischer Verlag, 1971.
Stordalen, T. *Echoes of Eden: Gen 2–3 and Symbolism of the Eden Garden in Biblical Hebrew Literature*. CBET 25. Leuven: Peeters, 2000.
———. "Genesis 2,4 – Restudying a *locus classicus*." *ZAW* 104 (1992): 171–73.
———. "The God of the Eden Narrative." In *Enigmas and Images: Studies in Honor of Tryggve N. D. Mettinger*, edited by Göran Eidevall and Blaženka Scheuer, 3–21. CB 58. Winona Lake: Eisenbrauns, 2011.
———. "Heaven on Earth – Or Not?" In *Beyond Eden: The Biblical Story of Paradise (Genesis 2–3) and Its Reception History*, edited by Konrad Schmid and Christoph Riedweg, 28–57. FAT 2. Reihe 34. Tübingen: Mohr Siebeck, 2008.
———. "Man, Soil, Garden: Basic Plot in Genesis 2–3 Reconsidered." *Journal for the Study of the Old Testament* 17, no. 53 (1992): 3–26.
Strong, John T. "Shattering the Image of God: A Response to Theodore Hiebert's Interpretation of the Story of the Tower of Babel." *Journal of Biblical Literature* 127, no. 4 (2008): 625–34.
Swiggers, P. "Babel and the Confusion of Tongues (Genesis 11:1–9)." In *Mythos im Alten Testament und seiner Umwelt. Festschrift für Hans-Peter Müller zum 65. Geburtstag*, edited by A. Lange, H. Lichtenberger, D. Römheld, 182–95. BZAW 278. Berlin: de Gruyter, 1999.
Takayoshi, O. "Near Eastern Fish Men and Women." In *Dragons, Monsters and Fabulous Beasts,* edited by J. G. Westenholz, 22. Jerusalem: Bible Lands Museum, 2004.

———. "The Snake-Dragon." In *Dragons, Monsters and Fabulous Beasts*, edited by J. G. Westenholz, 25–26. Jerusalem: Bible Lands Museum, 2004.

Tomasino, Anthony J. "History Repeats Itself: The 'Fall' and Noah's Drunkenness." *Vetus Testamentum* 42, no. 1 (1992): 128–30.

Trible, Phyllis. *God and the Rhetoric of Sexuality*. Overtures to Biblical Theology. Philadelphia: Fortress, 1978.

Tsumura, David Toshio. *Creation and Destruction: A Reappraisal of the Chaoskampf Theory in the Old Testament*. Winona Lake: Eisenbrauns, 2005.

———. *The Earth and the Waters in Genesis 1 and 2*. JSOTSup 83. Sheffield: Sheffield Academic Press, 1989.

Turnbull, J., ed. *Oxford Advanced Learner's Dictionary*. Oxford: OUP, 2010.

Turner, Laurence A. *Announcements of Plot in Genesis*. JSOTSup 96. Sheffield: JSOT Press, 1990.

———. *Genesis*. Readings: A New Biblical Commentary. Sheffield: Sheffield Academic, 2000.

———. "The Rainbow as the Sign of the Covenant in Genesis IX 11–13." *Vetus Testamentum* 43, no. 1 (1993): 119–24.

Uehlinger, Christoph. *Weltreich und „eine Rede": Eine neue Deutung der sogenannten Turmbauerzählung (Gen 11,1–9)*. OBO 101. Freiburg; Göttingen: Universitätsverlag; Vandenhoeck & Ruprecht, 1990.

Van de Mieroop, Marc. *The Ancient Mesopotamian City*. Oxford: Oxford University Press, 1999.

———. "Reading Babylon." *American Journal of Archaeology* 107, no. 2 (2003): 257–75.

Van Seters, John. *Prologue to History: The Yahwist as Historian in Genesis*. Louisville: Westminster John Knox, 1992.

Vanstiphout, H. L. J. *Epics of Sumerian Kings: The Matter of Aratta*. Edited by J. S. Cooper. WAW 20. Atlanta: SBL Press, 2003.

Van Wijk-Bos, Johanna W. H. *Making Wise the Simple: The Torah in Christian Faith and Practice*. Grand Rapids: Eerdmans, 2005.

Van Wolde, Ellen. *Genesis: Translation and Commentary*. New York: Norton, 1996.

———. "The Story of Cain and Abel: A Narrative Study." *Journal for the Study of the Old Testament* 16, no. 52 (1991): 25–41.

Von Rad, Gerhard. *Genesis*. Old Testament Library. Philadelphia: Westminster, 1972.

———. "The Theological Problem of the Old Testament Doctrine of Creation." In *The Problem of the Hexateuch and Other Essays*, 131–43. London: SCM, 1966.

Von Soden, W. "Etemenanki vor Asarhaddon nach der Erzählung vom Turmbau zu Babel und dem Erra-Mythos." *Ugarit-Forschungen* 3 (1971): 253–63.

Walker, Christopher, and Michael B. Dick. "The Induction of the Cult Image in Ancient Mesopotamia: The Mesopotamian *mīs pî* Ritual." In *Born in Heaven,*

Made on Earth: The Making of the Cult Image in the Ancient Near East, edited by Michael B. Dick, 55–121. Winona Lake: Eisenbrauns, 1999.

Walsh, Jerome T. "Genesis 2.4b–3.23: A Synchronic Approach." *Journal of Biblical Literature* 96, no. 2 (1977): 161–77.

Waltke, Bruce K. *Genesis: A Commentary*. Grand Rapids: Zondervan, 2001.

Walton, John H. "The Antediluvian Section of the Sumerian King List and Genesis 5." *Biblical Archaeologist* 44, no. 4 (1981): 207–8.

———. "Genesis." In *Zondervan Illustrated Bible Backgrounds Commentary*. Vol. 1: *Genesis, Exodus, Leviticus, Numbers, Deuteronomy*, edited by John H. Walton, 2–159. Grand Rapids: 2009.

———. *Genesis 1 as Ancient Cosmology*. Winona Lake: Eisenbrauns, 2011.

———. *Genesis*. Zondervan Illustrated Backgrounds Commentary. Grand Rapids: Zondervan, 2013.

———. "The Mesopotamian Background of the Tower of Babel Account and Its Implications." *Bulletin for Biblical Research* 5, no. 1 (1995): 155–75.

———. "The Sons of God in Genesis 6:1–4." In *The Genesis Debate*, edited by Ronald Youngblood, 184–209. Grand Rapids: Baker: 1990.

Warning, Wilfried. "Terminologische Verknüpfungen und Genesis 12,1–3." *Biblica* 81, no. 3 (2000): 386–90.

Warnock, Mary. *Imagination*. Berkely: University of California Press, 1976.

Waschke, Ernst-Joachim. "Der Mensch 'aus Staub' und 'Gottes Ebenbild' – Anmerkungen zu unterschiedlichen anthropologischen Perspektiven." *Hallesche Beiträge zur Orientwissenschaft* 42 (2008): 489–505.

———. "Zum Verhältnis von Ruhe und Arbeit in den biblischen Schöpfungsgeschichten Gen 1–3." In *"Gerechtigkeit und Recht zu üben" (Gen 18,19). Studien zur altorientalischen und biblischen Rechtsgeschichte, zur Religionsgeschichte Israels und zur Religionssoziologie. Festschrift für Eckart Otto zum 65. Geburtstag*, edited by R. Achenbach and M. Arneth, 69–80. BZAR 13. Wiesbaden: Harrassowitz, 2009.

———. *Untersuchungen zum Menschenbild der Urgeschichte. Ein Beitrag zur alttestamentlichen Theologie* (ThA, 43). Berlin: Evangelische Verlagsanstalt, 1984.

Weinfeld, M. "Sabbath, Temple, and the Enthronement of the Lord: The Problem of the Sitz im Leben of Genesis 1.1–2–3." In *Mélanges bibliques et orientaux en l'honneur de M. Henri Cazelles*, edited by A. Caquot and M. Delcor, 501–12. AOAT 212. Kevalear; Neukirchen-Vluyn: Butzon & Bercker; Neukirchener, 1981.

Wenham, Gordon J. "The Coherence of the Flood Narrative." *Vetus Testamentum* 28, no. 3 (1978): 336–48.

———. "Genesis 1–11 as Protohistory." In *Genesis: History, Fiction, or Neither? Three Views on the Bible's Earliest Chapters*, edited by Charles Halton and Stanley N. Gundry, 73–97. Grand Rapids: Zondervan, 2015.

———. *Genesis 1–15*. WBC 1. Waco: Word, 1987.

———. "The Priority of P." *Vetus Testamentum* 49, no. 2 (1999): 240–58.

———. "Sanctuary Symbolism in the Garden of Eden Story." In *"I Studied Inscriptions from before the Flood:" Ancient Near Eastern, Literary, and Linguistic Approaches to Genesis 1–11*, edited by Richard S. Hess and David Toshio Tsumura, 399–404. SBTS 4. Winona Lake: Eisenbrauns, 1994.

Westenholz, Joan Goodnick. "The Theological Foundation of the City, the Capital City and Babylon." In *Capital Cities: Urban Planning and Spiritual Dimensions: Proceedings of the Symposium Held on May 27–29, 1996 Jerusalem, Israel*, edited by Joan Goodnick Westenholz, 43–54. Bible Lands Museum Jerusalem Publications 2. Jerusalem: Bible Lands Museum, 1998.

Westermann, Claus. *Genesis 1–11: A Commentary*. Minneapolis: Augsburg, 1984.

———. "Der Mensch im Urgeschehen." *Kerygma und Dogma* 13 (1967): 231–46.

Whitt, William. *Genesis: A New Translation with Commentary*. Highland Park: The Middle Coast Press, 2019.

Wiggermann, F. A. M. *Mesopotamian Protective Spirits: The Ritual Texts*. Cuneiform Monographs 1. Groningen: Styx, 1992.

———. "mušḫuššu." In *Reallexikon der Assyriologie und Vorderasiatischen Archäologie*. Vol. 8, edited by D. O. Edzard, 455–62. Berlin: de Gruyter: 1993–97.

———. "Nin-ĝišzida." In *Reallexikon der Assyriologie und Vorderasiatischen Archäologie*. Vol. 9, edited by D. O. Edzard, 368–73. Berlin: de Gruyter, 1998–2001.

———. "Tišpak, his Seal, and the Dragon mušḫuššu." In *To the Euphrates and Beyond: Archaeological Studies in Honour of Maurits N. van Loon*, edited by O. M. Haex, Hans H. Curvers, Peter M. M. G. Akkermans, 117–33. Rotterdam: Balkema, 1989.

Wilcke, C. "Genealogical and Geographical Thought." In *DUMU-E2-DUB-BA-A: Studies in Honor of Åke W. Sjöberg*, edited by H. Behrens, D. Loding, and M. Roth, 557–71. Philadelphia: Occasional Publication of the Samuel Noah Kramer Fund, 1989.

Wilson, Robert R. "Between 'Azel' and 'Azel': Interpreting the Biblical Genealogies." *Biblical Archaeologist* 42, no. 1 (1979): 11–22.

———. *Genealogy and History in the Biblical World*. New Haven: Yale University Press, 1977.

———. "The Old Testament Genealogies in Recent Research." *Journal of Biblical Literature* 94, no. 2 (1975): 169–89.

Wiseman, Donald J. "Genesis 10: Some Archaeological Considerations." *Faith and Thought* 87 (1955): 14–24.

Witte, M. *Die biblische Urgeschichte. Redaktions- und theologiegeschichtliche Beobachtungen zu Genesis 1,1–11,26*. BZAW 265. Berlin: de Gruyter, 1998.

Wright, Jacob L. "Making a Name for Oneself: Martial Valor, Heroic Death, and Procreation in the Hebrew Bible." *Journal for the Study of the Old Testament* 36, no. 2 (2011): 131–62.

Wright, N. T. *The Climax of the Covenant: Christ and the Law in Pauline Theology*. New York: T&T Clark, 1991.

———. *The Resurrection of the Son of God*. Christian Origins and the Question of God 3. London: SPCK, 2003.

York, A. "The Maturation Theme in the Adam and Eve Story." In *"Go to the Land I will Show You"*, edited by J. E. Coleson and V. H. Matthews, 393–410. Winona Lake: Eisenbrauns, 1996.

Young, D. W. "On the Application of Numbers from Babylonian Mathematics to Biblical Life Spans and Epochs." *ZAW* 100 (1988): 331–61.

———. "The Influence of Babylonian Algebra on Longevity Among the Antediluvians." *ZAW* 102 (1990): 321–35.

Zenger, E. "Beobachtungen zur Komposition und Theologie der jahwistischen Urgeschichte." In *Dynamik im Wort. FS aus Anlass des 50 jährigen Bestehens des Kath. Bibelwerks in Deutschland*, edited by E. Zenger and J. Gnilka, 35–54. Stuttgart: Katholisches Bibelwerk, 1983.

Ziemer, Benjamin. *Abram – Abraham. Kompositionsgeschichtliche Untersuchungen zu Genesis 14, 15 und 17*. BZAW 350. Berlin: de Gruyter, 2005.

———. "Erklärung der Zahlen von Gen 5 aus ihrem kompositionellen Zusammenhang." *ZAW* 121 (2009): 1–18.

Ancient Sources

"Atrahasis." In *The Context of Scripture*. Vol. 1: *Canonical Compositions from the Biblical World*, translated by B. R. Foster, edited by W. W. Hallo, 450–53. Leiden: Brill, 2003.

"The Disputation between Summer and Winter." In *The Context of Scripture*. Vol. 1: *Canonical Compositions from the Biblical World*, translated by H. L. J. Vanstiphout, edited by W. W. Hallo, 584–88. Leiden: Brill, 2003.

"Epic of Creation." In *The Context of Scripture*. Vol. 1: *Canonical Compositions from the Biblical World*, translated by B. R. Foster, edited by W. W. Hallo, 390–402. Leiden: Brill, 2003.

"The Epic of Gilgamesh, standard version." In *Myths from Mesopotamia*, edited and translated by Stephanie Dalley, 50–135. Oxford: Oxford University Press, 2000.

Langham Literature, with its publishing work, is a ministry of Langham Partnership.

Langham Partnership is a global fellowship working in pursuit of the vision God entrusted to its founder John Stott –

> *to facilitate the growth of the church in maturity and Christ-likeness through raising the standards of biblical preaching and teaching.*

Our vision is to see churches in the Majority World equipped for mission and growing to maturity in Christ through the ministry of pastors and leaders who believe, teach and live by the word of God.

Our mission is to strengthen the ministry of the word of God through:
- nurturing national movements for biblical preaching
- fostering the creation and distribution of evangelical literature
- enhancing evangelical theological education

especially in countries where churches are under-resourced.

Our ministry

Langham Preaching partners with national leaders to nurture indigenous biblical preaching movements for pastors and lay preachers all around the world. With the support of a team of trainers from many countries, a multi-level programme of seminars provides practical training, and is followed by a programme for training local facilitators. Local preachers' groups and national and regional networks ensure continuity and ongoing development, seeking to build vigorous movements committed to Bible exposition.

Langham Literature provides Majority World preachers, scholars and seminary libraries with evangelical books and electronic resources through publishing and distribution, grants and discounts. The programme also fosters the creation of indigenous evangelical books in many languages, through writer's grants, strengthening local evangelical publishing houses, and investment in major regional literature projects, such as one volume Bible commentaries like the *Africa Bible Commentary* and the *South Asia Bible Commentary*.

Langham Scholars provides financial support for evangelical doctoral students from the Majority World so that, when they return home, they may train pastors and other Christian leaders with sound, biblical and theological teaching. This programme equips those who equip others. Langham Scholars also works in partnership with Majority World seminaries in strengthening evangelical theological education. A growing number of Langham Scholars study in high quality doctoral programmes in the Majority World itself. As well as teaching the next generation of pastors, graduated Langham Scholars exercise significant influence through their writing and leadership.

To learn more about Langham Partnership and the work we do visit **langham.org**

www.ingramcontent.com/pod-product-compliance
Lightning Source LLC
Chambersburg PA
CBHW051540230426
43669CB00015B/2673